PLAYER DEVELOPMENT
FOR
POSSESSION SOCCER

ESSENTIAL SKILLS FOR THE FIRST BALL GAME

by Martin Bidzinski

Library of Congress
Cataloging - in - Publication Data

Player Development for Possession Soccer - Essential Skills for the First Ball Game
by Martin Bidzinski

ISBN-13: 978-1-59164-252-7
Library of Congress Control Number: 2017942491

Diagrams created using Easy Sports Graphics
http://easy-sports-software.com/en/

Art Direction, Layout and Proofing
Bryan R. Beaver

Reedswain Publishing
88 Wells Road
Spring City, PA 19475
www.reedswain.com
orders@reedswain.com

Also by Martin Bidzinski (available at www.reedswain.com)

Paperback and E-Book

- The Soccer Coaching Handbook
- Smart First Touches - Developing the Skillful Player
- Developing the 360° Player

E-Book

- The Soccer Coaching Manual - The Most Effective Use of Space
- Soccer Coaching - Ergonomics

DVD

- Developing the First Touch
- Developing 1v1 and Dribbling Skills
- Developing the Two Footed Player
- Passing and Receiving to Create Time and Space
- Developing Reaction and Explosive Movement
- Match Fitness Training
- Developing the 360° Player
- Formal Training for Soccer Skills

Video Download

- Off the Wall - A Soccer Skills Masterclass

CONTENTS

INTRODUCTION

I did not believe that my first soccer coaching book titled 'The Soccer Coaching Handbook' published back in 1996 would cause me problems when I wrote about the coaching side of the game. I simply wanted coaches to understand the implications of the conclusions I made when I realized that most of what was taking place at the youth level of the game had begun to be politically orientated. I know it is difficult to comprehend that political and financial based decisions influence how the game is coached not only at the top international and club sides, but also at grass roots level, but that is sometimes how things work. I have written extensively about many coaching issues over the last twenty years but because the game has evolved so much in the last ten years alone, I realized that more work has to be done if the coaching side of the game is to be understood more widely against a background of expectations that are now also more in keeping with commercially driven policies.

1 - THE BIRTH OF THE SECOND BALL GAME

As a young man I loved the game of soccer and enjoyed working in and playing the game until that moment when the game of soccer began moving away from its own reality and into the world of politics and the power of money. This influenced what took place on the training ground in many a club. It is true that when it came to my neck of the woods, the continent of Europe as a whole, I have experienced all sorts of factors which affect the way the game of soccer is played. For example, one reason for England failing to win the World Cup since 1966 is the fact that the game in England changed from one of skilful play before the nineteen sixties to one of a more physical game. With hindsight, the physical approach to playing soccer in England had begun to take place more or less just after 1963/64 with the appointment of Alf Ramsay as England manager. I believe that this appointment was based on a political decision, one which has had its consequences to the game of soccer right up to the present day. In plain terms, team England's defeat in 1954 at the hands of the Hungarians was the cause of a long lasting political backlash. I believe that the establishment of that fateful time didn't want a repeat of the negative experience that befell England against the Hungarians back in 1954 given the political reality of the cold war at that time and the implications of it on the relationship between East Europe and the Western alliance. It was not a surprise that the establishment chose Mr. Ramsey to be the England manager prior to the World Cup of 1966. In Coach Alf Ramsey the powers that be saw a man who was full of passion for his country and his Nationalism was more than obvious. For one thing, Mr. Ramsey's credentials for the England's manager post could not have been more appropriate. After all, Mr. Ramsey served as an officer in the 'British Army' during the Second World War. On leaving the army Mr. Ramsey played professional soccer and followed this up by working as a manager in the game with some success. Mr. Ramsey's success as manager was based on his playing philosophy which was set in a forward moving mentality that came from his personal experience gained in his army days. When the soldiers went to fight in foreign lands during the Second World War, they were trained to run forward at the enemy, head on.

THE RAMSEY LEGACY

As manager of England he did a wonderful job by leading the team to victory and winning the World Cup in 1966. However, the consequential effect of his playing philosophy ultimately resulted in a different approach to playing the beautiful game. From then on the game in England became more direct, an example of the so-called forward moving game. In copying Sir Alf Ramsey's team shape of 4 - 1 - 2 - 3, the coaches of the beautiful game did what coaches do and simplified what Ramsey's team shape actually was. By doing so, they gave birth to the team shape known as the 4 - 3 - 3. I can't imagine that the people running the establishment, the soccer associations back then, knew anything of the consequences that the 4 - 3 - 3 team shape would create when it came to the skills side of the game, namely that it started the systematic reduction in the skill level of home grown players. In fact, there exists in England today such a dearth of home grown talent that in 2015 the English FA was negotiating, somewhat unsuccessfully I might add, with the home clubs to play more home grown players and not sideline them out of the team, as was the case in some of the top clubs in England during the 2015/16 season, where in fact only a handful of home grown players took part.

2 - A QUESTION OF BILATERALITY

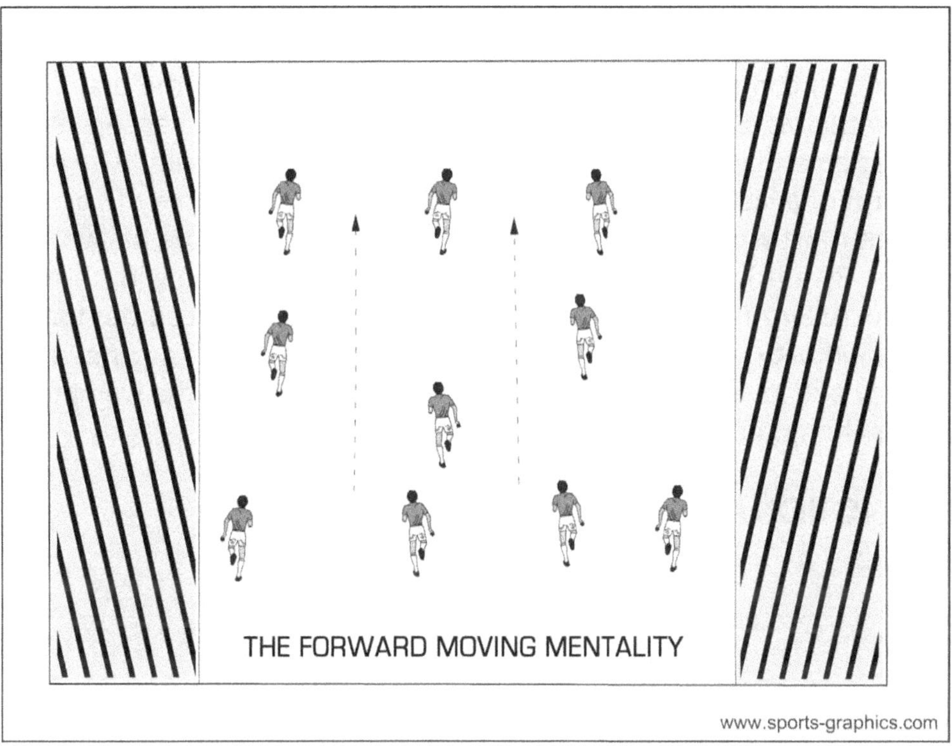

THE BILATERALITY IMPLICATION

Was Sir Alf Ramsey aware of the many implications that arose from his forward moving direct line of attack? Did he know anything about the concept of bilaterality at that time in the human evolution story? I don't know the answer to that question and of course none of us can ask him because he is no longer with us. I suspect though that having served in the British Army as a Captain he would have had to know quite a lot about the concept of conformity, which is an integral part of the way the army operates. In any case, one of the most serious consequences of this forward moving mentality when it came to the game of soccer can be seen in his decision not to have wingers in his team. This created a system of play that was more forward moving, direct and without any need for lateral thinking, which left the players in his charge with one and only one objective, to go forward, forward and nothing but forward.

WHAT IS BILATERALITY?

What do we know about bilaterality and its implications to the game of soccer? Medical science informs us that when a player primarily develops the use of the right foot, he naturally develops the left side of the brain more so than the right side of the brain, and vice versa. Where there is a lack of ability on the weaker side of the human being, there is a lack of bilaterality, or if you prefer to put it another way, a lack of collaboration between the right and the left side of the brain and the left and right hand side of the physical being. Under such circumstances the sum total of the make-up of the brain doesn't work together as a single unit, nor does the physical body, hence a lack of collaboration and therefore a lack of lateral ability - bilaterality. The major implication of a lack of bilaterality when it comes to the game of soccer is the effect that most who use the right hand will naturally kick the ball with the right foot. By ensuring the lack of bilaterality in his team (no width - no wing play as such) Sir Alf Ramsey, knowingly or otherwise, enforced the forward moving mentality on the game of soccer and did away with any need for bilaterality and its implications which are consequential to the way the game of soccer should actually be played.

THE FUNCTIONAL GAME
THE 4 - 3 - 3

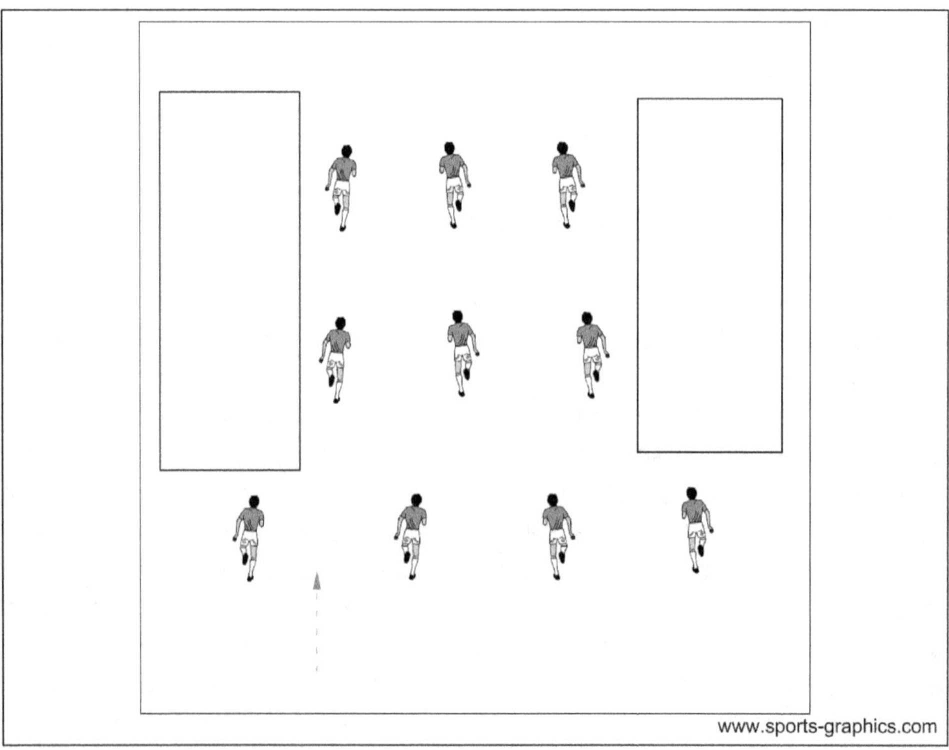

THE WINGLESS WONDERS

The lack of bilaterality in the coaching domain meant that most players ended up being predominantly right footed and only able to use that one good foot with any reasonable measure of skill. This became the accepted reality in the development of the individual player and it was never questioned. Consequently, neither was the effect of the 4 - 3 - 3 playing shape, which was to give birth to a different type of game to that of the skilful game soccer that existed prior to 1966. By the early 1970's, the mind set of everyone either playing or coaching the game of soccer was now firmly set to a forward moving mentality and one based on the big, strong, one-footed player.

TAKING CONTROL OF THE GAME

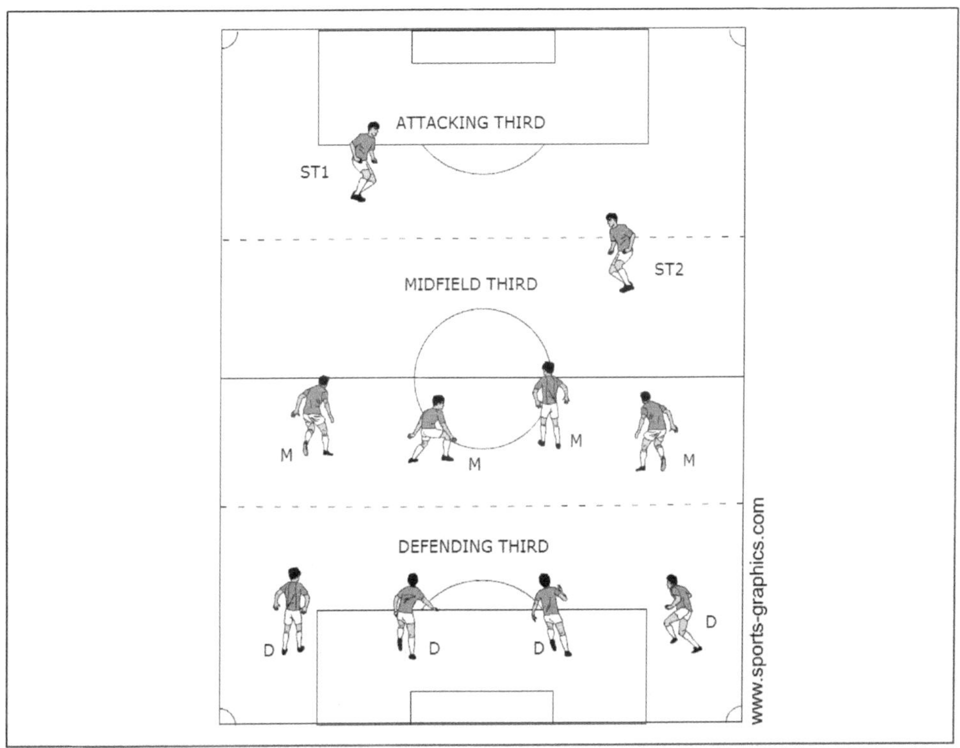

THE THREE AREAS OF CONTROL

Taking control of the way the game is played was achieved by dividing up the field of play (the soccer pitch) into three sections. Knowing what kind of playing attributes are required in each section of the field of play gives the manager the opportunity to control the game. Therefore, the simplest way of taking control of the game is to select the type of playing attributes that would fit in and comply with the playing requirements in a particular area of the pitch, which could be set according to the manager's playing philosophy. The forward moving direct style (no bilaterality) requires a physically superior player, one that is either big and strong or full of running or both. Because of this, the England manager, in keeping with his forward moving mentality, had simplified what a soccer player should be and this helped to change the perception going forward. No longer were coaches looking for skilful players like Sir Stanley Matthews, but instead began to favor bigger and stronger players who could hoof the ball up the field and run and battle for it against equally physical opponents.

THE BIRTH OF THE FUNCTIONAL GAME OF SOCCER

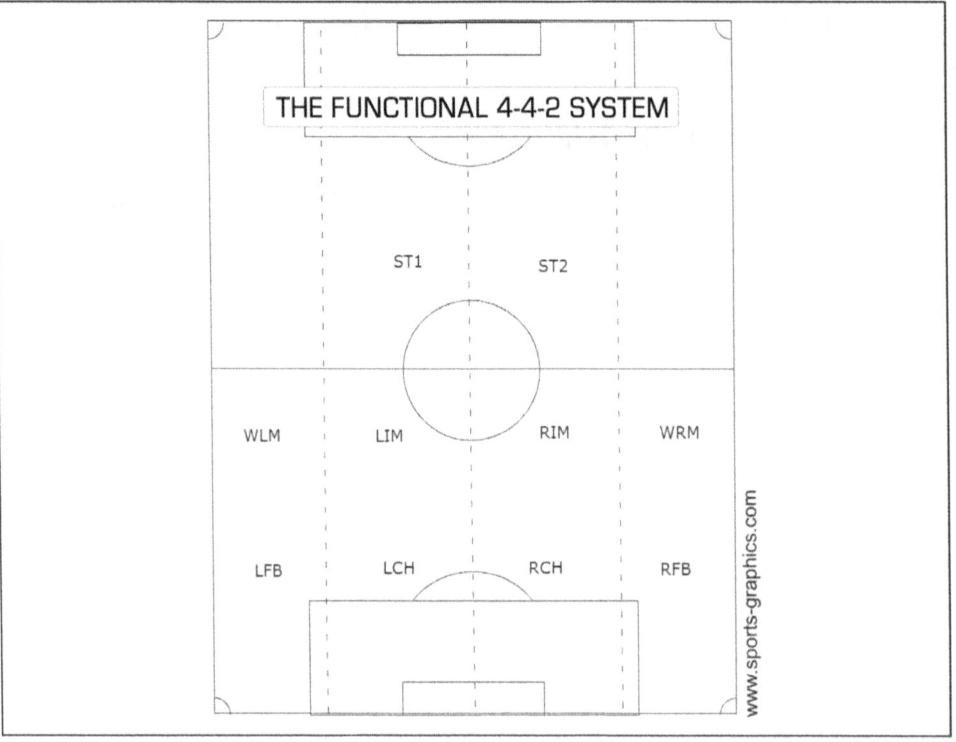

One ex-goalkeeper of a famous English club once made a comment in my direction, "Well, are you into them X'S and O'S?". I suppose he was asking if I was still writing my coaching books. I have to say that I am, as he put it, into them x's and o's, and for a good reason! I remember very well the brutal tackles that took place in the game of soccer in the early seventies and did not want the game to go that way. Back in the early seventies the 4 - 3 - 3 playing system was failing the game. The fans didn't like the way the game was played without wingers and in protest stopped coming to watch soccer in droves. In fact, at one point in the seventies the game of snooker was more popular on television. In my quest to improve the coaching side of the game I realized that none who worked in the game would question anything and as the game evolved more and more, prior to and during the early years of the Premiership and even after its conception in 1992, I realized that some managers in the game continued to enforce a forward moving mentality and the more aggressive approach to the way the game is played. I always remained loyal to the real game of soccer and have never approved of the long ball game, which was based on political interventions on behalf of what can only be described today as the corruption of the beautiful game on behalf of different vested interests.

THE 4 - 4 - 2: GIVING RISE TO THE FUNCTIONAL GAME

The 4 - 4 -2 team shape was implemented after the 4 - 3 - 3 team shape had run its course and was favored by such English managers as Don Revie of Leeds United. Coach Revie was keen to promote the 4 - 4 - 2 in the hope that it would create a more exciting game, which would hopefully promote the more skilful game and bring interest back to soccer. In some ways the 4-4-2 team shape at the time of his reign as England's manager did change the game for the better for a while and the people did return to support the game, because in some ways the game of soccer became more exciting to watch. However, by this time certain coaching methods such as conditioning the players to two contacts with the ball had already become common practice and this would prove to be counter-productive to the development of skilful players. It was thought that conditioning the players to take two contacts to the ball would improve their skill level, but on closer examination the reality was exactly the opposite. In fairness, I am sure that Coach Revie had good intentions and the way he saw the game was different to that of the coaches who came after him, but he in effect had simply continued to enforce the physical game on the players with methods of coaching that ensured the creation of what can now be described as 'A second ball game mentality'.

THE SECOND BALL GAME

The 4 - 4 - 2 team shape became the most effective method of player control that one could imagine because the 4 - 4 - 2 at the hands of the second ball game coach became a playing structure that enabled him to take control of the individual player to the extent that each player played in his designated area on the pitch and had no chance of expressing his individual ability. Rather, he was assigned a specific function to be carried out in his designated area on the pitch.

THE PROBLEMS WITH FUNCTIONAL EXPECTATIONS

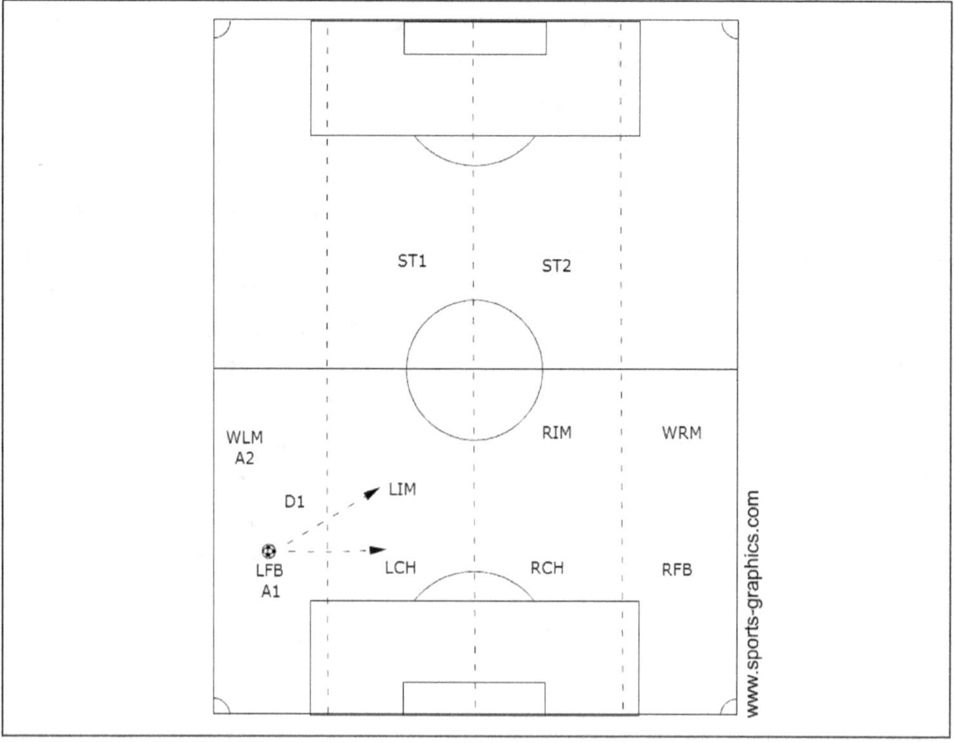

In a functional game of soccer, it is not unusual for the coach to allocate a playing position based on which foot the player uses to solve his playing problems. The continued acceptance of the facts surrounding the lack of bilaterality in the player's development program and the consequential inability to use both feet effectively can be observed in the above diagram. The lack of 'Two footedness' in the functional reality, as demonstrated by the left full back's role as illustrated in the diagram does create its problems. Here we see a 4 - 4 - 2 team shape with the left full back in possession of the ball. The effects of the player's lack of 'Two Footedness' can be clearly seen. In practical terms, the player's one footedness (in this case he is left footed) restricts him to certain angles of play, in which case we can see him shying away from making the pass to A2 down the sideline. When the player is only able to pass the ball with his left foot in the left full back role, then even the touchline will have its implications. In this case, the easiest pass options for the left footed player in this left full back functional role are shown by the black arrows. As a consequence of functional roles and the resulting one footedness of the player, we can observe what type of game is actually being played and it is not just as a result of the limitations I have described in relation to the players' physical options. If the manager keeps his players in the functional role, the full back will not even think about any of the problems I have highlighted here, because in the functional reality when the player is pressed by any opposing player, he will simply hoof the ball long, down the line. The above example may not be appreciated in terms of the implications until you realize what the implications are. If the player is not two footed he is restricted to play the game to the angles shown and if that is the case then the player cannot possibly play the game of soccer to the first ball game expectations where the name of the game is to keep the ball and create counter attacking moves from the back of the team shape.

If the long ball is seen as a priority option, none of the players involved will have much time on the ball and this has its implications when it comes to the all-around development of any player. There are serious reasons for not keeping any player in the functional role, especially one that is based on functional expectations. If a player is kept to only the functional role and the input into the player's development is without any form of lateral development, that player will become strong on one side of his physical being, both mentally and physically, and as a result will have serious playing limitations.

THE IMPLICATIONS

The next examples highlight some of the more serious implications that result from the long ball game where the 'One footedness' of the player is not considered to be a problem. Only when you examine the effect of the functional game of soccer on the development of the player will you be able to recognise what is actually taking place. One of the most obvious places to see the lack of collaboration between the right and left side of the brain is in front of goal, where a player fails to score because he can't bring the ball onto his weaker foot. Some of the points I am making may sound trivial until you realize what the lack of 'Two footedness' actually means. For one thing, it means the lack of collaboration between the right and the left side of the physical being which can be seen in areas of the game such as the midfield, for example, where the opponents can determine the direction of play. This is shown by the diagrams below where the nearest challenger for the ball can expose the reality of a lack of two footedness and actually take control of the game.

THE HIDDEN PROBLEMS

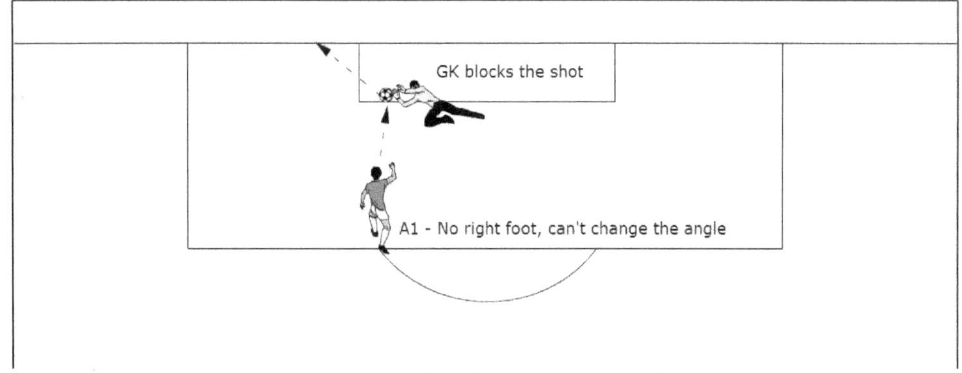

THE DEFENSE IS IN CONTROL OF THE DIRECTION TAKEN BY THE ATTACKING PLAYERS

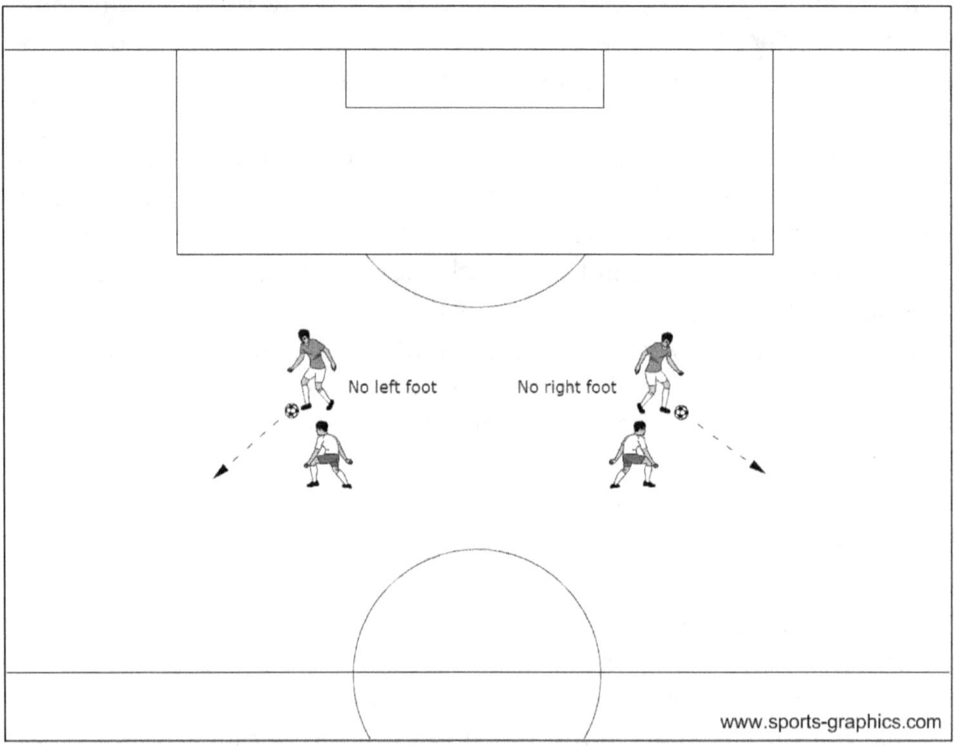

TEAM A - ONE FOOTED - NO COLLABORATION

The hidden problems of one footedness actually contribute to a lowering of playing standards, which is the point raised by the above reality. These issues have simply been ignored for many years in the name of second ball game interests, even when the quality of the work on the field of play was obviously inadequate. Worst of all is the reality that the one footedness of the player was never questioned, but was in fact hidden by coaching solutions such as the drill format that is shown in the next diagram. This type of coaching solution is totally devoid of any concerns for the one footedness of the individual player, or his lack of skills. By applying the drill format to the coaching regime, the coach can enforce a second ball game philosophy, in which case the players are subjected not only to keeping their functional role, but will also have additional constraints imposed on their game. The additional constraints can involve such methods as conditioning the players to make a specific number of contacts/touches with the ball, i.e. one-touch or two-touch drills.

THE DRILL

GOING THROUGH THE MOTIONS

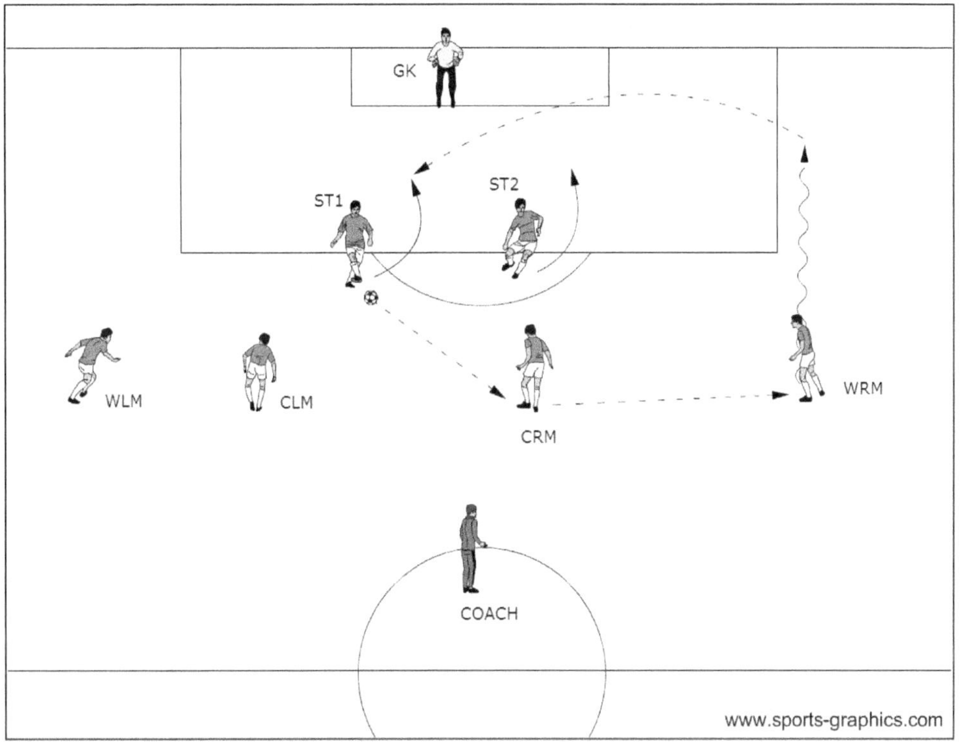

In this type of coaching method the players are only expected to fulfill their functional role. It is essentially like a boxer practicing shadow boxing, with no opponents on the pitch. The word drill does nothing to actually describe this way of working because all it is, in practical terms, is the practice of a pre -set pass and move pattern to a working sequence that is not concerned with the technical details. The players simply do their best to follow instructions and work the ball to the pre-set patterns determined by the coach, as shown by the following examples.

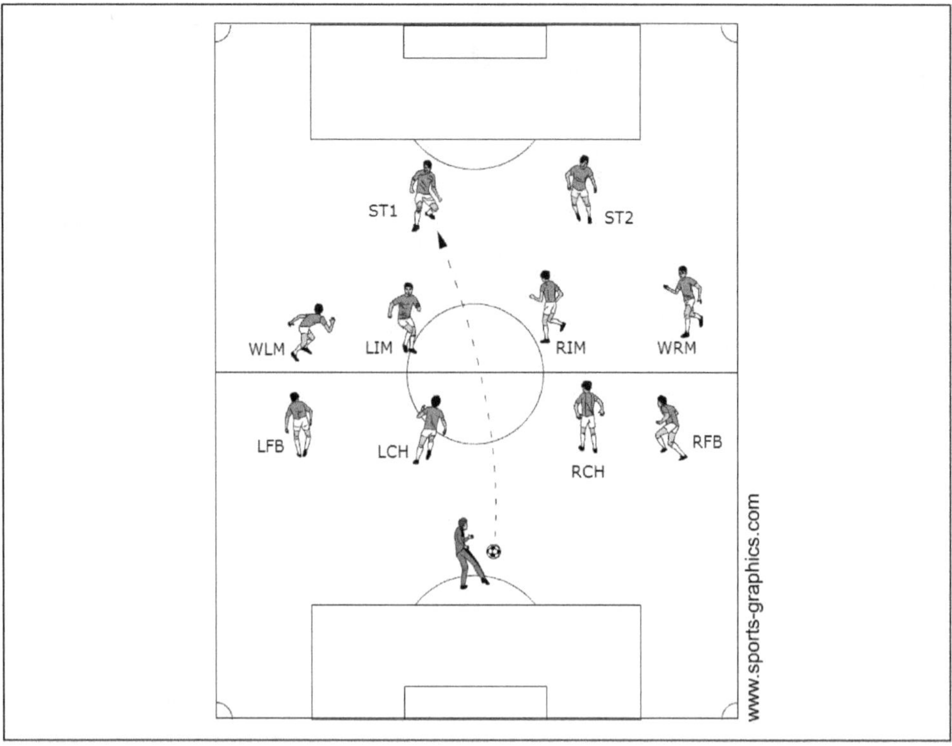

MOVEMENT PATTERN

The coach can plan a movement pattern which can vary to whatever he wishes. Here is a sample of what the Coach has planned. In this one the Coach begins the moves by playing the long ball to one of the strikers, let's see how the game plan unfolds:

NEXT
LAY THE BALL BACK

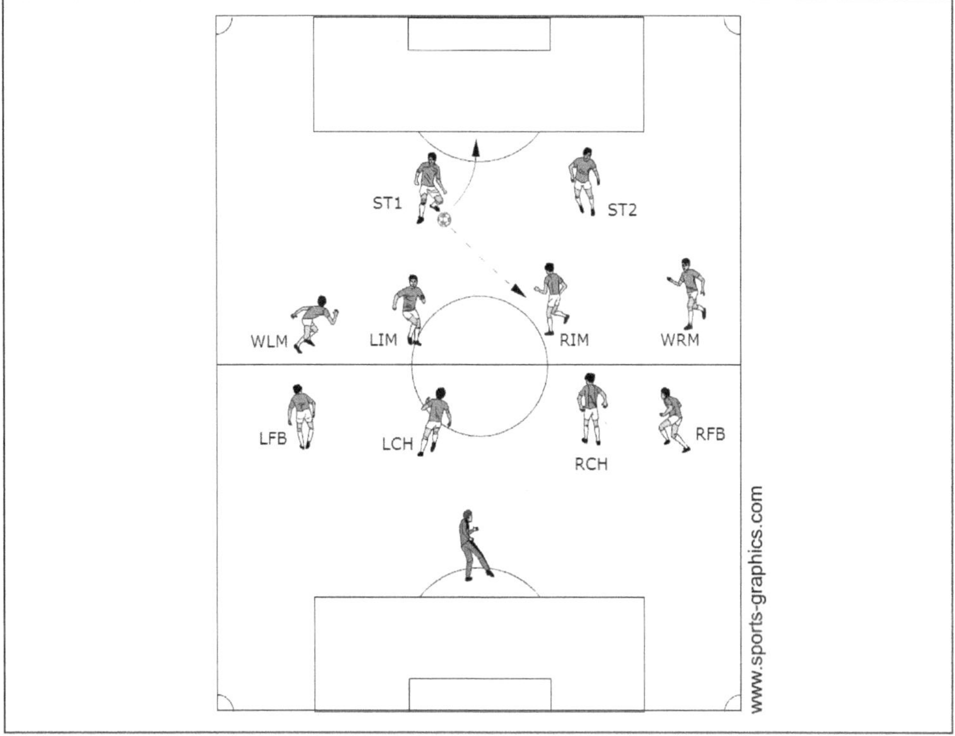

It is simply accepted that the STR1 (Striker) can control the ball on his first touch and has the ability to keep the ball long enough to make good use of it. With his next move, he plays the ball to the right center midfield player and turns away, moving off to the direction of the opponent's penalty area.

Note - Playing to the functional expectations, the striker at this point is not expected to interact with the midfield player but to simply turn off the pass and move to the direction of the penalty area, where his next function will be to hopefully get on the end of the cross into the box.

NEXT

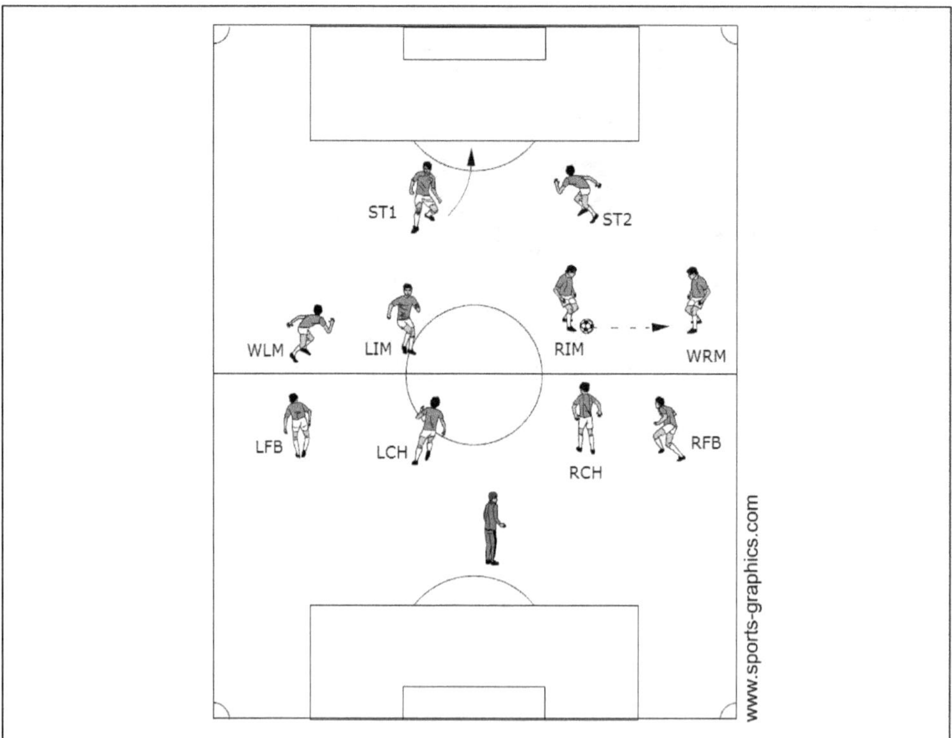

On receiving the ball from the striker, the right central midfield player RCMP plays the ball out to his wide right side midfield player, at which point he also has completed his functional role and will simply let events unfold.

NEXT

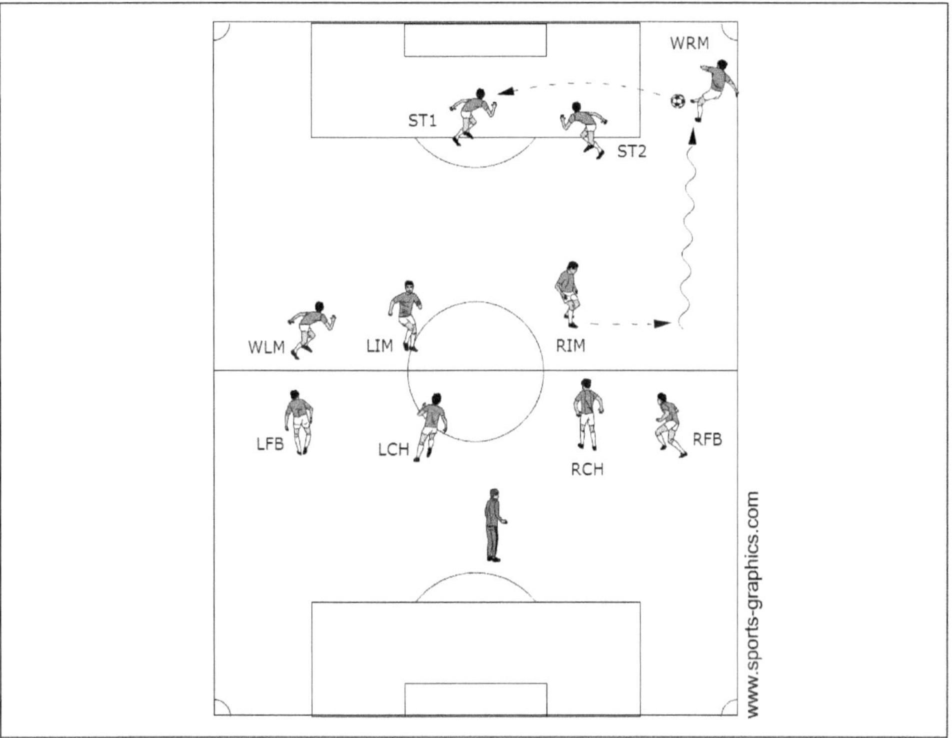

Events unfolding - The wide right midfield player takes up the ball and begins his run down the channel. At some point in the run (can be determined by the coach) he will attempt to cross the ball into the penalty area to the striker.

NEXT
THE END PRODUCT

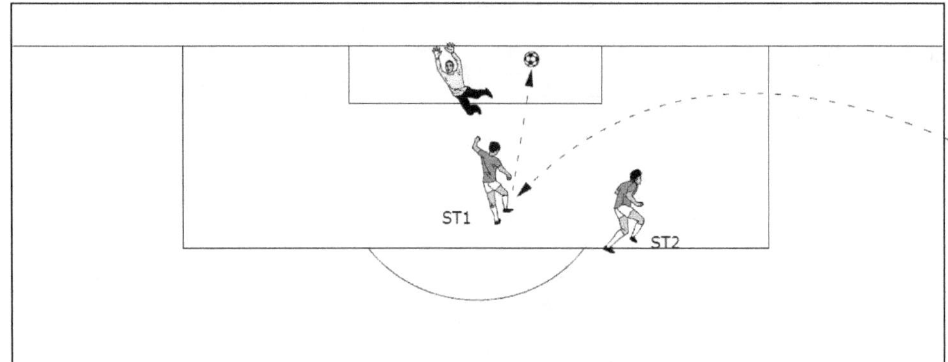

The striker's functional role - The end product is to get the strikers on the end of the cross of the ball into the box and to score a goal. The hope is that the right wide midfield player will send a decent cross into the opponent's penalty box and the strikers will get on the end of the cross and score a goal.

Note - In a pre- planned movement pattern such as this, the players not directly involved with play keep the rest of the team shape in place, which is obviously the functional reality. However, not being involved has its downside too, because doing nothing contributes to no development.

The more obvious names for the player within the team shape. Just a reminder that in order to keep things simple, depending on the topic for discussion I will at times just have the letter A for the team in possession of the ball and the letter D for the team that doesn't have possession of the ball. The letter A therefore can stand for the player/team in possession of the ball. The letter D can stand for the defender nearest to the player in possession of the ball and therefore for the team in the defensive phase of the game.

3 - THE CONTROLLED ENVIRONMENT

The above reality brings me to reflect on the manager and his role in this functional game of soccer. There are managers in the game, even today, who prefer to work with players who accept the reality of the functional role. Some managers even prefer players who don't have a great deal of talent but are big and strong and will run all day long. The coaching priorities for the functional role can be defined as the development of strength, fitness, competitiveness, running with the ball, hard work ethic, battling attributes and so on. I do concede that some of the above working objectives can't be faulted. I have given a mark out of ten for each of the main attributes a functional player will have. Believe it or not, the benchmark for the functional defender when it comes to the resulting playing attributes applies to all the functional players, no matter what position in the team they aspire to. The forward moving mentality, together with the long ball game, ensures this to be the case. Please note that so far I have not mentioned the goalkeeper. This is because in a functional training session the goalkeepers usually work separately from the rest of the players in the team and are only included when the coach organizes a game of soccer, or if the coach decides to work on crosses of the ball and finishing etc. The result of functional training on the individual can be observed in the physical and technical playing attributes which are as follows:

ATTRIBUTES OF THE FUNCTIONAL PLAYER (out of 10)

HEADING ABILITY	-	6
TACKLING ABILITY	-	6
KICKING THE LONG BALL	-	10
PASSING THE BALL SHORT	-	5
BALL CONTROL SKILLS	-	5
THE FIRST TOUCH ABILITY	-	5
A COMPETITIVE ATTITUDE	-	10
CONCENTRATION	-	10
TEAM GAME MENTALITY	-	10
PASSING THE BALL LONG	-	10
CREATIVITY	-	5

There are logical assumptions here in terms of the marks given for certain aspects in the game to the functional player. Playing like with like will produce a similar game, in which case the defender will have to deal with lots of crosses into his defensive area and when in possession of the ball have the ability to kick the long ball out of the defensive third. In a functional game of soccer the player doesn't need a high level of ball control skills as such.

THE RESULTING ATTRIBUTES

Keeping the players to a minimalistic forward moving functional role that ensures a certain level of competence and results in making the game look busy is actually very simple. The coach just has to employ a functional training session.

DESCRIBING THE FUNCTIONAL TRAINING SESSION

A functional training session begins with a warm up. In preparation to the training session, the warm up can involve the following examples of physical movement patterns. In keeping to the functional expectations, and therefore to the team spirit of the functional game, the warm up will take place in a group setting. In a functional training session the players gather together in a group at the outset of the training session and go together to do the warm up, in which case they can implement the following movement patterns if they wish into their warm up routine. The diagram also explains the type of general fitness/running patterns used in a typical functional training session.

PHYSICAL FITNESS FOR THE FUNCTIONAL GAME

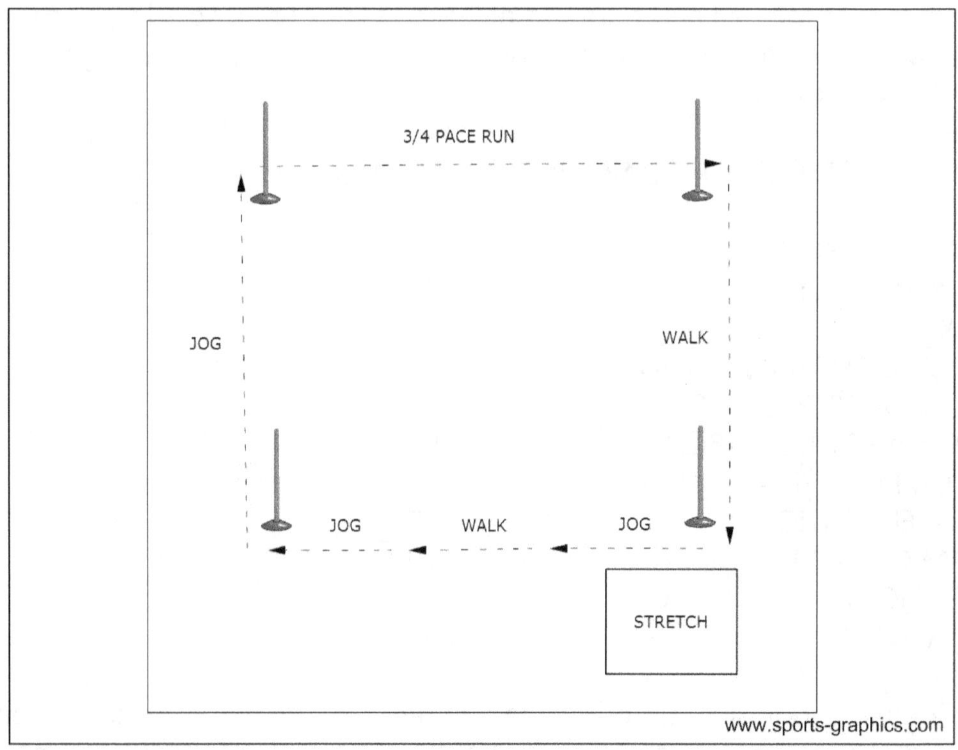

THE STANDARD SOLUTIONS

The group approach does instill a feeling of togetherness which is not a bad thing in its own right and is obviously helpful in situations where the players lack the skills to keep the ball long enough to control the game. The time taken to do a warm up in a group setting can be as little as fifteen minutes.

PART 2 OF THE FUNCTIONAL TRAINING SESSION

The introduction of the ball into the working equation takes place in part two of the functional training session. The principles of work keep in line with the expectations of the functional game where the player is not expected to keep the ball at his feet (save for the recent coaching idea which is to run with the ball in the attacking third of the field of play) but to move the ball on. In this group work, the players make up a circle about 15 yds across. The players who make up the circle practice passing the ball to each other while under pressure from the two players inside the circle, whose job is to try to intercept the ball. The level of effort here is in keeping with the minimalistic approach, in which the eight players that make up the circle do very little while the two inside the circle do the hard work.

GROUP ORIENTATED SOLUTIONS

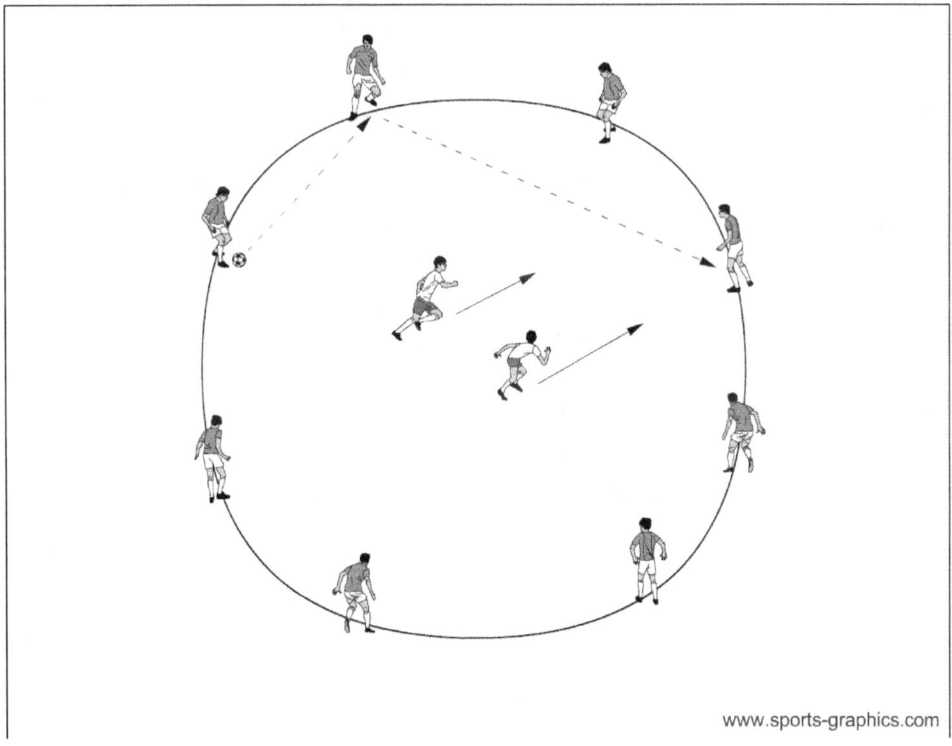

AN ALTERNATIVE TO PART TWO

Format B

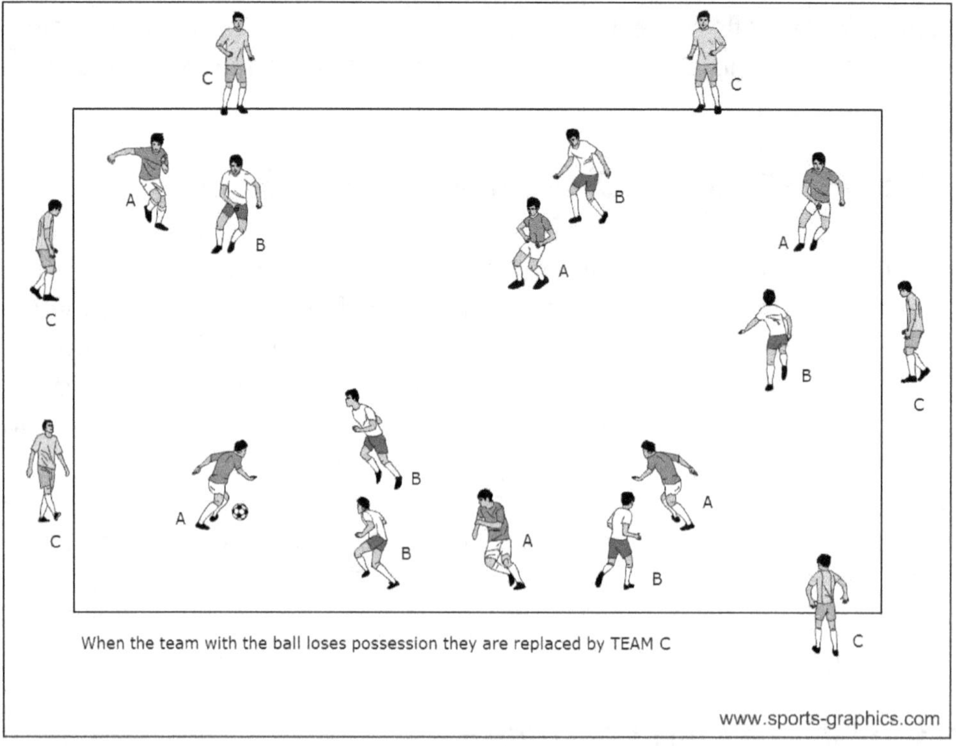

The level of effort is usually dependent on what takes place during the working week. If, for example, the team is coming off a competitive match day and a subsequent day off, part two of the functional training session would be based on the easy option, in which case the coach would employ the above mentioned circle format. If, on the other hand, the coach is concerned about the players' fitness levels for the upcoming match, then part two of the functional training session would involve a more fitness orientated endeavour, an example of which can be seen in Format B. Format B is a contrived game, not a proper game of soccer as such, but a game where the players are only permitted to take two contacts with the ball, which is inclusive of the actual pass to a teammate. A simple game of keep ball - Team A tries to keep the ball and Team B tries to take the ball away. When team A loses the ball to team B for whatever reason, Team A steps down and Team C steps in to compete for possession of the ball against Team B.

PART THREE OF THE TRAINING SESSION

PRACTICE PLAYING THE GAME OF SOCCER

THE FULL SIDED GAME ON A SMALL PITCH

The training session can end with yet another contrived reality. In part three of the training session the exercise can be a proper competitive game of soccer. However, there are artificial conditions imposed on the players that will make it very difficult for them to actually play the game. The contrived reality this time around is created by having lots of players packed into a tight working area and once again conditioning them to two touches. The objectives set by the tight playing area and the conditions imposed on the players regarding the way they have to work with the ball is not a part of any quest to develop the skilful player. On the contrary, conditioning the players to a minimum number of contacts with the ball in this type of game is directly related to the needs of the functional reality and therefore the needs of the second ball game. The objectives for the functional game of soccer come naturally in this type of reality because it creates a busy game, where the competitive mentality, hard tackling, running and physical strength come to the forefront of the players' endeavours.

THE BATTLING CONTRIVED GAME V THE FUNCTIONAL STRUCTURED GAME

Having worked the players in a chaotic environment, with imposed conditions in a tight area, the Coach can change the format and introduce the actual structured functional game of soccer. In the above example, most of the players try to keep the shape while the coach works on getting his left sided full back to move forward and overlap the midfield and run forward with the ball at his feet into the attacking third.

Note - In addition to the work that I have described thus far, it is not unusual for the players to work with weights in the gym or even play five a side or even organise a game of head tennis. Set pieces, like the taking of free kicks in the final third, is something that happens at the end of the training session from time to time. Probably because it is a skills orientated reality and one that requires individual input, most free kicks are designated to the one player in the functional team that can kick the ball to the quality that's required.

4 - THE CREATION OF THE HYBRID GAME

FROM THE FUNCTIONAL TO THE HYBRID

THE COMPROMISE SOLUTION

In England there is now another version of the game which is neither a functional game nor a first ball game. I call this new game the hybrid game. How did the hybrid game come about in some countries of Europe, in particular in England? The answer to that question is simple, football (soccer) is BIG business. With the influx of foreign billionaire ownership, clubs are able to bring in the best players in the world and are no longer limited to home grown talent, talent that in the case of England is more often than not a product of functional development and less skilful players. The mix of home grown players with these foreign players and managers, who generally aspire to a more skilful game of soccer, has led to this hybrid reality.

BUILDING THE HYBRID TEAM

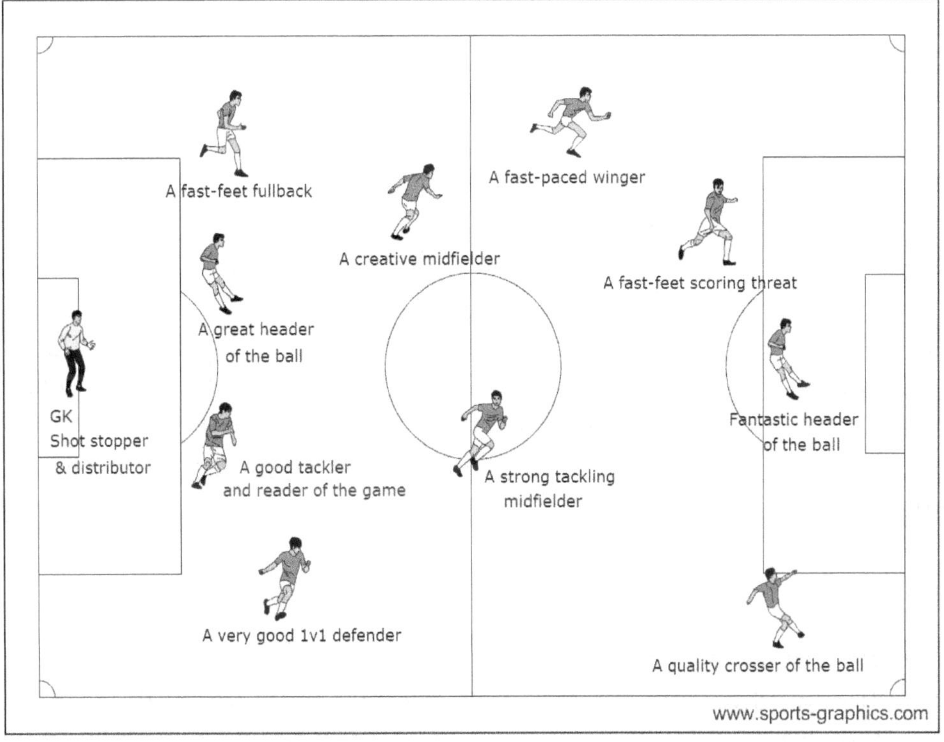

THE FUNCTIONAL GAME V THE HYBRID GAME

When the team is made up of players that are not of the same mould and are different from each other in terms of their abilities, the result is a game of soccer that is not functional but one of a hybrid reality. Of course, how big a change to the way the game is played is all down to what a quality player is all about. For example, what is meant by such reference points as a 'goal scoring talent' or a 'creative midfield player' etc. Below you can see the playing attributes that can change the way the game is played. These have been given marks out of 10. Examples of hybrid teams in England would be Manchester City, Arsenal, and Chelsea. All have bought impact players that can change the game from functional to skilful, and therefore hybrid, in an instant.

ATTRIBUTES OF THE HYBRID PLAYER (out of 10)

HEADING ABILITY	-	10
TACKLING ABILITY	-	7
KICKING THE LONG BALL	-	8
PASSING THE BALL SHORT	-	8
BALL CONTROL SKILLS	-	8
THE FIRST TOUCH ABILITY	-	8
A COMPETITIVE ATTITUDE	-	10
CONCENTRATION	-	10
TEAM GAME MENTALITY	-	8
PASSING THE BALL LONG	-	7
CREATIVITY	-	8

The playing attributes vary in players. Some of the players, like the striker for example, may be a 10 at heading the ball but only an 8 in other respects. The same reality applies to all the players in a hybrid team. The point is that each player is different and it is this difference between them that makes for the hybrid game of soccer.

THE HYBRID GAME OF SOCCER

When it comes to raising the playing standard in England, and in most countries of Europe, the best that anyone can do under the present circumstances is to create the hybrid game. There are exceptions to this, the most obvious being the country of Spain and in particular Barcelona FC. Barcelona FC play the first ball game. But for the most part, the hybrid game is the best that most can aspire to because there are teams that still use a structured formation and this has its own implications. It is, for example, not realistic to ignore the fact that in the English Premiership, some of the teams have players that are functional to such an extent that they hardly ever venture beyond the halfway line and keep most of the team shape behind the ball. Since most of the teams resort to a rigid defense structure and use a double bank of four to five players in their defensive line up, everyone keeps to a team structure that can match any team shape, especially during the defensive phase, when any team, no matter what type of game they represent, can be vulnerable to counter attacking play. Given the mixed bag of realities in the English Premiership, for example, the team shape must cover for both the attacking phase and the defensive phase of the game and so the team shapes as such have not changed much in recent years. When it comes to the playing standards, therefore, these have been raised to the hybrid level by the quality of the players selected for certain positions in the team shape and it is this that has made the difference to how the game is played.

IMPLEMENTING THE PLAYING ATTRIBUTES

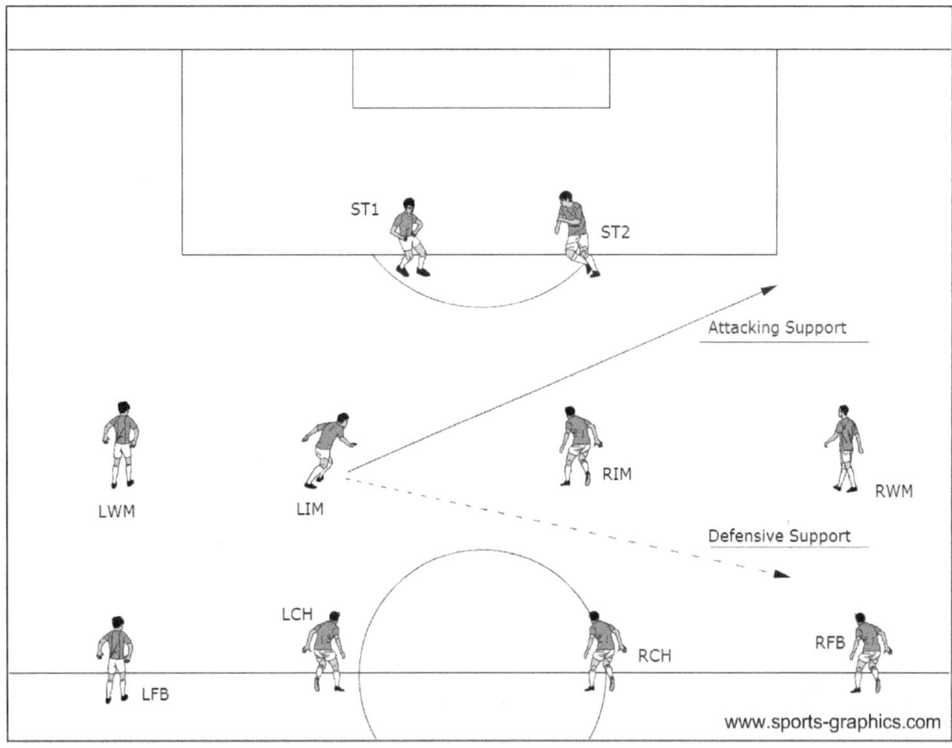

LEFT SIDED MIDFIELD PLAYER WORKING THE DIAGONAL LINE

The tactical patterns for the individual player as seen here and in the next couple of examples are not new to the game of soccer. However, they do point out things the manager can do to implement changes to the main team shape as a result of having skilful options. In this example, the left sided midfield player is instructed to work along a diagonal line of action in both the attacking phase of the game (see the solid arrow) and the defensive phase (see the dashed arrow). Working the diagonal line in the attacking phase has its aim, which is to destabilize the opponent's defensive team shape by creating a 2v1, especially useful if the opponent uses a zone type defense. On the other hand, when the team has lost possession of the ball and is on the defensive, LSMP can track back to help protect the front of his defense, right up to his right full back.

PLAYING WITH WIDTH

Having two skilful wide players with plenty of pace and the ability to send quality crosses into the opponent's penalty area can make a big difference to the manager's game plan. The idea would be to get the midfield players to play the ball to the wide left sided player or the wide right sided player and for the wide players to then move the ball beyond the opposing full backs in order to get as many crosses into the penalty area as possible.

If the wing back players possess a fantastic level of stamina, the game plan is based on both wing backs working up and down the channel on the left and right of the team shape. They take part in the attacking phase of the game when the team has possession of the ball and in the defensive phase of the game when the team loses possession of the ball.

A SUMMARY OF THE HYBRID GAME

Unlike the rigid functional roles of the second ball game, the hybrid team uses specialised players in different positions who can be given a license to implement their technical know how into the unfolding reality of the game. In a hybrid team, most of the players are unlike the simple functional player because whether they have a specialised role or not, all of them can contribute more to the team as a result of having the better skills base and the better technical playing repertoire than those who have played predominantly in the second ball game, where the ball is likely to be more in the air than on the ground.

THE NOT SO COMFORTABLE TRUTH

A game plan can only be effective if you have the right players behind it with the right physical and technical attributes to carry it out. Some experts on the game of soccer talk up the team shape as if it is the magical combination to unlock the door to victory, failing to mention anything about the quality or the lack of quality players in the game. Sometimes, we can see the politics of it all played out prior to a game of soccer on the television pre-game shows. One false perception sold by some punters who have a clear interest in the second ball game is this idea that the Barcelona game is based on the 4-3-3 team shape. This is totally misleading! - No mention of the goalkeeper in the team shape, for example (more about that reality in a minute).

In England, the players interpret the 4-3-3 team shape according to a set of functional roles. Most of the players maintain the rigid formation of the 4-3-3 throughout the match, in both the attacking phase and the defensive phase. For a first ball team such as Barcelona, on the other hand, the 4-3-3 team shape is simply a general description of their starting positions before the ball is kicked into play. The Barcelona players don't play to any rigid team shape, no matter what the phase of the game. In reality it is difficult to state exactly what shape the Barcelona players create because the shape changes constantly when in the attacking phase of the game and they only resort to constructing a team shape when they have not managed to win the ball back quickly (within five or six seconds). The major difference, therefore, lies in the reality that Barcelona do not keep to a rigid team formation during the game and this is more than obvious when they lose possession of the ball and because their team shape is so fluent they generally win the ball back with numbers within five or six seconds. They will most certainly not employ, for example, a zone marking defense as such. We will look at the way Barcelona defend in a minute. For now, the point is that talking up the team shape as if it's the solution to everything, rather than talking about the quality of the players in the team shape, lends itself to some handy misinterpretations of the realities on the field of play.

THE GOALKEEPING IMPLICATION

Take, for example, the hidden reality within the above diagram with its lack of information that is not so readily given by the punters on television. When the punters describe the team shape of Barcelona as the 4-3-3, you never hear any of them describe it as the 1-4-3-3. In other words, the Barcelona goalkeeper, as far as they are concerned, is not worthy of a mention. For me it is interesting to note just why that is the case because it's important to the understanding of the coaching mentality. Why anyone would omit the goalkeeper from the team shape is actually an interesting question. I can begin to answer it in the following way: In reality the 4-3-3 team shape played to the functional expectation is very much different to that of the first ball game interpretation of the same team shape. In the functional role the goalkeeper does not often interact with any of his back four defenders. When it comes to describing the expectations of the goalkeeper in a functional game of soccer, he has two primary roles: 1 - To stop the shots on goal and, therefore, prevent the opponents from scoring a goal and 2 - To kick the long ball down the pitch as far as he can.

5 - COACHING THE FIRST BALL GAME

My coaching philosophy was born on the realization that the first ball game is not a forward moving functional game of soccer. When the first ball game team works the ball to a sequence of short and even longer passes of the ball, this means having the appropriate skills to be able to do that and the correct numbers of players in the vicinity of the ball, which enables the team to play the more creative game of soccer. It is also true that the number of players in the vicinity of the ball gives the first ball game team the ability to win the ball back quickly should they lose possession of the ball. The following diagrams will show how a first ball game team wins the ball back and how they go about keeping the ball, not only to take control of the game but also to create goal scoring opportunities. The following examples come from an actual game between Italy and Spain in the European Championship of 2012, but could equally well apply to the way Barcelona play. The first example shows the Spanish players moving in on the midfield player for Italy who is in possession of the ball from almost all directions and winning the ball back.

SPAIN WIN THE BALL BACK - NOT IN ZONE DEFENSE MODE DEFEND IN NUMBERS

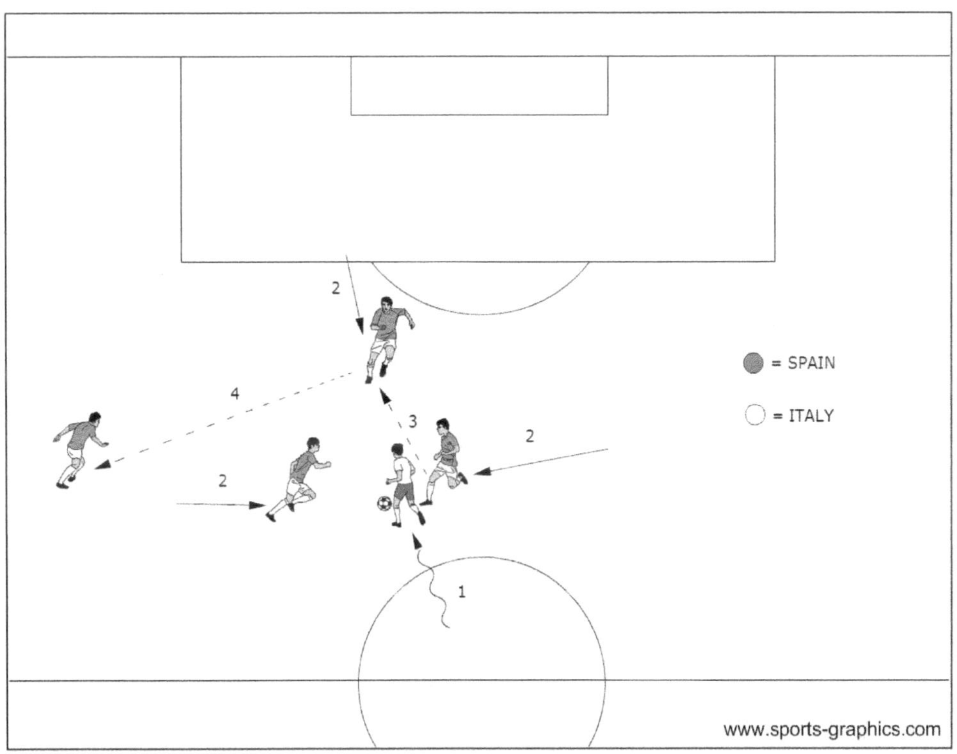

Unlike the zone marking system that has crept into the more functional game of soccer in recent years, the first ball game team brings into action the proper defense strategy which is based on 'Nearest man to the ball' - In the first ball game, the nearest man to the ball puts immediate pressure on the opponent who has the ball at his feet. This pressure is always supported with help. When the ball is won, it is immediately played to the player outside of the immediate vicinity of the ball, usually to the second man in free space. The team then kicks into gear and goes again into the attacking phase of the game. Unlike what takes place in the functional game of soccer, the playing direction will not be just forward moving, because the ball doesn't always go forward no matter what, but can just as easily end up going back to the goalkeeper. What matters most is not giving the ball away cheaply.

A SKILLS BASED REALITY

When playing the first ball game, the ball often ends up with the goalkeeper who, unlike in the functional game of soccer, is actually an integral part of the game plan.

THE WORKING PHILOSOPHY : WIN IT BACK - KEEP IT. DON'T GIVE THE BALL AWAY CHEAPLY!

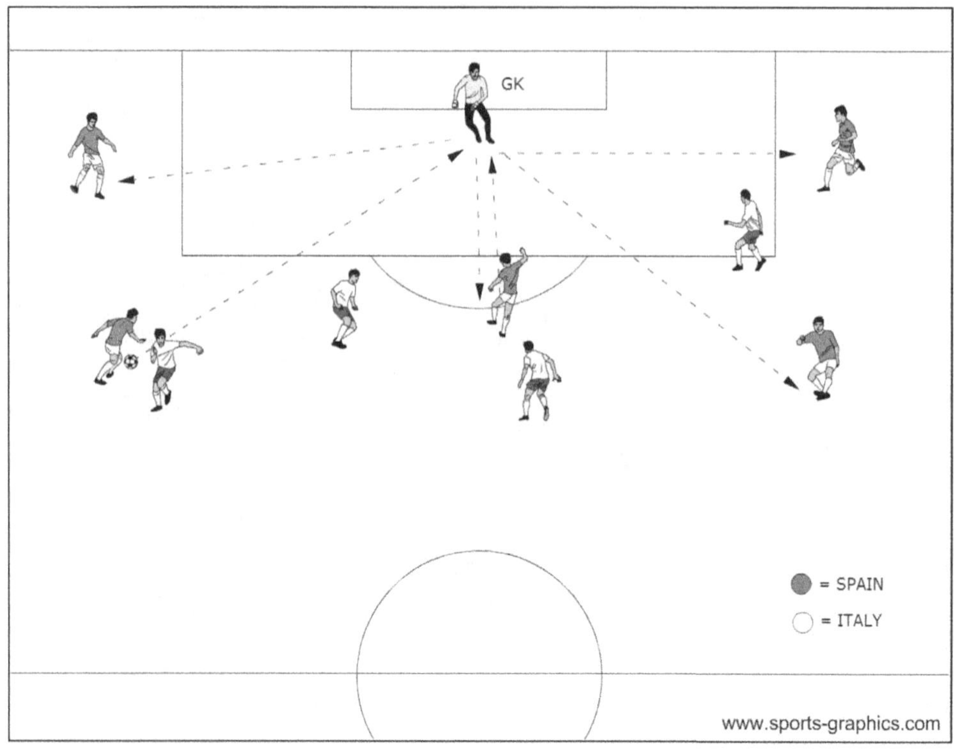

When the first ball game goalkeeper receives the ball, he is expected to use the ball skillfully and to in effect be an outfield player as well as a goalkeeper and help the team to begin the counter attacking moves by working the ball to any of the players to the front or side of his position. Describing the reality here for the first ball game goalkeeper and the team as such is actually one of the best ways of recognizing the difference between the first ball game and the functional game of soccer.

In the above diagram the goalkeeper in effect acts as an extra player and therefore has the license to play the short or the longer pass option to any of his teammates. The expectations require the goalkeeper to be a proper skilled player and the same applies to the players in front of his goal area and beyond. The finish to one of the typical counter attacking moves can be seen in the next diagram. This diagram shows what happens when one team employs a zone marking mentality, which is the most vulnerable way of defending.

SPAIN - THE COUNTER ATTACKING MOVES CREATING A GOAL SCORING OPPORTUNITY GOAL FOR SPAIN!

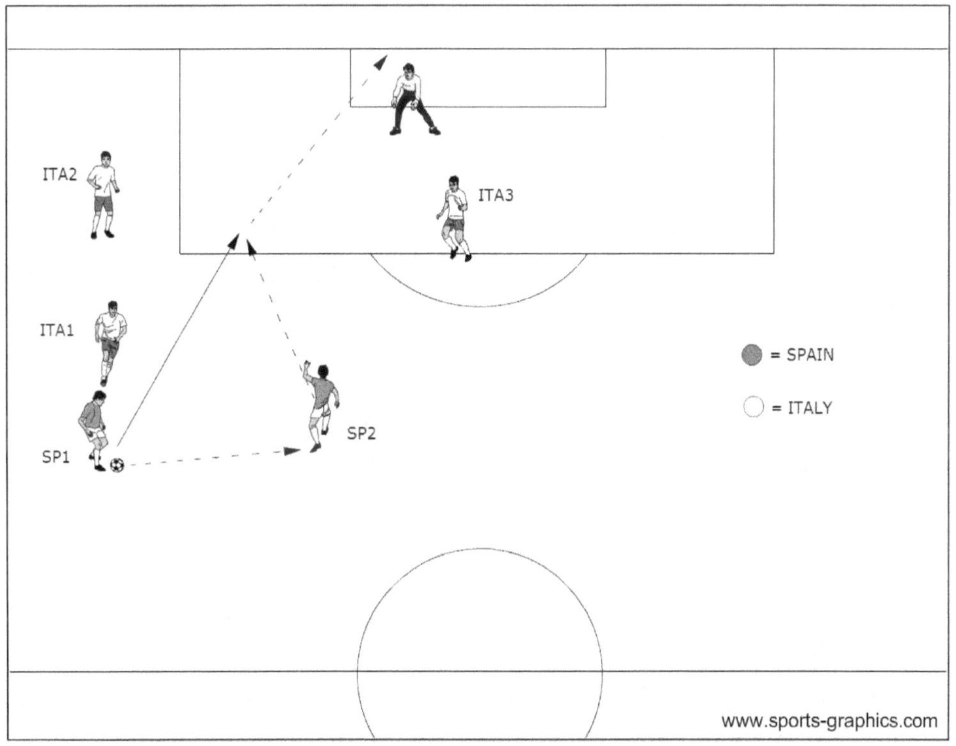

In the above example of a goal scoring opportunity for Spain, the reality unfolded around a simple truth: the principles of defense based on the nearest man to the ball as far as the functional game of Italy was concerned, didn't exist. In the unfolding drama, player ITA1 for Italy should have gone with the runner, in other words, he should have challenged SPN1, but because he was zone marking his designated area, he did not respond in any way to the run by SPN1. In fact, nobody did! SPN1 plays the ball to SPN2, moves quickly forward, and takes up the return pass from SPN2. He then moves to the inside line of attack, leaving ITA2 (the right full back of Italy) now on his left shoulder, and moves forward free as a bird to strike the ball home. Goal to Spain! Spain faulted recently in the European Championships of 2016 when it was Italy's turn to gain the upper hand and put Spain out of the competition.

THE RESULTING FIRST BALL GAME MENTALITY

The truth is simple, playing the ball out from the back requires a great deal of skill in both the defensive ability to win the ball back without fouling the opponent and in keeping possession of the ball. The examples here show the proper way of playing soccer. The punters would have you believe otherwise and keep quiet about the difference between hoofing the long ball down the field of play and working the ball out from the back of the team shape. This is because they know that the difference is all down to the ability of the players. None of them mention the goalkeeper in the team shape because they know that working the ball out from the back requires skillful players, whereas hoofing the long ball does not. The choice of how to play the game of soccer is down to the coach. I am not going to make that choice for anyone, but I do know that I personally would never work with any player in a way that makes him a second ball game player, under any circumstances. The forward moving mentality with its functional player role, backed by coaching solutions such as drills and conditioned games, takes away the opportunity for any young player to be a first ball game player. All functional training solutions result in a heavy set player, and a heavy set player has the type of physical attributes that have their limitations when it comes to the skilful game of soccer.

THE FIRST BALL GAME TRAINING SESSION

When it comes to the first ball game, the first thing to understand is the effect of any form of training on the physical being. When it comes to the first ball game, the coaching method is based on a different reality to that of the functional one because the work is directly relevant to the first ball game. Just one of the most important considerations from a first ball game point of view is the well balanced development of the physical being. By balanced, I mean the correct balance between the fast and slow twitch muscle forms. It is this balance that makes all the difference to the player in terms of his playing qualities. Not everyone appreciates the fact that functional training favors the development of slow twitch muscles, and if the physique is built on slow twitch muscles, this does result in a heavy set player and a heavy set player will not be as agile or as mobile or as effective on the skills side of the game as a player who has a more balanced physical reality, one that ensures the development of fast twitch muscle forms to the correct proportions in relation to the slow twitch muscle forms.

THE GIVEN DIFFERENT ENVIRONMENTS

The science can point to the fact that most human beings have a 50 - 50 make up between the slow and fast twitch muscle forms in the body. That may be the case under normal sedentary circumstances, but when you examine what happens to participants in certain sporting endeavours then clearly the ratio of 50 - 50 changes. I believe that it is possible to alter the ratio of muscle composition with either the aerobic or the anaerobic state of being and for me the all important factor in terms of what type of development takes place is all about the ratios of work between the aerobic and anaerobic states. The science factors indicate that activities which promote normal oxygen intake, such as sitting down in a classroom, watching television at home, playing games on a computer and, get this, even participating in training sessions where the actual effort is sporadic, the participant can end up with a dominance of slow twitch muscle forms and the problem of carrying too much fat around the body. A physique built on slow twitch muscle forms will often be big and strong, but when it comes to performing the actual skills of soccer this predominantly slow twitch, unbalanced body type is most certainly not the ideal reality.

6 - DEFINING THE SKILLS OF SOCCER

The easiest of moments during the game of soccer to note the difference between a bad player, a good player and a great player, is when the player takes control of the ball and after that single moment what he does with it. What end product can the player put into action? Will it benefit the team? Can it create something special, like a pass that opens up a goal scoring opportunity, or even a goal itself? Whatever the outcome, the sequence of events will unfold from a single touch to the ball, the touch that can make anything possible.

There is a hidden reality that is rarely talked about and yet every coach should know about it's consequences. Namely, it is the lack of 'Two footedness'. It so happens that in the majority of players (over 90%) it is the right foot that is favored. Why this is the case is a matter of development.

DEVELOPMENT CONSIDERATIONS

Allow me to use the following analogy: Every child is born with a brain that is not programmed. It is like an empty computer disk. But given the input from its surroundings, the disk will be full of all sorts of information and ideas that will result in development, on both the physical and the mental side of the human being. The initial development of the brain takes place as a result of the child interacting with family members and this development goes hand in hand with the development of the physical being. The two are inarguably linked. When the interaction with the family members takes place naturally, most people will develop the use of the right hand and therefore the use of the left side of the brain and with that reality the predominant use of the right side of the physical being. Many coaches fail to see the hidden implications of the natural consequences. If the training method ignores the lack of 'Two footedness' and supports the use of the right foot only, the player will simply be in a training environment that will continue to develop the left side of the brain and as a result there will be no effective collaboration between the left and the right side of the brain. The lack of collaboration in the brain leaves players, through no fault of their own, in the wrong development program, one that will have the hidden effect of a lack development on one side of the physical being, which will then impact on the overall physical balance, which will in turn ensure weak points within the physical being, such as a weak, left foot/hand etc. If you are a coach that supports the functional game of soccer, and therefore the long ball game with its forward moving mentality, then none of this will matter to you, when it actually should! Someone taking up the game of soccer at a young age should never be exposed to a reality where the two footedness issues are ignored. Ignorance in these matters is not bliss, it is simply wrong! The first ball game development program pays attention to the development of the two sides of the brain, because that reality has it's implication to the development of the physical side of the human body. You can argue all you want about whether someone is or is not naturally right handed or one footed. The truth is that when it comes to playing the more skilful game of soccer, there is no choice but to work on the development of the collaboration between the left and the right side of the brain, because that quest is relevant to the development of the physical ability, without which the player could not possibly implement many of the type of skills that are required to create the first ball game. Any counter argument based on natural tendencies doesn't wash, because left to the natural state, the player will only be a one footed player. When the work is specific to the first ball game, the development of both the brain and the physical power of the human being is concentrated on two important areas that make the first ball game possible:

(A) THE FIRST TOUCH

1. MOVING THE BALL OFF THE LINE - THE LATERAL ANGLE IMPLICATION
2. THE EXTENDED TOUCH OPTION - A MULTI ANGLE IMPLICATION
3. THE SET UP TOUCH - OPENING THE ANGLE UP FOR PASSING THE BALL
4. THE REVERSE TOUCH - THE TURN OF THE BODY
5. THE DINK TOUCH - LIFTING THE BALL OVER AN OBSTACLE
6. THE ROLL TOUCH - MOVING THE BALL TO THE BACK OF THE OPPONENT

(B) PASSING TECHNIQUE

1. THE PASS OF THE BALL WITH THE LACES OF THE BOOT - A LONG PASS
2. THE PASS OF THE BALL WITH THE INSIDE INSTEP - A SHORT PASS
3. THE PASS OF THE BALL WITH THE OUTSIDE OF THE BOOT - ANGLED AND SHORT
4. PASSING THE BALL TO THE FORWARD ANGLE OPTION AND THE DIAGONAL ANGLE OPTION.

The structure of the first ball game training session covers all the angles. The first ball game theory is backed by special solutions. In the following diagrams we can note the position of the player A1 at the center of each solution. The position of the player at the center of the four cone placement, for example, is significant to the requirements of the first game, because it shows the balanced approach that ensures no bias towards the use of the right or the left foot. The angles shown by the arrows to the side, forward and back of the player, for example, require the use of both feet and are relevant to the above first touch options which we will mostly certainly discuss in detail in the appropriate chapter. The ability to play the game of soccer to the first ball game standard, as shown by Barcelona, for example, is actually dependent on the player's ability to perform the first touch options described on the previous page, none of which would be possible without proper development.

THE FIRST BALL GAME - CREATING THE 360 DEGREE CAPABILITY

The first ball game training session is obviously going to be different to that of the functional training session, where in practical terms, there was a three stage general approach to the player's development. Most of the work in the functional training session didn't, for example, concern itself with developing collaboration between the right and left side of the brain because it didn't need to. The first ball game is different. In the first ball game the players are expected to possess a wide range of playing skills, to be two footed and possess an excellent range of first touch options. We will look at the problems related to the lack of two footedness in more detail later, but for now you can see that there are a number of first touch options available to any player who is able to play the ball effectively with either foot. In addition to the above first touch skills repertoire for the first ball game, we can break down the qualities of each player and assess his development. One of the reasons for assessing the player is because the first ball game is very dependent on the reliability of the individual. Every player in the team has to perform to the best of his abilities all of the time and be on top of his game. If that is not the case and any player falls short of the mark, the team will falter. There is a fine line between failure and success and the first ball game player has to be able to perform to as near on a perfect mark out of 10 as possible.

ATTRIBUTES OF THE FIRST BALL PLAYER (out of 10)

HEADING ABILITY	-	8
TACKLING ABILITY	-	7
KICKING THE LONG BALL	-	8
PASSING THE BALL SHORT	-	10
BALL CONTROL SKILLS	-	10
THE FIRST TOUCH ABILITY	-	10
A COMPETITIVE ATTITUDE	-	10
CONCENTRATION	-	10
TEAM GAME MENTALITY	-	10
PASSING THE BALL LONG	-	10
CREATIVITY	-	10

High aspirations? Not really! The first ball game is demanding. It is not a game for the player who doesn't want to work hard on his game. The bench mark is a 10. Of course, it is a high mark that will almost be impossible to achieve in each of the areas stated. The point though, is that this bench mark is something that every young player should work towards. The first ball game is based on the player who reaches such levels of excellence, maybe not in every field of endeavour but most certainly in the majority of what is involved in the make up of the first ball game. Every player needs to deliver excellence in the areas shown, otherwise the team will falter.

Given the reality of the expectations of the more skilful game of soccer and therefore of the first ball game, the training session is much more involved than anything that is provided for by any functional training session. In order to achieve the many objectives of the first ball game, the training session is actually made up of a six stage approach. The aim of the training session is to cover as much of the make up of the first ball game as possible. By the make up of the first ball game I mean the type of physical attributes and skills required to play the first ball game.

SUMMING UP THE REALITY

When the training concepts are based on the forward moving mentality, it enforces the use of the one good foot to the ball. Just as serious is the reality that when working to the 'forward moving' dimension, there is no need for lateral thinking. Here are some important reasons for getting away from the functional reality and from the implementations of coaching solutions that simply cater for the use of the one good foot.

IGNORING THE OBVIOUS

If the training method ignores the issues of a lack of bilaterality, it is simply impossible for the players to play the game of soccer to the first ball game standard because a one footed player cannot apply the full range of first ball game touches to all possible angles of play. In functional training, with no lateral input in the working equation, the players end up one footed and unable to play the ball effectively on the one side of the body.

WITH COLLABORATION - DEVELOPING TWO FOOTEDNESS

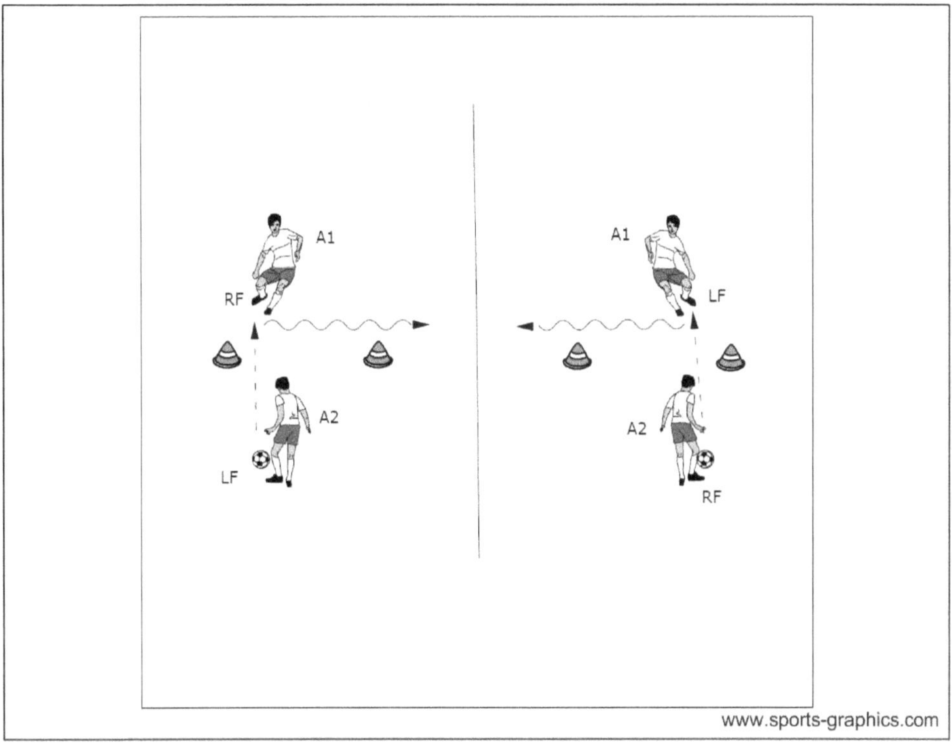

The above example of the skill known as moving the ball off the line contributes to the explanations of some of the major differences between the functional game of soccer and the first ball game, from again a playing point of view and also the coaching point of view. Moving the ball off the line is a first ball game touch option that opens up the angle of play to the front of the player. If the player is developed to a forward moving reality, he will not have the technical skills to perform this touch to the ball to all the angles possible. The touch discussed here, just like many of the first touch options that I have mentioned previously, requires development in training solutions that seriously employ the lateral based solutions that we will look at in the appropriate chapters on this subject.

THE BUILDING BLOCKS OF THE FIRST BALL GAME

The development of the first touch options for the first ball game cannot be achieved without first laying down the foundations for the physical ability to implement the first touch options to the ball. It would simply be pure nonsense to condition the players to two contacts and see that way of working with the players as a means of developing the first touch. For starters, there is no such thing as a single touch option, there are, as I have already pointed out, more than one touch option and even then some of the first touch options can be played to a number of directions, not just the one. You can be certain that conditioning the players to the two contacts of the ball will never develop the real first touch options to the ball. In order to achieve many of the first ball game objectives, of which, the first touch options is one, the player needs to be subjected to a training regime that must ensure the correct development of the physical and technical side of the first ball game.

THE 360° PLAYER

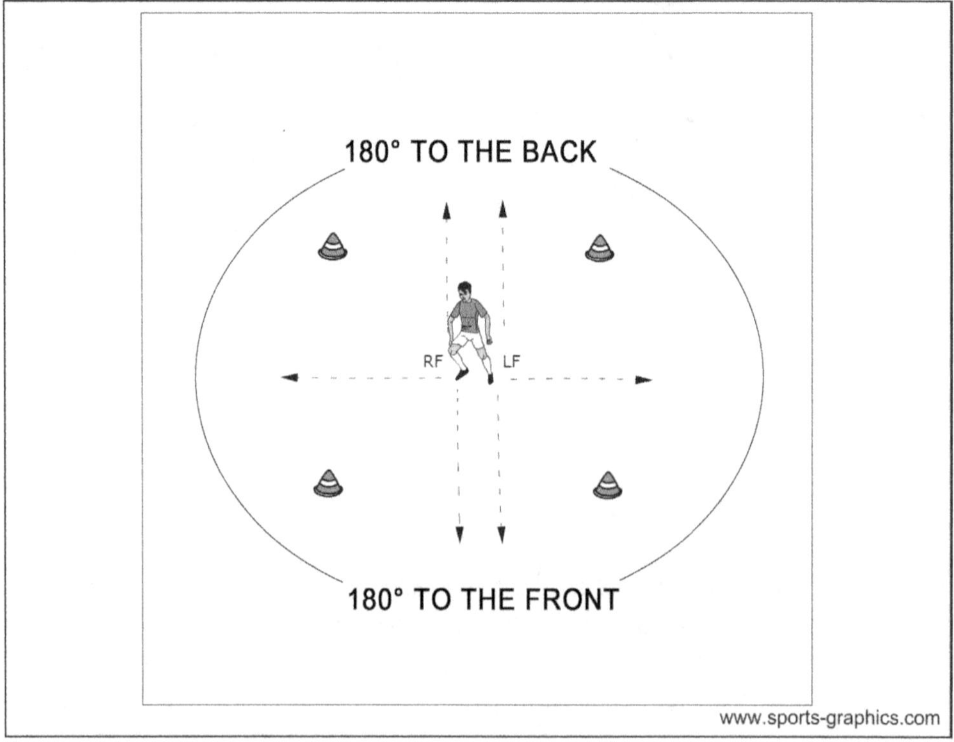

7 - THE DYNAMICS OF THE FIRST BALL GAME

The first ball game training session has a six stage approach. The reason for the six stage approach is that, unlike the functional game of soccer, the first ball game is based on players with a much greater range of soccer skills. The training solutions have to consider the reality that there are two types of physical actions that make up the first ball game of soccer, explosive and sedentary. It can be said that the explosive activities use the fast twitch muscle more so than the slow twitch muscle and, the sedentary activities use the slow twitch muscle more so than the fast twitch muscle. Therefore, it is important to note which activity is explosive and which is sedentary. The word explosive is perhaps somewhat over the top, but also appropriate, because it describes any fast physical movement with or without the ball. On the other hand, the word sedentary describes physical actions such as walking or standing still. The sedentary and the explosive actions are opposite extremes and of course there are moments which are in between the two, jogging being one example. It is logical to say that when the player receives the ball and has the ball at his feet, such a moment can be physically different to and much more challenging than any moment where the player does not have the ball. Trivial observations perhaps, but actually seriously important to the understanding of the coaching system I am about to introduce for the creation of the first ball game. The first ball game is not simply a forward moving game, where the forward running gate is the dominant physical movement feature. It is rather a game of soccer that is almost without limitations, where there are lots of movement forms involved, and in all directions.

A DIFFERENT THOUGHT PROCESS - AEROBIC TO ANAEROBIC

When a player receives the ball, the physical reality can change very quickly from an aerobic state to an anaerobic state. When it comes to the skilful game of soccer, where the ball is shared a lot because the game is based on keeping possession of the ball, the players will experience more of the anaerobic state of being than the aerobic. Keeping this in mind, the training session has to consider the development of the ability to cope with the most taxing of all physical conditions, namely, the anaerobic state of being, hence the different approach to the players' development.

STAGE ONE - THE WARM UP

I believe in the warm up, for all sorts of reasons, least of all because it is essential to the preparation of the work that follows. However, I don't believe that the warm up should be more than twenty minutes. In my training session, the warm up is very much controlled to make sure that it is injury free. The work begins with some static stretching work, concentrating on the hamstrings and calves. The players can then do the more dynamic work in the warm up, groin kicks - high leg kicks - jumps and so on. In addition to the static and dynamic stretches, the players can add more natural movement forms such as walking or light jogging.

THE CONTROLLED WARM UP FORMAT

The best way to control the warm up is to place the players in a circle and the circle itself can be made up of cone placements. The cone placements can be applied to instructional purposes. Each player, for example, is allocated a cone placement as his/her home base. Players listen to instructions and react accordingly - From cone to cone placement - jog one, walk one, this instruction is repeated until the coach changes his instructions - players listen for the next call. If the Coach calls 'Home base 1' - The players jog up to the center circle cone placement and back to their home base and stop to listen for the next call/instruction. Coach should work players in both directions. At the end of the warm up, the coach can create a little competition between the blue players and the red players.

THE WARM UP - IN CONTROL

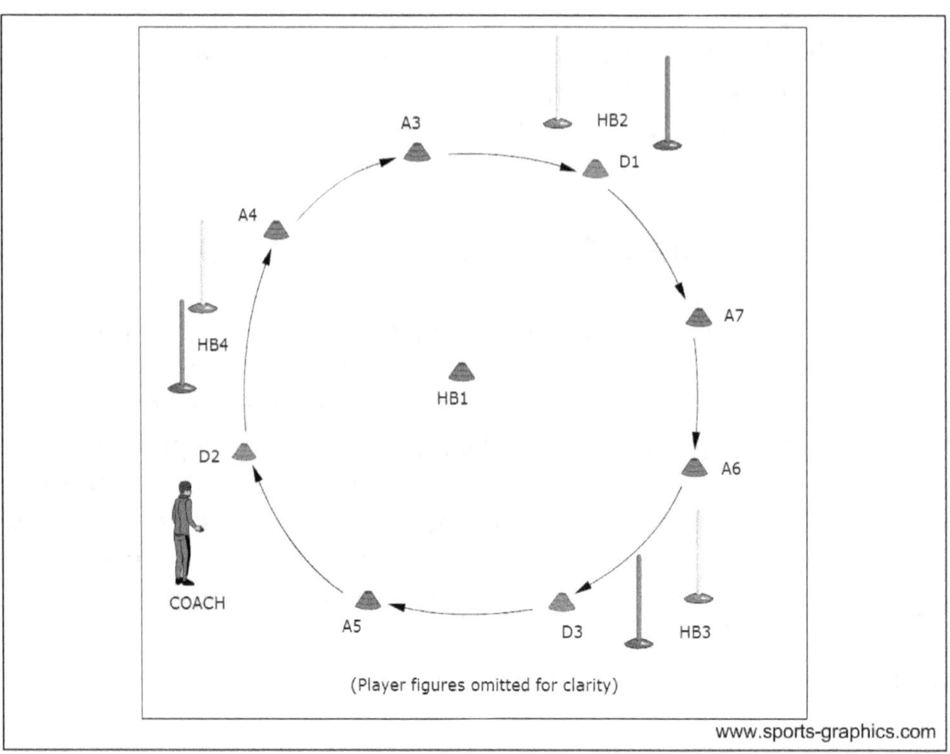

In this format, the range of coaching instructions to the players has almost no limitations. The coach is free to make up the instructions on the hoof (as he goes along). At the end of the warm up, the players can be asked to do some running because it is good to stretch the legs out.

STAGE TWO - SOCCER SKILL DYNAMICS

In stage two of the training session, we apply dynamic movement forms, ones that reflect the physiological changes from the anaerobic state to the aerobic state of being. This first example of dynamic work is relevant to all sorts of realities found within the first ball game. One such reality is the fact that playing the game of soccer can, without the right physical intervention, cause a shortening of the hamstring, simply because the running patterns are not sufficient to ensure the flexible conditioning of the muscles in that part of the leg. The counter to the lack of flexibility in the muscles is the work in stage two of the first ball game training session. The dynamic work is not just about ensuring the flexibility of the muscles, it is also a training solution that looks to work on the development of inner core strength and endurance, not to mention the small matter of the all-important leg movement coordination.

EXAMPLES OF DYNAMIC AGILITY WORK

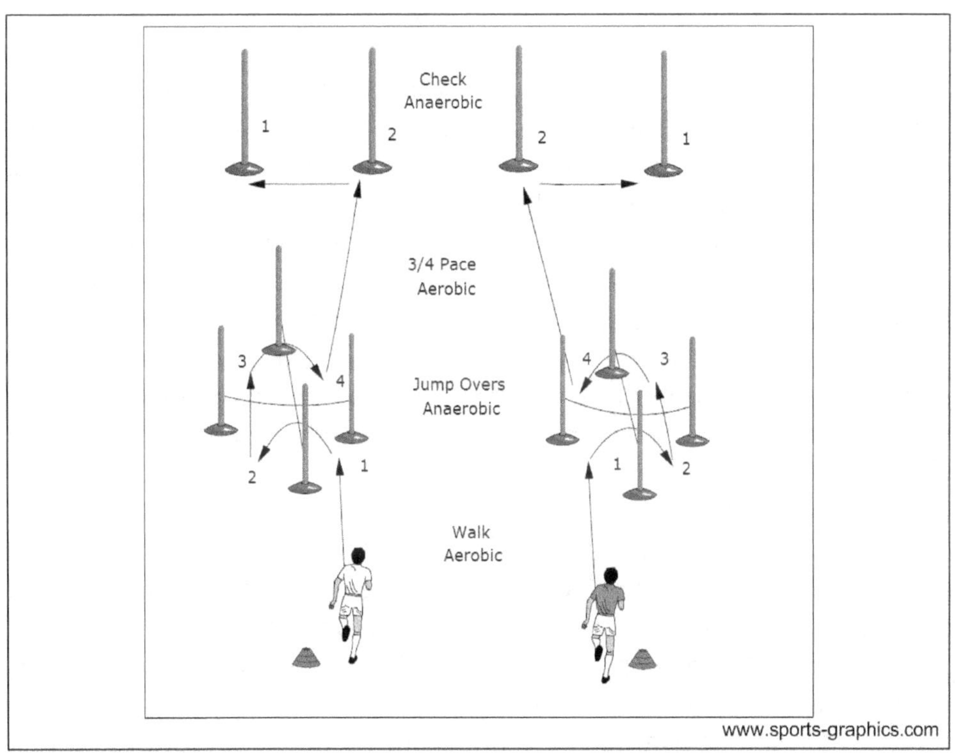

THE ANAEROBIC & AEROBIC STATE

In Competition - In the above format, two players compete against each other to be the first to finish the set task. The set task comes in a simple call out instruction by the coach. For example, from the starting position the coach could call out "1,2,3,4, 2&1 - Go!". What does 1,2,3,4, 2&1 mean? It means - run forward - jump through the stick formation keeping the movements going to the working sequence given, then run up to the next stick placements, touch stick 2, finishing the working sequence on stick 1. The next time around, the player could finish the working sequence on stick 2.

THE WORKING OBJECTIVES
THE ANALYSIS

The human body is made up of two types of muscles, slow twitch and fast twitch. The two types of muscle are linked by connective tissues to the bone structure.

THE MUSCLE STRUCTURE

What are the implications of the muscle groups to the above working format? The objective of any first ball game training routine is to give the player the opportunity to work with fast twitch muscle forms more so than slow twitch muscle forms. The design of the routine ensures that this is the case. The fast twitch muscle works when the player is under pressure physically. The minute the human body tenses up it is the fast twitch muscle that comes into its own because it is this part of the muscle that gives the power for the tension in the physique that in turn makes it possible to move a limb. The fast twitch muscle represents the power base, the inner core strength of the human body. The slow twitch muscle is a protective muscle for the fast twitch muscle and is the back up, if you will, that enables the human body to function in less active moments. We know the difference between players that play in the functional game of soccer and players that plays in the first ball game of soccer and so it requires a powerful and yet a much leaner body and so the main objective of any training routine is to target the development of the inner core (the fast twitch muscle) because it is the power base and when we target the development of the fast twitch muscle we can maintain a leaner body and a physique that is more mobile - agile - skilful. In the examples of dynamic work, the players experience the anaerobic state at the points in the exercise where the bigger effort is required. In the above example, the anaerobic experience, for example, takes place in the agility jump through and at the check-out point at the top of the format.

IN FAVOR OF THE FAST TWITCH MUSCLES

The working formats for the first ball game must ensure that the level of anaerobic experience matches the needs of the first ball game player. Most of the dynamic formations can therefore touch the base of the anaerobic state, more so than the aerobic state.

The dynamic solutions will always have a greater effect on the physical development of the player than any work in the weight training room because when it comes to the strength development side of the equation, the dynamic movement forms of training that touch the base of the anaerobic state are exceptionally effective. Anaerobic work is difficult and so the effort is based on a rotation of players taking turns. This way of working can ensure adequate rest time for each player. A two minute effort is more than sufficient. The coach should monitor what goes on at all times.

DYNAMIC - LATERAL AGILITY
ANAEROBIC - INNER CORE STRENGTH

Tape height 14"

These tried and tested formats are extremely effective when it comes to the needs of the first ball game. In the above format we can get the player to work on higher levels of stamina (on the development of the inner core strength) by getting him to work his body sideways on in an agility based exercise. There is nothing better than to employ the use of the player's own body weight to train up the fast twitch muscle forms because it is simply impossible to train the wrong muscles in relation to the movements required for the first ball game. The above lateral movement performed by the player (sideways-on skip-over's) is very anaerobic, which means that we are in effect targeting the development of the inner core strength.

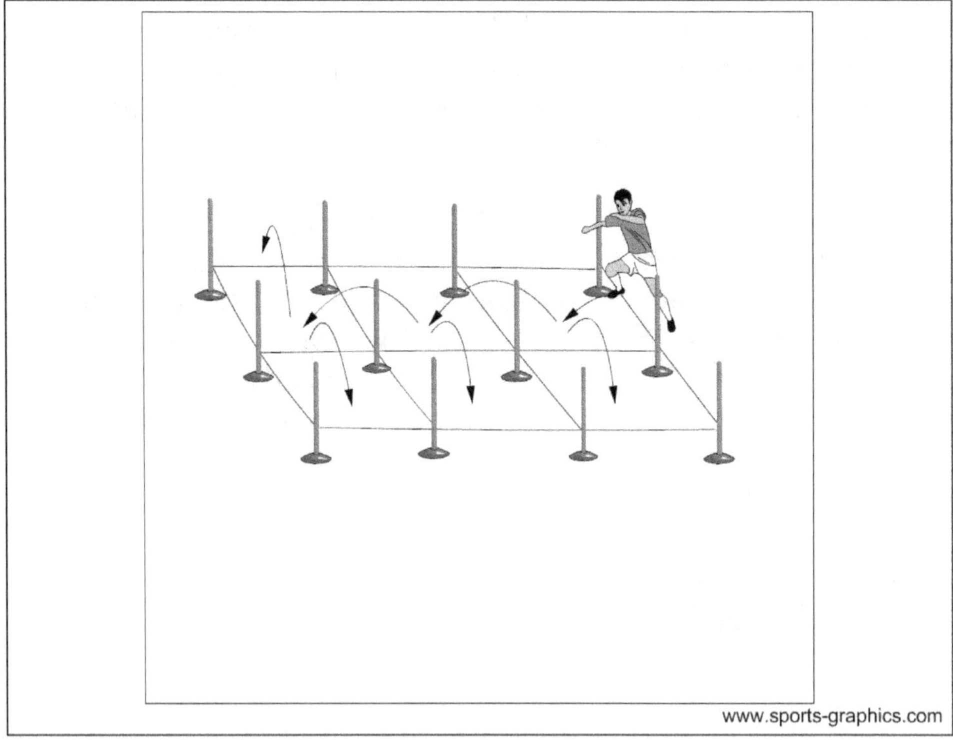

THE MAZE FORMAT

One example - The player enters the boxes with a forward high foot lift jump over and from then on is instructed to jump through the boxes and work his way out of the box through the red gate.

AGILITY LEG WORK

There are lots of reasons why the player needs to do this type of work. The game of soccer is deceptive in many ways. For example, during the game only the players in the vicinity of the ball, and in particular the player on the ball, are active physically. The majority of the players are relatively inactive. Given time, in the reality, the ratio of work in a game of soccer would not sustain the flexibility in the muscles of the leg/upper body required to be skilful, so the only way to maintain flexibility - agility - is to use the dynamic agility type formats.

DYNAMIC - AGILITY - FORWARD AND LATERAL ROTATIONAL - THE ANAEROBIC FORM

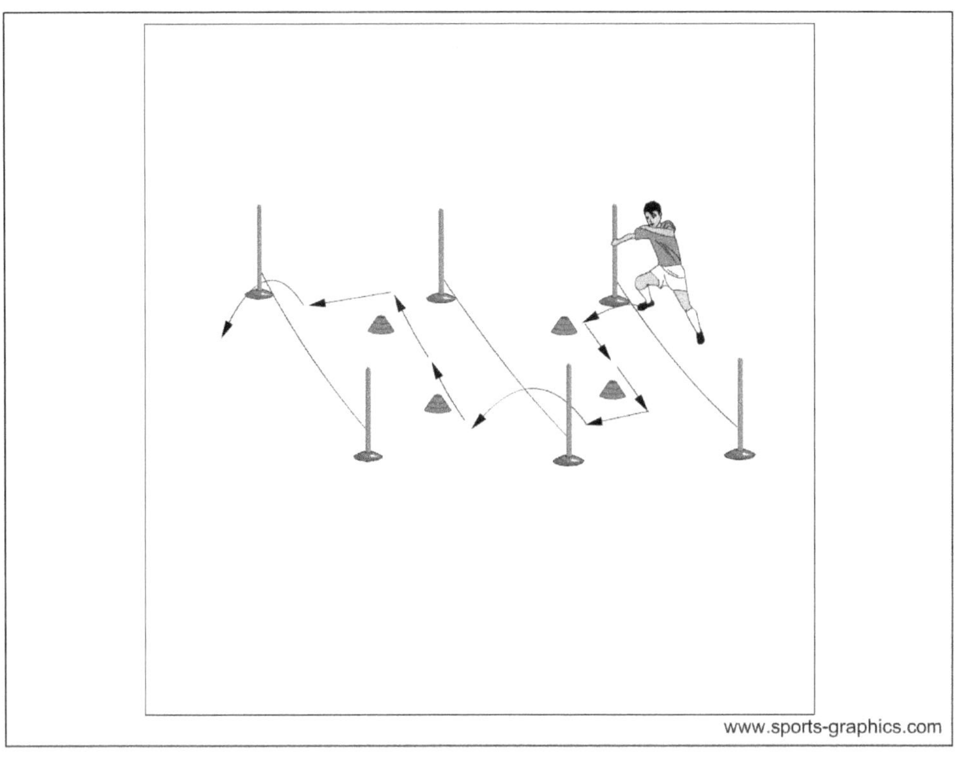

The above format may look far removed from the skills of the first ball game, but a closer examination proves otherwise. The jump-overs and the lateral movements (the two cones to the front of each jump-over - face to the cones - sideways straddle feet action) is what is required for developing the fast feet ability that helps the player retain possession of the ball in one on one situations.

Example: Player A1 does the lateral fast feet inside instep to inside instep shuffle and moves the ball out of the defender's (D1) reach.

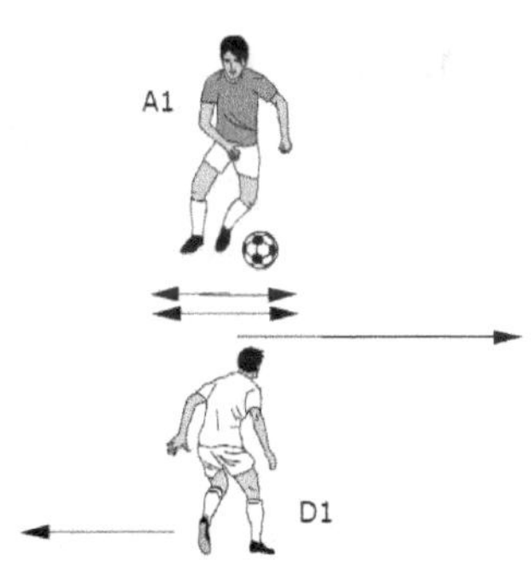

DYNAMIC - THE MAGIC ROUNDABOUT

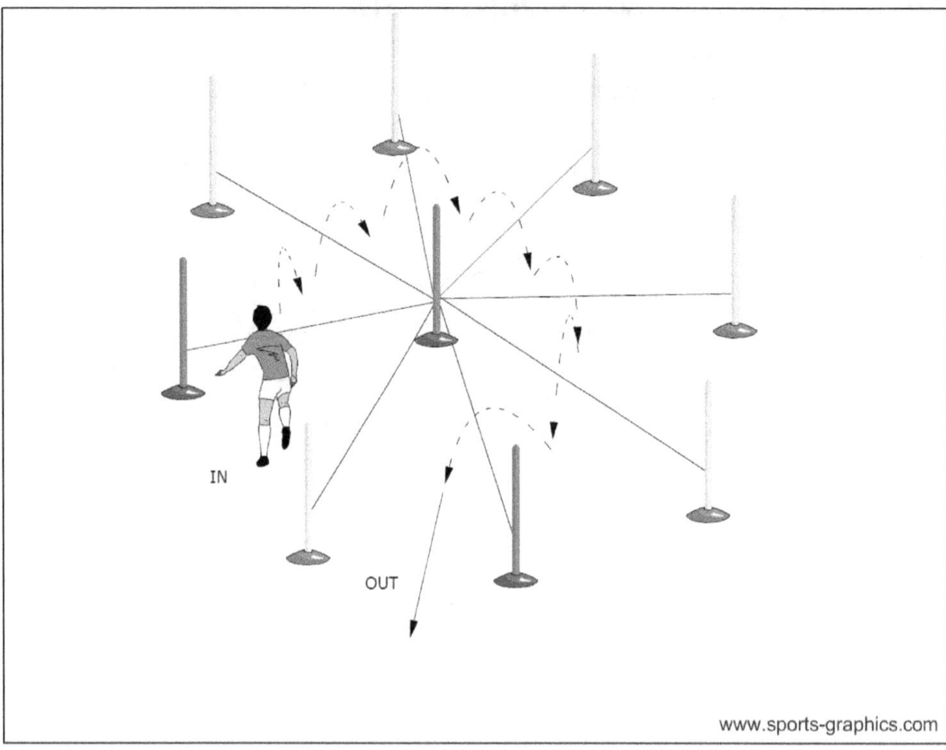

In many respects, it is a magic roundabout because of what can be achieved within its structure. Because the player uses his own body weight to work with, he experiences the correct proportional development of his physique between the lower and upper part of the body. The work generates the proper type of physical effort that strengthens the inner core, making the player stronger and less prone to injuries. To achieve the objectives mentioned, player A1 moves around the circle beginning at point A1 and performs a jump-over with either the right or the left foot leading (depending on which direction he is working: clockwise = right foot leading, counter-clockwise = left foot leading) over the segments (safety tapes obstacles). Kicking the leading foot/leg over the safety tapes develops the strength in the upper part of the thigh and the core and contributes to the overall conditioning of the player in terms of his stamina. In this format, the player does just a few circles of this work and comes out of the format. Rest period - 2 min in a repetition of 2 x 3 circles - Rotate the players through the format.

TARGETING THE INNER CORE - THE ANAEROBIC & AEROBIC CIRCUIT

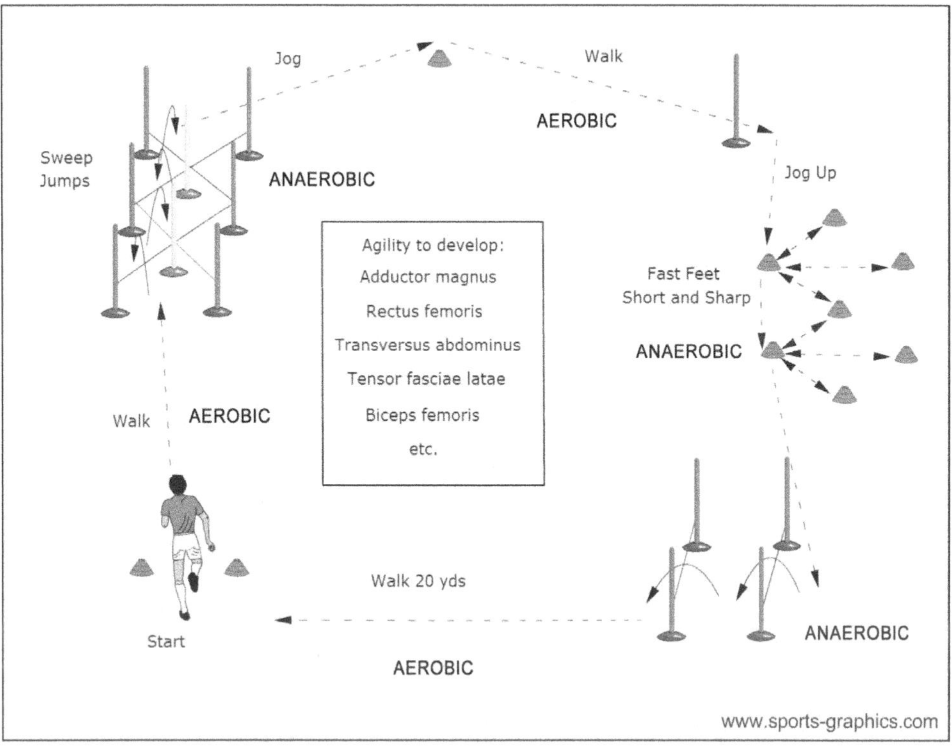

In the above example, we have three stations of 'Anaerobic' work with three 'Aerobic' breaks in between.

STAGE THREE - THE DEVELOPMENT OF FOOT TO FOOT COORDINATION

In stage three of the training session, we use formats that implement the lateral component into the working equation. The design of each format still keeps the player in touch with the dynamic agility aspect of his development, but the main effort here will focus on developing the ability to move the legs - feet - in a coordinated and therefore controlled manner, so that the player can perform the specific movement patterns that are both fundamental to the development of inner core strength and to the overall ability and quality of performance that make the first ball game possible.

IN THE FIRST EXAMPLE - LEG TO LEG COORDINATION

In this first example, for the development of foot to ball coordination (no ball required at this point), I have set the cone placements up in a way that enables the player to work on the diagonal movement options with the feet (the two footedness approach) and we also have the physical square-on position to the cone placements that enable the player to work the ball inside instep to inside instep. This type of training enables the player to develop fast feet and the ability to deal with situations during a match where taking the ball past a defensive position is required.

MULTI DIRECTIONAL IMPACT

It is the accumulation of all the work put in that makes the player who he is. The input into the player's development when it comes to the first ball game is a lot different from that of any functional training solution. The working formats, for example, will endeavour to focus on the lateral implications, because without the implementation of the lateral work, the player would not be able to develop the coordinated two footed capability, nor the ability to work the ball in a creative and skilful manner to a wide range of movement options (skill options with the ball or simply physical). The dynamics here are inclusive of the development of the fast twitch muscles and. From a technique development point of view, for example, the emphasis here is to work on the distinction between the square-on short inside instep feet movements and the short diagonal inside instep feet movements, both of which are relevant to the ball skills side of the game.

DYNAMIC - FOOT TO FOOT - SKILL COORDINATION
DYNAMIC - TWO ANAEROBIC - TWO AEROBIC

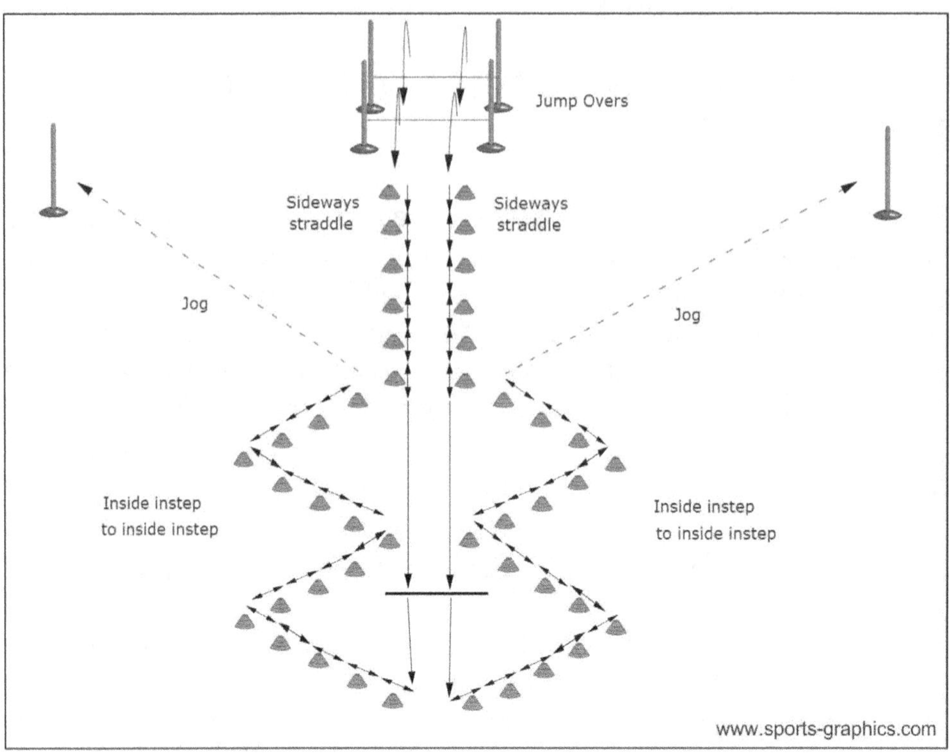

The two anaerobic stations generate a lot of tension from the effort involved and this more than adequately covers the anaerobic state. There is also a point in the format where the players jog back to the starting position, but this is just to loosen up any build-up of lactic acid and is a good way of reducing the tension and promoting normal blood circulation and recovery time.

DYNAMIC - LATERAL TO FORWARD ACTION WITH SWEEP OVERS

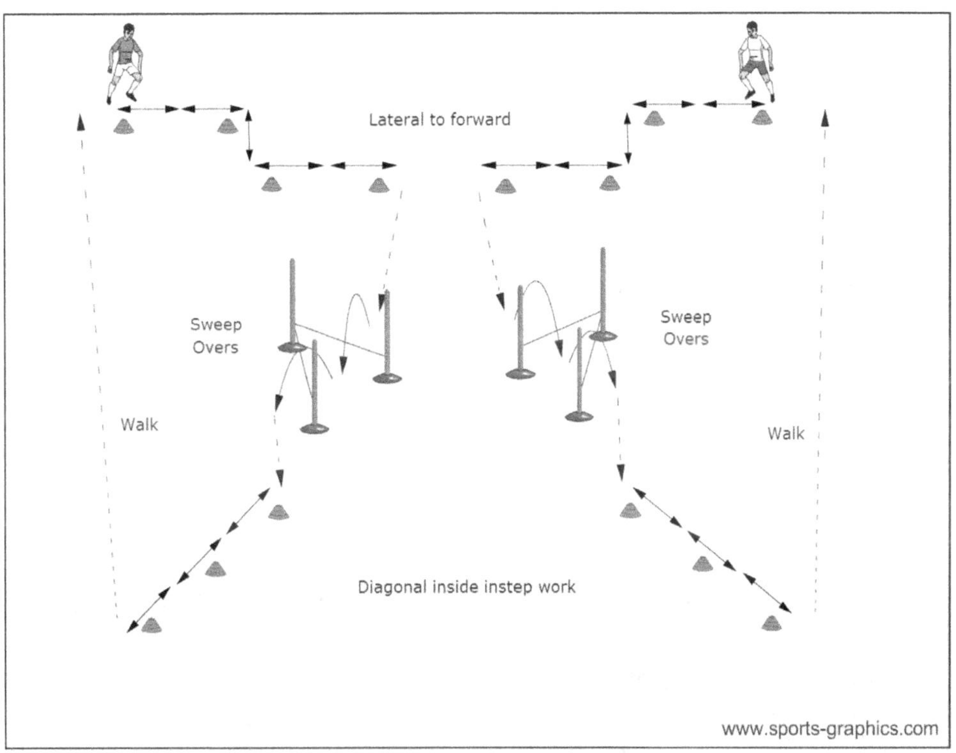

The different physical movement patterns indicated by the cone and stick placements show how we can generate the anaerobic state of being. Every single movement option here is also directly related to the skills side of the first ball game. For example, the lateral to forward inside instep movements, with the player staying square-on to the action, promote the development of physical balance between the left and right side of the body.

DYNAMIC AGILITY - SWEEP JUMPS & SWEEP OVERS NEXT EXAMPLE

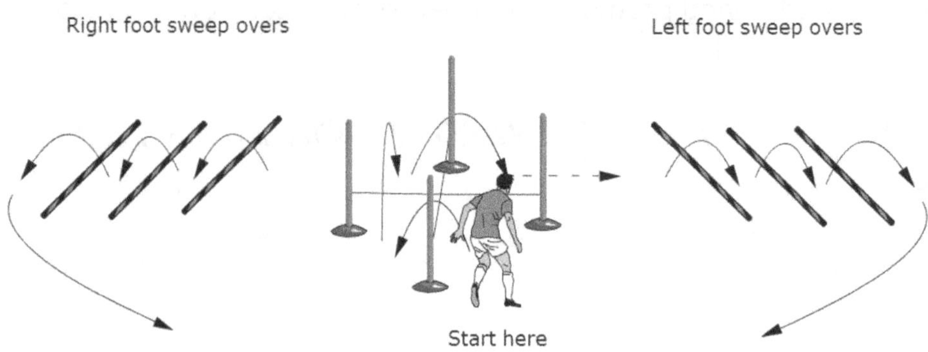

There is every need to work on the type of movements that create the first ball game of soccer. I would recommend short durations in every format because what we want to see is as much of the movement experience that creates the first ball game as possible in any training session, rather than to work on any one thing that takes an hour or so of the player's time. For example, a two mile run is, for the purposes of developing players, a waste of time and something I would not recommend. The same is true of playing a five a side game for half an hour. Match fitness for the first ball game is different to that of the functional game because during the first ball game the anaerobic state comes into the working equation, so the fitness level has to be specific to the requirements of the rapid changes in the physical efforts required. In other words, the physical movement patterns have to be specific to the needs of the first ball game. A two mile run would simply never give you the right type of working physical patterns that make up the first ball game or its fitness requirements. From a practical point of view, there is no need to dwell for long periods in any of the working formats because these are tough solutions that are most effective when they are used to either a set rep format or a set time. When the training session is made up of a six stage approach, the work takes care of all the players' needs.

Note - An example of the layout for the first ball game training session using the format examples here will be shown towards the end of this book.

DYNAMIC POWER UP & SPRINT UP

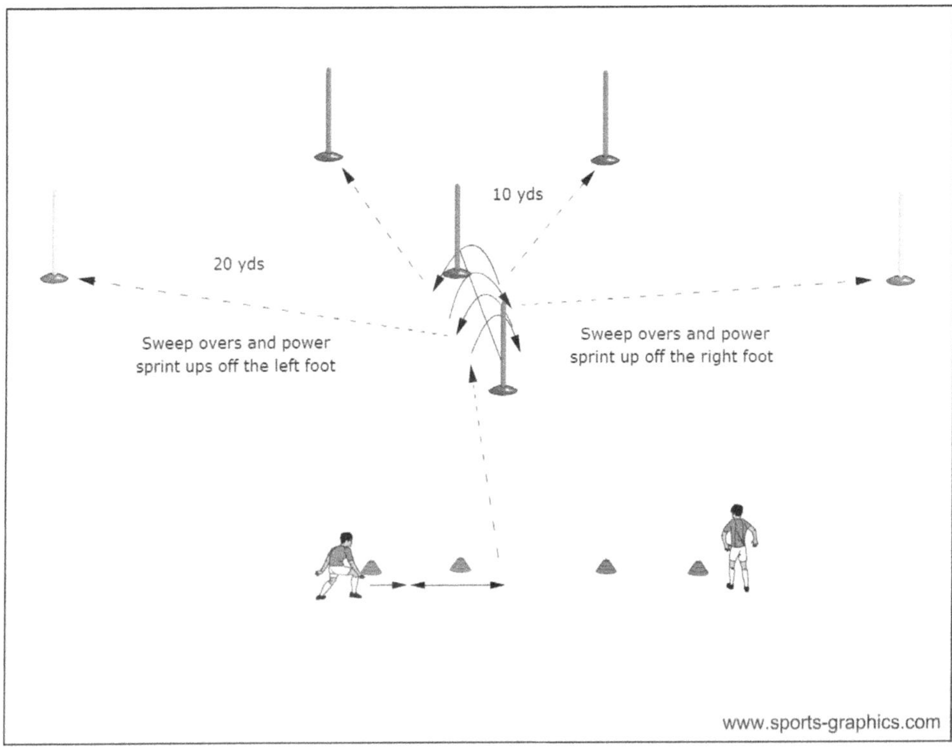

The changes in the state of being, from the anaerobic state to the aerobic, take place depending on whether the player is working on explosive power or for his endurance for sustaining energy for the overall requirements of playing the game of soccer. The work on stamina (slow twitch) is achieved by creating a working solution that makes the player do the work efficiently but keeping the physical effort just under the anaerobic state.

UNDER THE ANAEROBIC RADAR - THE DEVELOPMENT FORMAT FOR STAMINA

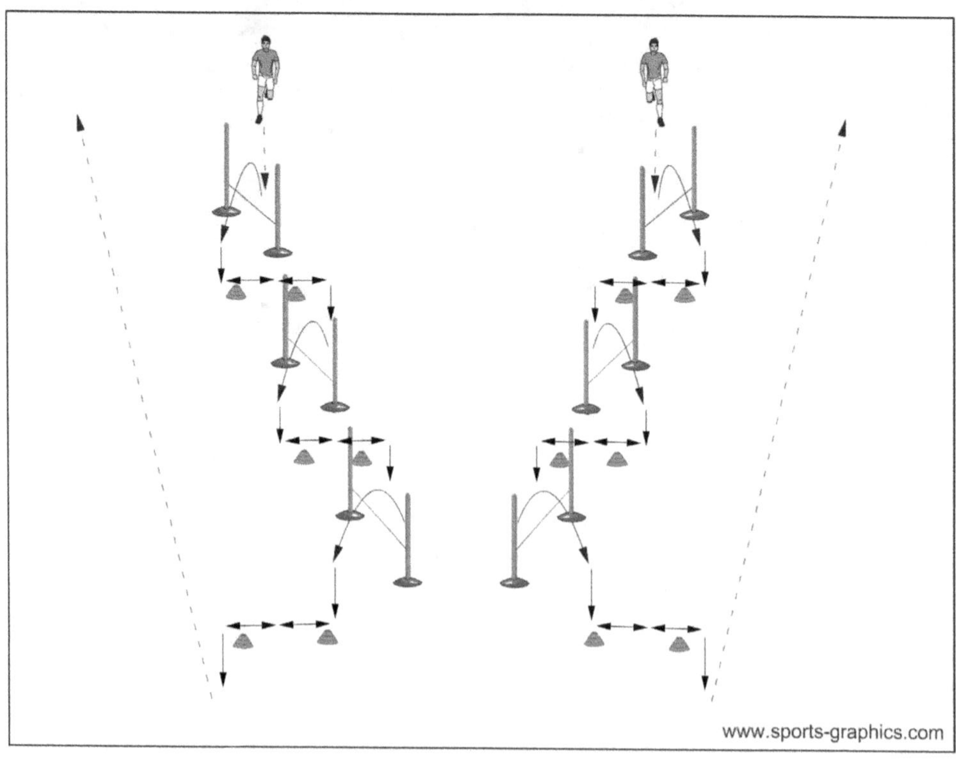

NOTE - IN THE ABOVE FORMAT - RFL = RIGHT FOOT LEADING - LFL = LEFT FOOT LEADING THE LATERAL MOVEMENT ACTION.

FAST FOOT WORK - A DIFFERENT STRUCTURE

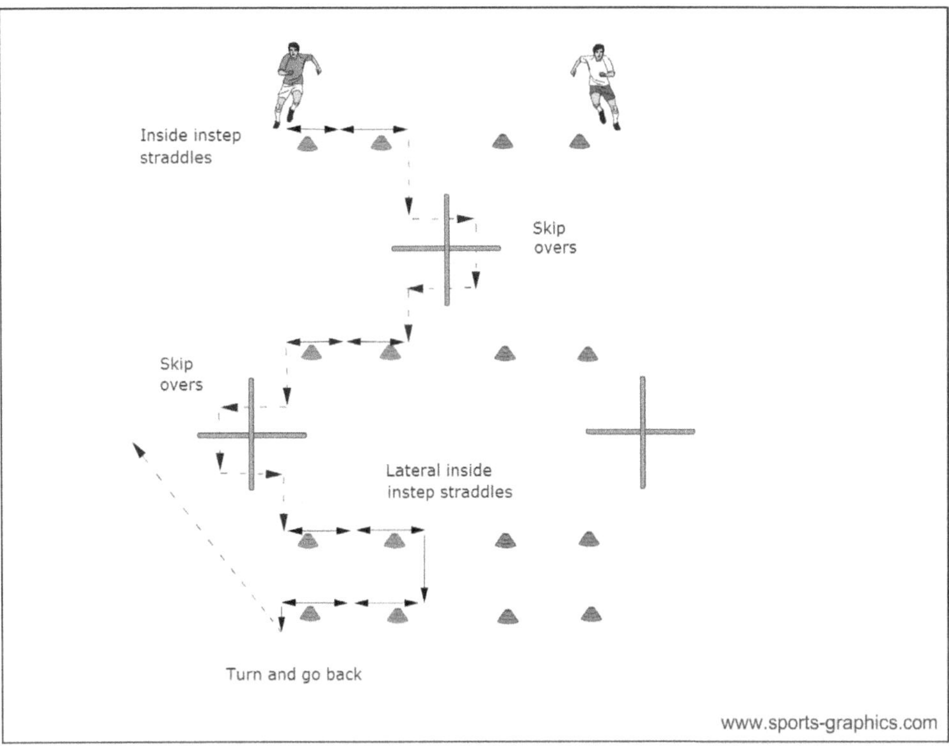

The sticks are lying flat on the ground. Players perform skip-over jumps to the three corners, always landing on one foot, then move forward to the next cone placements. The idea here is to move the feet precisely to the set objective but as fast as possible. In this way, the players work to develop the fast twitch muscles and therefore their fast feet ability.

FAST FOOT WORK - LATERAL TO FORWARD

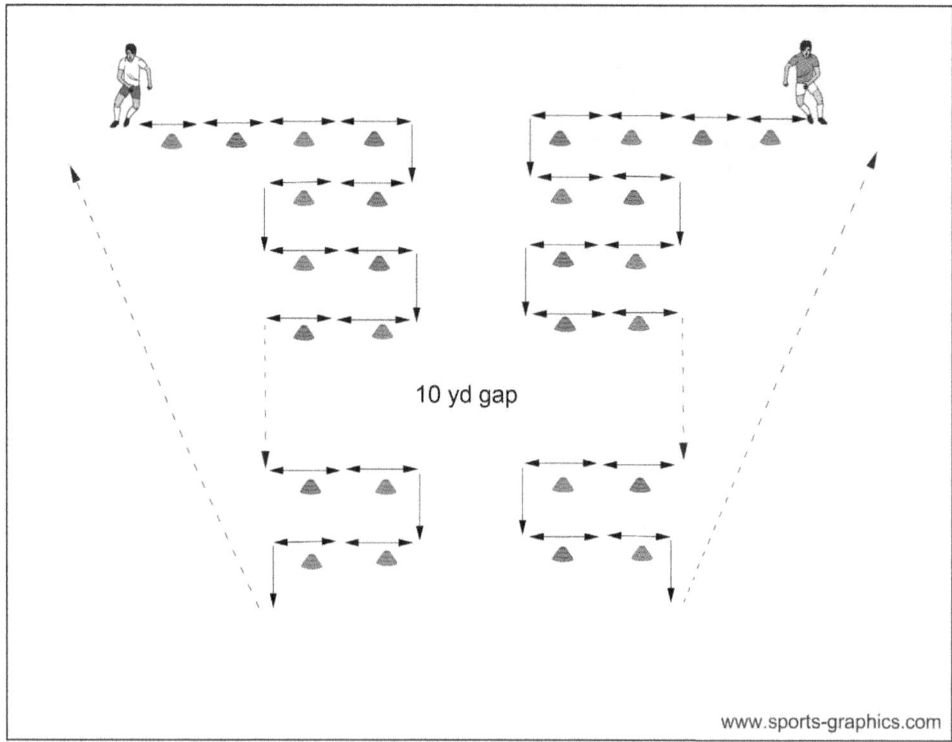

The players start on the left and the right side, facing the cone placements. The inside instep lateral movements should be precise, one foot placed after another to the designated place, which is shown by the arrows. The movement with the feet should be rhythmic but not laboured. In other words, the players should be light on their feet. When the players move into the two cone placements, this is the area in the format where the fast feet action is required and the players will experience a change in the state of being, from aerobic to anaerobic. Moving on - The 10 yard gap relaxes the players a little, but on reaching the last two positions in the format the players again work the fast feet action. On finishing, the player turns and moves back to the starting position with a gentle walk or jog.

ORGANIZATIONAL ASPECTS OF THE WORKING FORMATS

The working principles can be simplified. If, for example, the working format has a long line of cones, the work can be slower and that then generates a different reality to one where the movements are very short and sharp. We can say that when the physical movement is short and sharp, the fast twitch muscles are targeted.

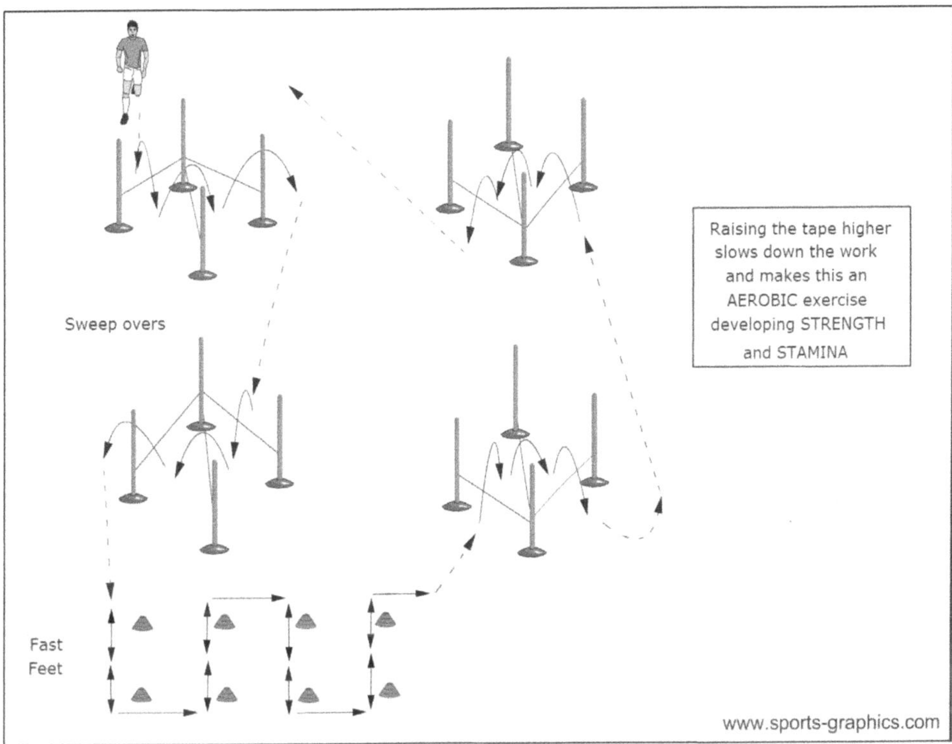

Here, players work the inside instep to inside instep movement without the ball at their feet, because this stage is preparation for the use of the ball. This inside instep to inside instep movement works to develop inner core strength as well as specific muscles such as the inner groin, thigh and calf. When it comes to the make-up of each format, the set distance between the cone placements is a matter of practical sense. When moving forward to the next cone placement, whether it is with or without the ball, the distance is approximately 4 feet. If a cone placement consists of more than one cone, the distance between them is approximately shoulder width. The leading foot to the action in any cone placement depends on the working direction. These are rotational type formats, which means that the coach can have players moving in and out of the format for as long as he wishes. That being said, when the training session is based on a six stage approach, the time spent in any format should be relatively short.

THE SLOW TWITCH MUSCLE FORMAT

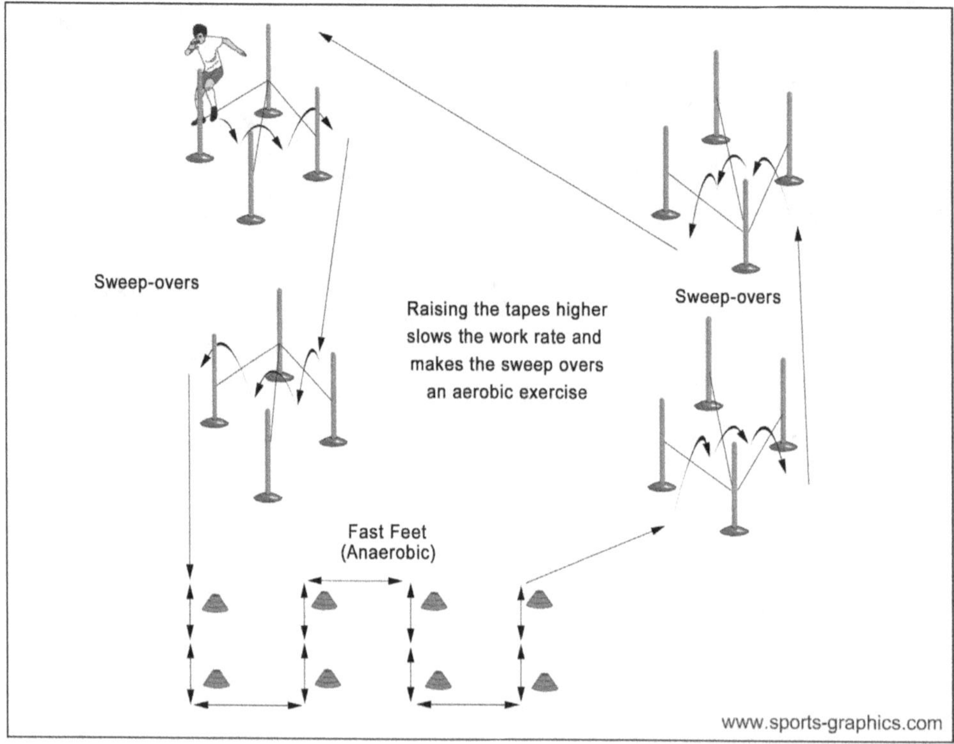

I will always emphasise the work related to the fast twitch muscles because that gives the player the better source of power. Having said that, the above format shows that it is possible to design a format that has a specific effect on the player. In the example, the effect is aerobic, because the length of the format and its design can change the speed of the action.

THE SECRET FORMULA

To determine whether an exercise is aerobic or anaerobic, the coach can ask himself the following two questions:

1. Is the player taking in oxygen when he is performing a string of physical movements?
2. How fast is he moving when working any part of the format?

If the answer to question 1 is **NO**, it can only mean that the action is **anaerobic** and therefore fast twitch muscle orientated.

If the answer to question 1 is **YES**, it can mean that the player is performing under the **aerobic** state, in which case he is using the slow twitch muscles.

If the answer to question 2 falls on the side of **SLOW**, it can mean that the player is performing under the **aerobic** state of being.

If the answer to question 2 is **FAST**, it can mean that the player is performing under the **anaerobic** state of being.

THE AGILITY SIDE OF THE WORK

A training session has to incorporate agility work because most of what actually takes place in the game only touches the agility base. For example, when the players compete for the high ball (heading) or perhaps when they have to jump over the goalkeeper or another player. This is a problem because when players simply play the game with movements that don't call for agility, it will ultimately ensure a lack of proper development. It is inevitable that there will be moments in a game when a player will need sufficient agility to solve a playing problem. For example, they may have to jump over the goalkeeper or another player. If this sort of agility is not specifically developed in training, the player may be unprepared physically to meet the challenge. This is the main reason that the term "hamstring injury" is so prevalent in the game today! In a six stage training session, stage three brings the solution to the above problem. It addresses not only agility but also all the other physical realities that I have mentioned. Keeping the player supple, mobile, agile, and fast feet orientated is not something that can be ignored. In England we have players on the injury list for a long time and I often wonder what is missing from their training routines. I believe that the first team players in the most famous clubs can be wrapped in cotton wool too often and don't do enough agility work in training.

FAST TWITCH ORIENTATED EXAMPLES WITHOUT AGILITY STATIONS

In the next few examples, the work is very fast twitch orientated and the aim of the working format is to develop the player's brain power to think and react to any given situation during a game. The word 'react' describes the overall ability of the player to engage a practical solution to any problem quickly. The next few examples of fast twitch formats are also relevant to stage three of the six stage training session.

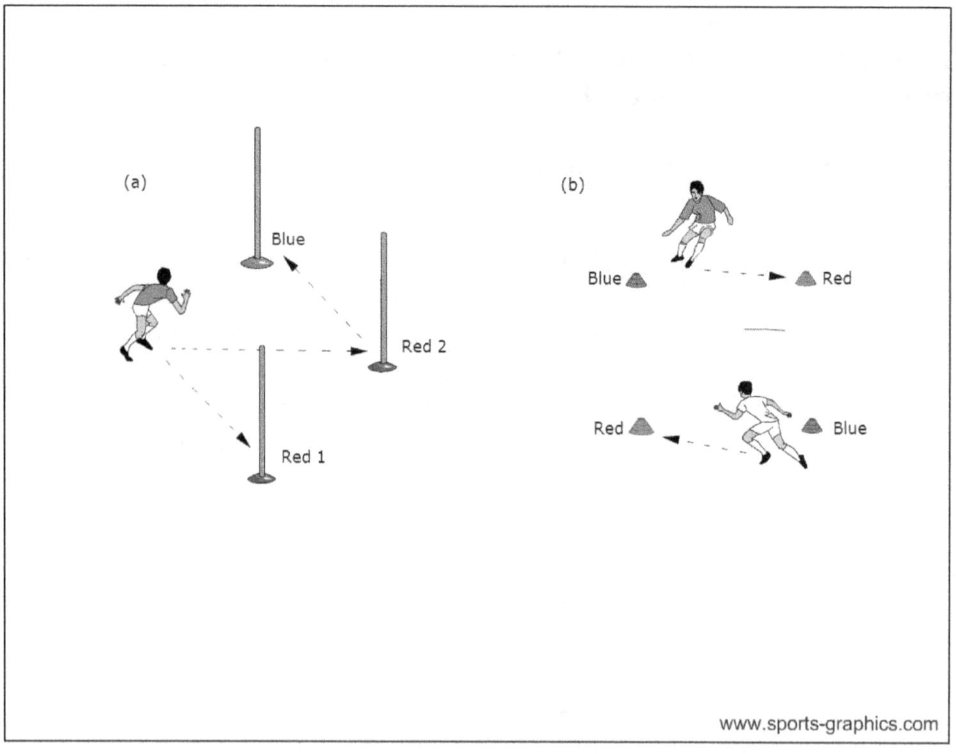

ANAEROBIC - A TWO THOUGHT ACTION

FAST CALLS - For fast feet (a) - The instruction for this type of format is very simple: touch red 1, touch red 2, out on blue or red 2, red 1, out on blue.

Touching the anaerobic state, developing explosive power, this format is used to sharpen up the player's wits.

For (b), we can maintain the anaerobic state for two minutes if we want to achieve the anaerobic effect, that is, any longer than two minutes and it becomes more in tune with the work on stamina. Players react to quick calls of: "Touch red cone", "Touch blue cone", "Change places!". Simple, but effective!

LOOKING UP

Thinking and visualizing can lead to good decisions! In the above format the players didn't have to think too much, but in this next example if they don't think they will get things wrong.

IN COMPETITION - THINK - REACT

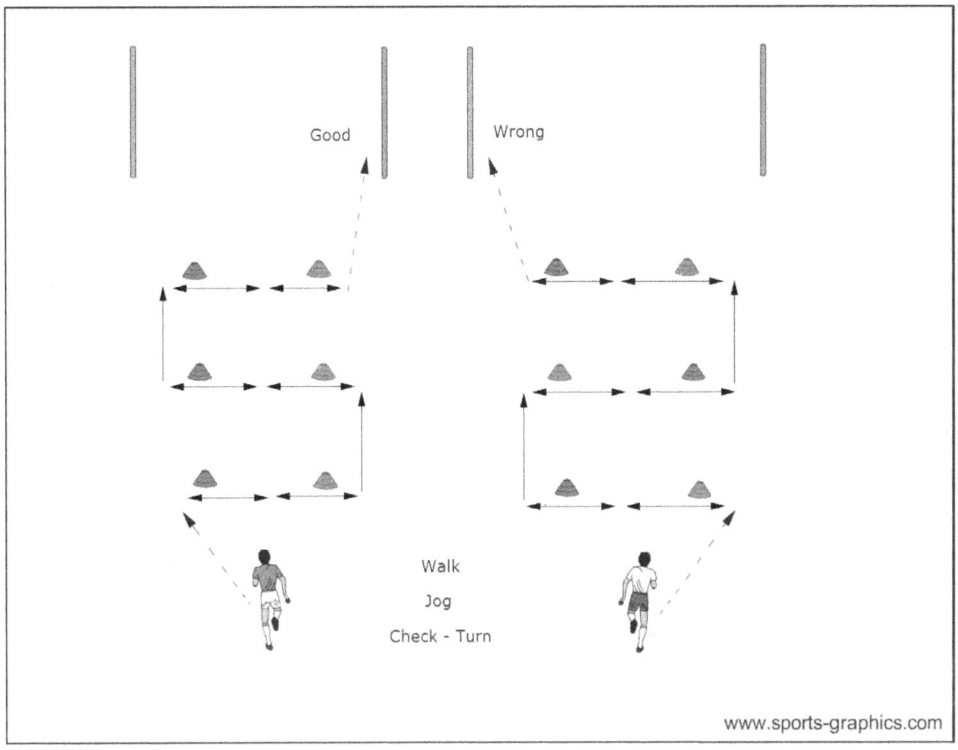

ANAEROBIC - A LOT GOING ON

The call is simple enough, namely, "Out on blue!" or "Out on red!". The players must work their feet through the cone placements and finish up on either the blue or red stick placement at the end of the format. What makes this task difficult in terms of decision making is what happens prior to the players moving up the format to the stick placement. Prior to moving through the cone placements, the players have to work out to a sequence of calls made by the coach, such as "walk", "jog", "check" etc. The last call by the coach finishes one working sequence. The out call ("Out on blue" or "Out on red") is given first, before the player begins. The players must start from the correct side of the first two cones in front of them, because if they don't they will come out of the cone placements on the wrong side to the colored called. Mistakes don't win prizes!

THE WORKING DURATION

In the above format, the coach can keep the players in the anaerobic state for a couple of minutes by giving the players just a handful of calls prior to the last call to finish the working sequence.

On the other hand, he can keep them in the freelance section for much longer and therefore work on stamina, to then release the players up the format. In this way, the players can touch the anaerobic state for approx 30 seconds.

NEXT EXAMPLE - ANAEROBIC

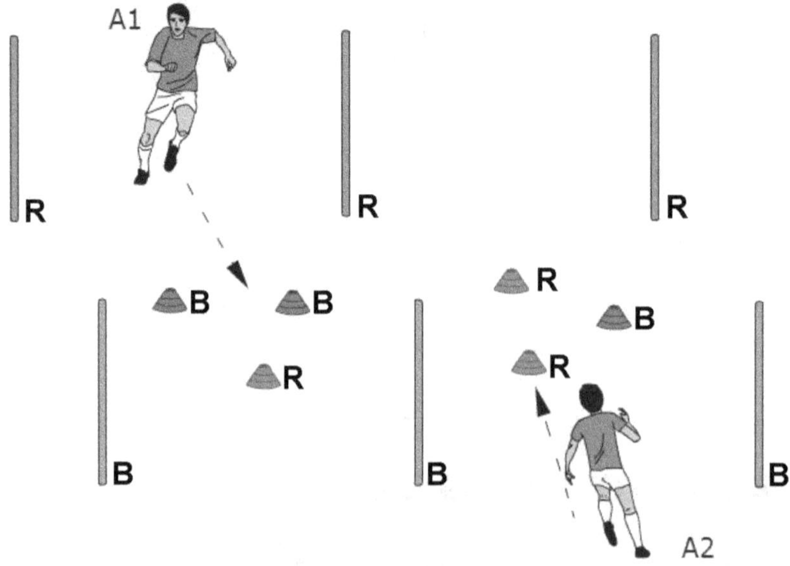

In the above format we have two competing players facing each other. The distance to the cones is 2-3 feet. The objective is simple : on "Go!", be first to slot your color cones to the correct home base(stick). 3 Red Sticks = 3 Red cones - 3 Blue sticks = 3 Blue cones.

THE DURATION OF THE WORK

The players can complete the set task in just a few seconds, nonetheless its good training, on both the reaction time and on the decision making side of things too. This type of work can be done to a set target of 3 x 1 reps per player.

NEXT EXAMPLE
FAST FEET - FAST REACTIONS

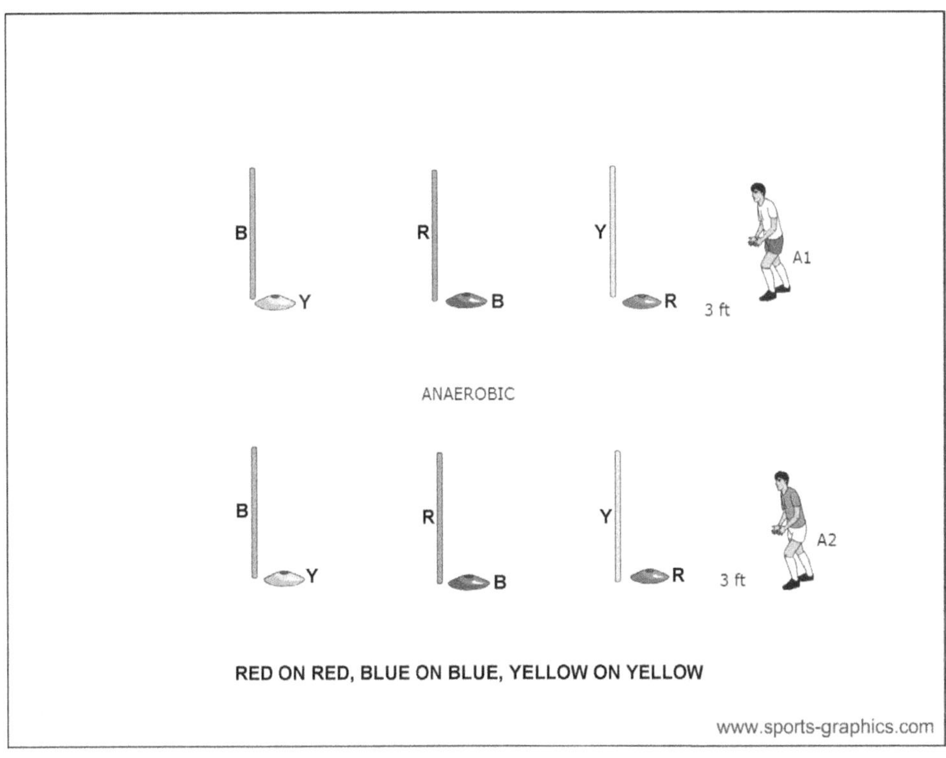

MAKING THE RIGHT DECISION

The above task looks simple enough and yet what looks simple can be anything but. This one is also about being first to place the cone on the matching colored stick. Being first to complete the task is dependent on which cone is picked up first. Sometimes going for the nearest cone doesn't win. By doing reps, the players touch the base of the anaerobic state without any bad effect on their physical being, but only acquire the positive effect of having a faster reaction time and the physical means to move quicker.

In this next one we extend the duration of the anaerobic state to ensure the development of a certain determination and a mental toughness that can sustain the player's competitive ambition to do well. The format is again based on a very simple cone and stick placement format and once again the objective is not complicated. Each player has a home base color, only this time the objective is not to place your color cones into your home base color but into the opponent's home base color, hence the name of this format **'BLUE AND RED BLOCKERS'**.

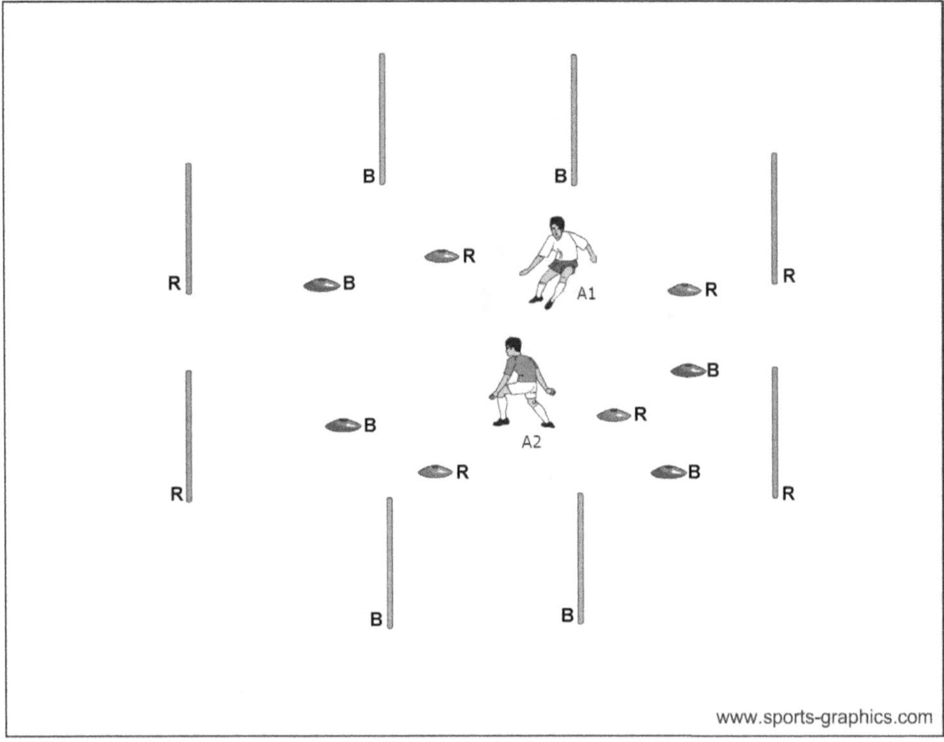

BLUE ON RED - RED ON BLUE

Very competitive and very anaerobic and, therefore, not easy to achieve the set objective. However, once again the format is for building up the inner core strength of the player, together with a competitive attitude. Again, we use the colors of the cone placements and the stick placements to create a working format for the development of not only fast reaction times but also good foot to foot - brain to brain (collaboration) and brain to foot physical movement coordination.

PROTECT YOUR HOME BASE - ANAEROBIC

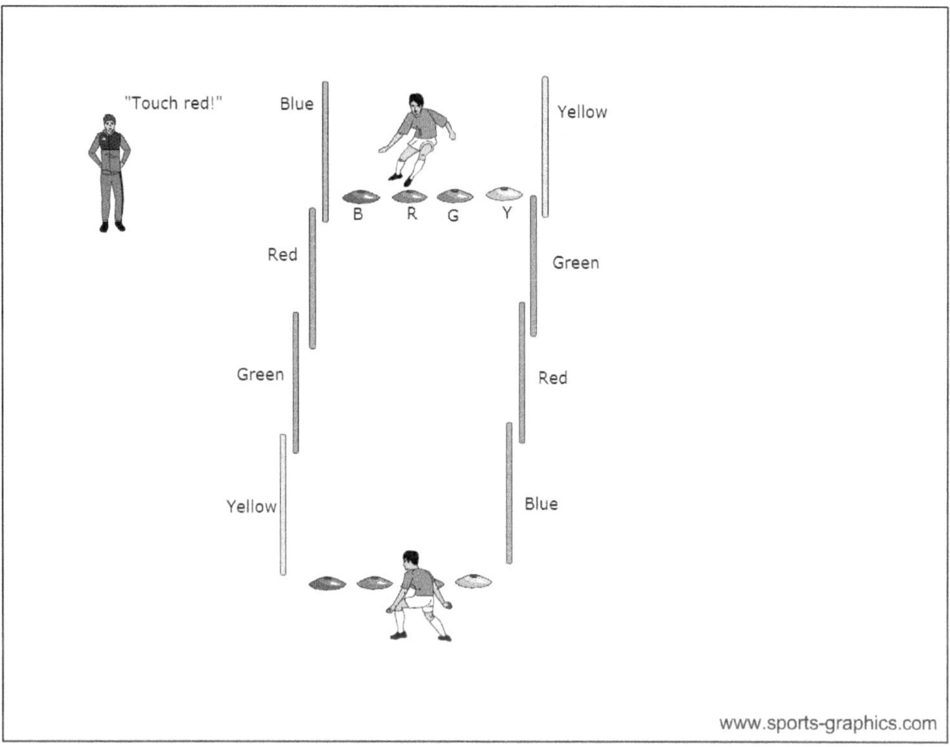

In this one, the Coach controls the timing of the competitive moment. There are colored cones at the feet of both players and the first objective of both players is to listen to the colors called by the Coach. On hearing the color called, each player bends down to touch that color and stands back up quickly. Touch red - touch blue - touch green etc. At some point in the working sequence the Coach will shout out the instruction 'Protect your home base'. On this instruction both players grab the red cone and rush to place the red cone into the home base stick, which is the red stick. The home base stick for each player is on his right. Once the red cone is slotted onto the red stick, both players must endeavour to be first to place the rest of the colored cones into the correct colored matching sticks.

FAST FEET DEVELOPMENT - THINK & REACT ANAEROBIC

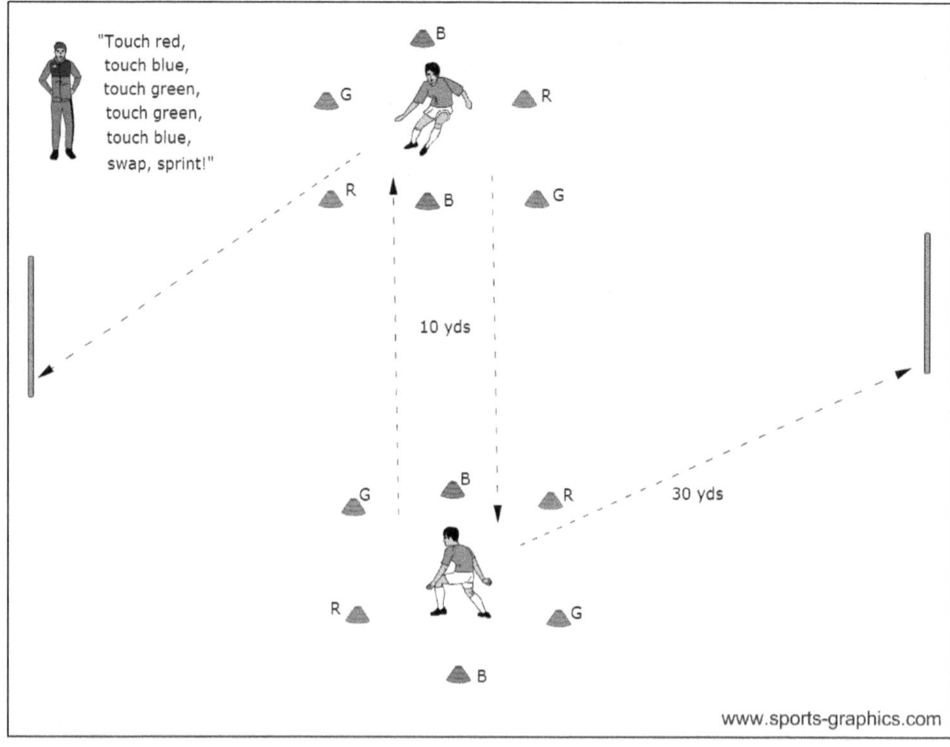

The Coach stands wherever he wishes and instructs the players. In this one the Coach calls out the following working sequence and both players react to the calls given. The last call is the word 'Sprint'. The working sequence could be as follows: Touch Red, touch blue, touch green, touch green, touch blue, touch blue, touch blue, swap places (players move to the other side, always moving up on their left hand side) - in place - continue - touch blue, touch red, tough green, sprint! On hearing the word 'Sprint' the players make the 30 yard sprint up to the stick marker assigned to them. Such formats are very fast twitch orientated but in line with the needs of the types of movements that are foundational to the next level of coaching. In stage three of the training session it is all about doing reps and developing the fast twitch muscles, using the anaerobic state of being to improve the inner core strength of the player. Keeping things simple and to a set time of short durations creates the right effect for conditioning the anaerobic state. Long bouts of effort move the player into another reality altogether, one of an aerobic state. We don't have to worry about the development of the aerobic state of being (slow twitch muscle forms) because that happens anyway in terms of proportionality of work when we put the sum total of the work together. It just happens to be true that most of what takes place in every day endeavours takes place in the aerobic state of being.

FITNESS TRAINING FORMS - SPRINTS & TURNS ANAEROBIC

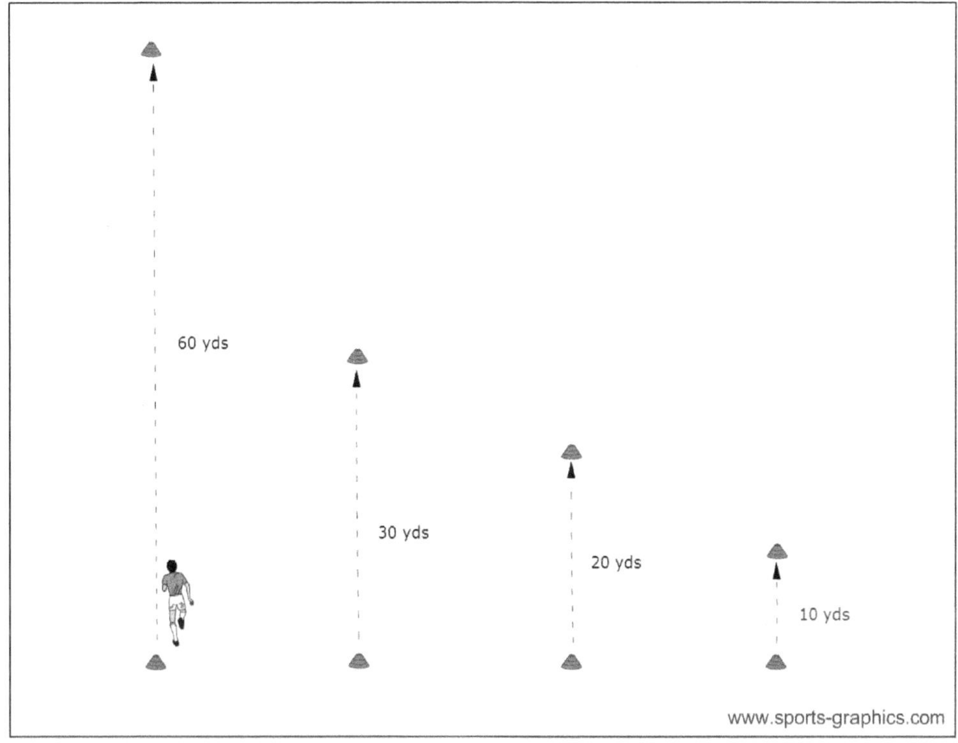

Sprints and checkouts are always a part of the work but just like everything else in the training session, everything is done in proportion to all the other needs of the player. In this example, the sprint out to the length shown is done to a set repetition. The player can, for example, do 3 times each length.

SPRINT WITH CHECK OUTS AND TURNS ANAEROBIC

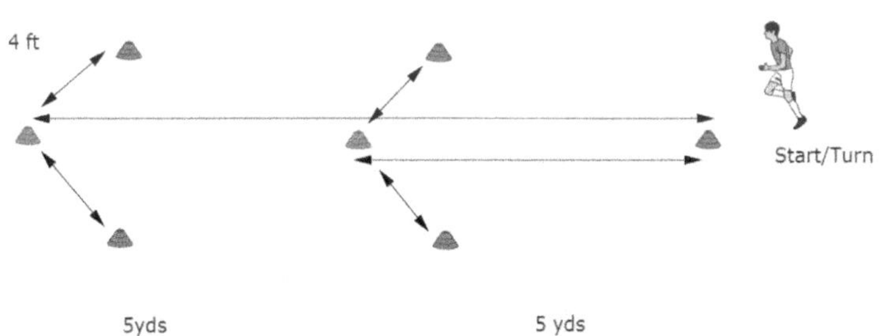

WINNING THE BALL BACK QUICKLY

During the forward moving game the running pattern is similar to what we see here. However, the first ball game team doesn't play the long ball and so when they do lose possession of the ball, winning the ball back is done differently to that of simply competing for the 50/50 ball. The first ball game team keeps the ball, which usually means that they have lots of players in the vicinity of the ball when possession is lost, so they are in a position to win the ball back quickly. The point is that winning back the ball is achieved by skilful means rather than by hard tackling. Here are examples of more movement forms for the development of the ability to win the ball back quickly.

FAST FEET

Let's take a look at the type of movements the player needs to work on in order to solve problems in defense and therefore develop the kind of playing attributes that will help him win the ball back. What is maybe not so obvious is that it's not just about 'fast feet' but also about the angle of the movements of the feet. A check out point in the run up to the opponent could have other implications, meaning that in terms of adjusting the defending position in relation to the opponent with the ball, the sideways check out movements could be just one or two sideways steps. It is not beyond the realm of possibility that the defender at the check out area, having made the first move to the side, is still not where he should be in relation to the position of his opponent and so an extra shuffle of the feet may be the solution.

LATERAL CHECK OUT POINTS - CHECK OUT TO THE LEFT AND RIGHT

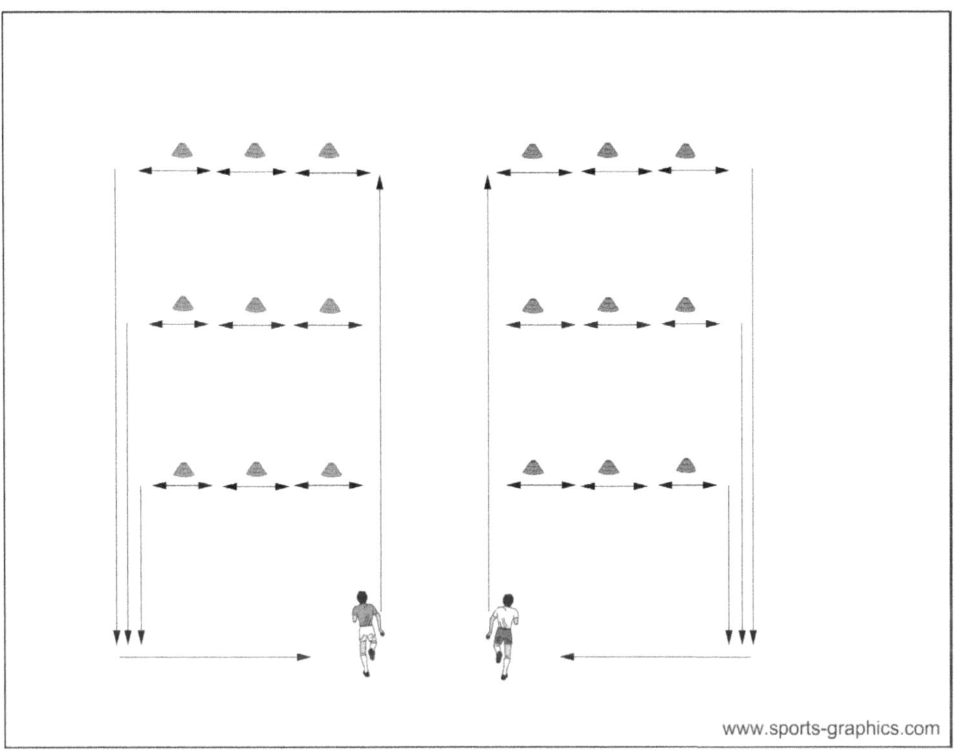

ANAEROBIC

In the above example, the player works on developing the sideways (square on) check out movements to the left and right of the check out point. The formats, therefore, include the run up and the check out points. These formats are also designed in a way that caters for a number of practicing players. The players run up to the check out points and work the feet to the lateral angle - then jog back. The total distance of the run ups is not more than 20 yards split into smaller sections by the set of cone placements. When the nearest man to the ball needs to close his opponent down, his run up could be to any distance so on the training ground we average this distance out and simply set it to a split reference section of 10 yds x 3 to the appropriate angle.

WINNING POSSESSION OF THE BALL - GIVING GROUND ANAEROBIC

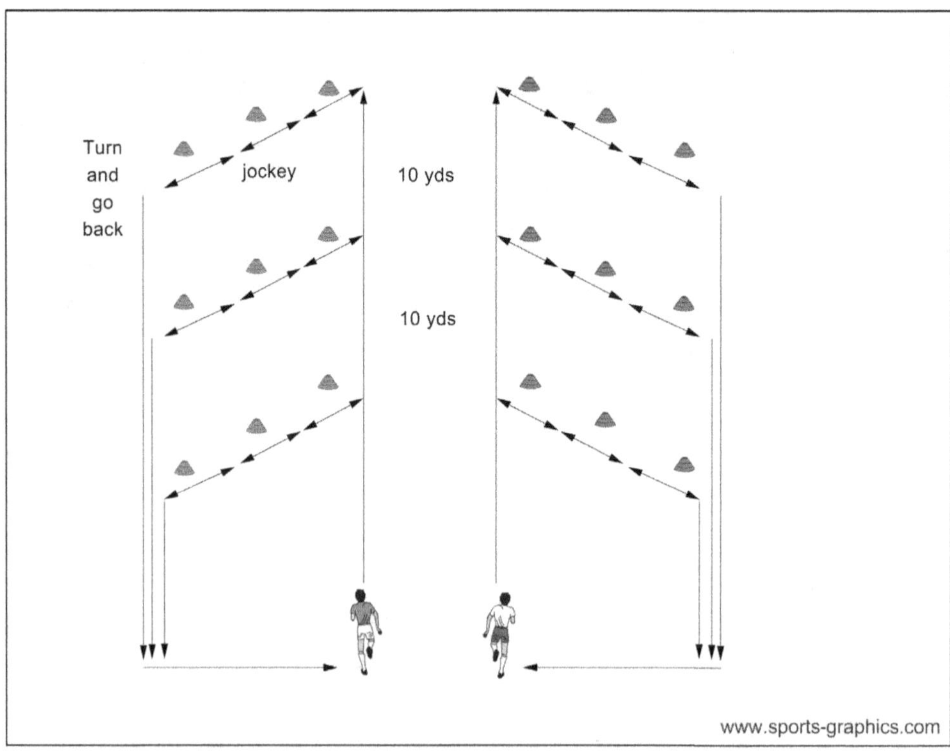

The above format shows how to work on the physical shape that enables the player to practice his turns off the right or left shoulder to the diagonal angle, also known as jockeying. The call to the first challenger can be in the form of a simple instruction - "On the left shoulder!" - "On the right shoulder!" - "Left shoulder down!" - "Right shoulder down!" - "Stay on your feet!".

NOTE - A lateral check out is for working on staying square on and adjusting to the position of the oncoming opponent, whereas the diagonal check out deals with establishing control of the opponent's movements by applying a give way skill known as jockeying, on the left shoulder or on the right shoulder - with no cover.

THE COMBINED FORMULA
PRACTICE LATERAL TO JOCKEYING MOVEMENT

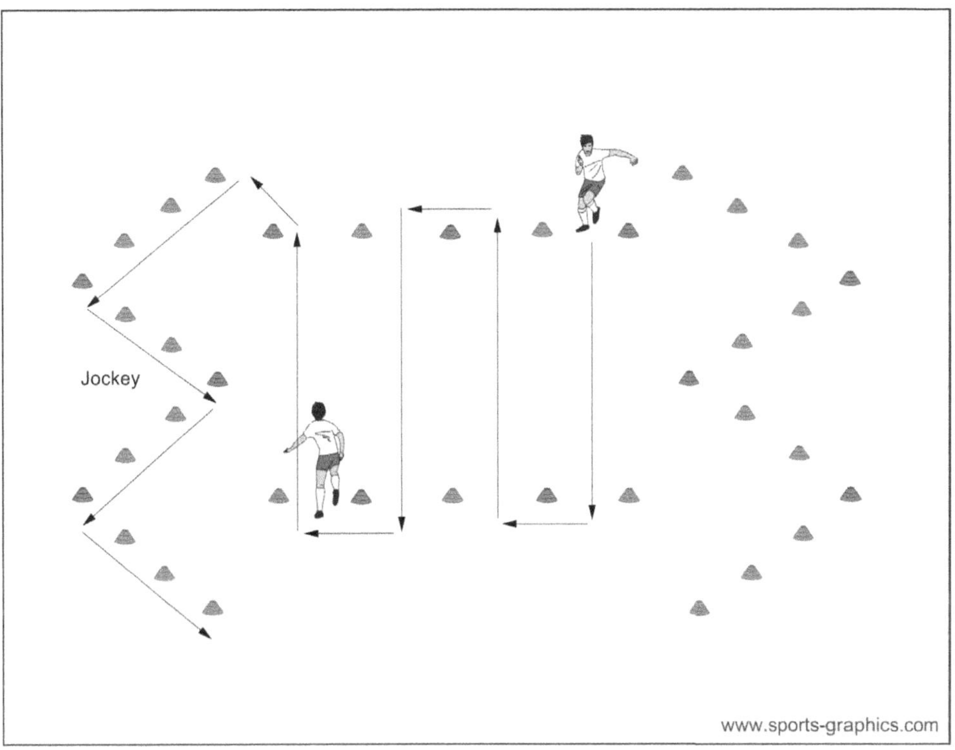

The above format puts the sum total of the movements together and in this way we can narrow down the movements to the relevant issues that enable the player to move up short to the opponent in possession of the ball, adjust his position quickly by first moving to the lateral angle and then forward and into the jockeying position, which should enable him to take control of the opponent's movements in a way that can send the opponent to the direction of choice. The diagonal movements can also create the opportunity to slow down the opponent's forward moving progress. The sum total of the lateral plus diagonal movements establishes the first challenge to the ball position, which can then be backed up by other players in the team in the form of cover etc.

INTRODUCTION TO STAGE FOUR

THE FORWARD MOVING AND FUNCTIONAL GAME

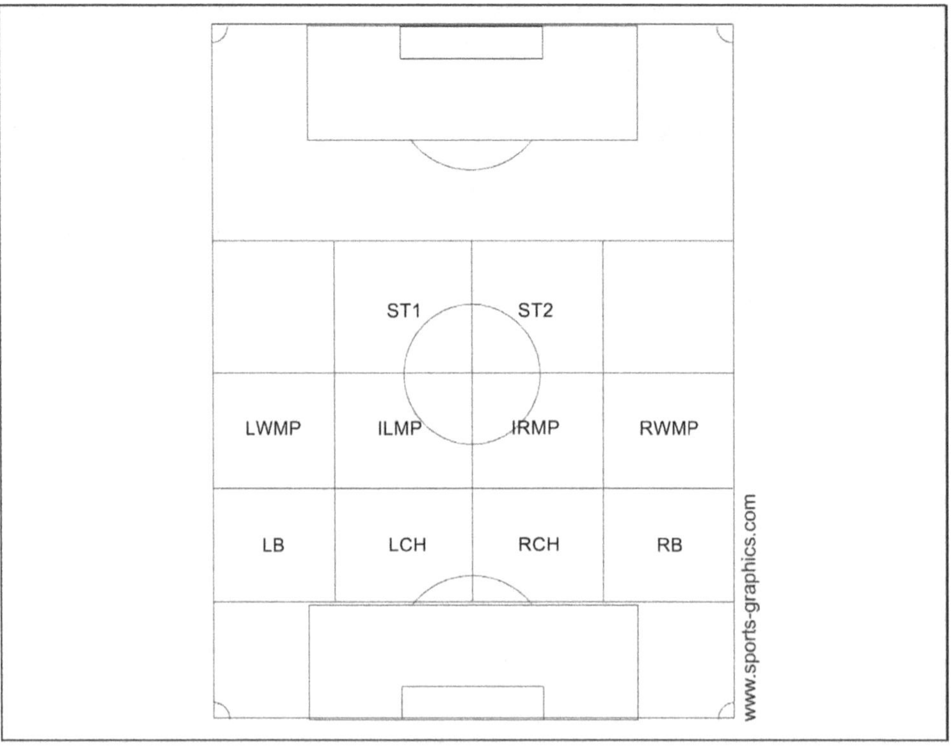

MY PERSONAL COACHING PHILOSOPHY

My personal coaching philosophy is a counter to the second ball game. I have always questioned the functional game of soccer, where the players don't have the right to express their game but are expected to work to a set of rules that actually confines them to their minimalistic roles in the team. I have observed the latter reality in some soccer academies where the men in charge are more concerned about having control over the games than coaching the young players to be the best they can be. What is even more absurd as far as I am concerned is the reality that when some academies fail to produce players of talent and quality, they resort to selecting the 'Big & Strong' battling type player because they have the second ball game to fall back on. This reality raises many questions for anyone interested in player development - "Do I want my players to be caged up in little boxes?", "Do I want them to play soccer to the forward moving mentality?", "Do I want them to play the long ball out from the back just to create a more physical game of soccer suited to bigger and stronger players?", "Do I want my players to be less than skilful, just so that they can give the ball away and create a 'busy' game of soccer?". The answer to every one of these questions is: **NO!**

STAGE FOUR - THE DEVELOPMENT OF TWO FOOTEDNESS & THE FIRST BALL GAME SKILLS

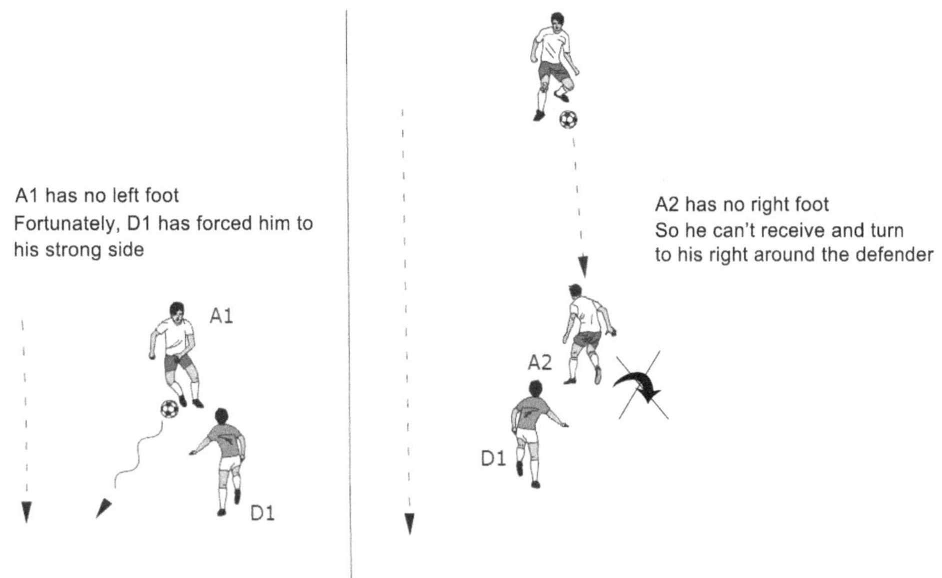

To understand the implications of having players who are out and out one footers, let's take a look at what happens in the most important area of the field of play, namely the penalty area. The goalkeeper's job is to protect his goal against any goal scoring effort and so he tries to close the angle down between himself and the opponent with the ball in such a way that the attacker has as little of the goal in his sight as possible. The player in possession of the ball, on the other hand, will naturally try to outwit the goalkeeper and score a goal. Simple enough! Except for one thing - even in today's professional game of soccer, some of the most highly regarded players in the world are left wanting in this situation and fail to outwit the goalkeeper because they are unable or unwilling to utilize their weaker foot.

DESCRIBING THE REALITY!

In the above detailed examples of a lack of 'Two footedness', the first challenger D1 closes player A1 Down on his left foot, leaving A1 no option but to move the ball to his strong side, which is his right foot. Nothing wrong with that you might say, until you consider that the choice of playing solutions is not down to the player in possession of the ball but down to the defender. The same applies to the second example where the player A2, on receiving the ball, can't turn around on his right foot because he is only left footed. Such a reality may be considered a minor detail until that is you realize the implication here, which actually shows that a right footed turn could place the player in a better attacking position but since he is a left footed player he doesn't have that option, moreover, if he did turn around on his left foot this would put player A2 in a bad situation and in danger of losing possession of the ball to the defender D1 which is actually a problem. The above examples of 'One footedness' are not seen as problems in many circles of the game, where such issues are ignored, when actually they do make a massive difference to the way the game is played, from a number of important realities, one being the difference between the first and second ball game. Would I want my players to be one footed and have all sorts of problems on the field of play as a result? OF COURSE NOT!

MY COACHING METHOD THE DEVELOPMENT OF 'TWO FOOTEDNESS' & THE FIRST BALL GAME SKILLS

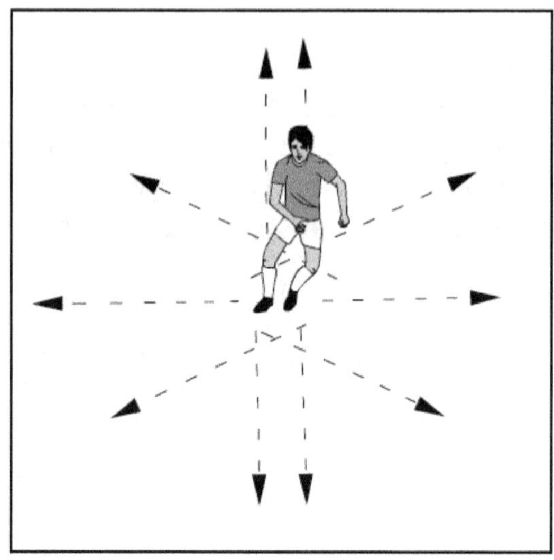

I have spoken at length about the need to favor fast twitch muscle development when it comes to the more skilful game of soccer, but this is not the only area of concern for those involved with player development. Let us go back for a moment to the reality I highlighted at the start of this book, that normal every day activities are governed by the forward moving reality, which happens to influence almost everything that human beings do. It is important to understand the implications this has on player development, because when the human being is always kept in this forward moving reality, the chance of developing collaboration between the left and the right side of the brain is minimal. This is not something that we should ignore. The coach should understand that human beings are creatures of habit and that the practical experience of everyday life shapes these habits. Considering the simple fact that everyone has to eat in order to survive, it's not surprising that the hand a child eats with is the hand that child will favor in all endeavours. This reality can create a lack of collaboration between the left and right side of the brain from an early age. When a young person takes up the game of soccer at the age of six, as an example, this lack of collaboration in the brain can be observed in the lack of ability to work the feet in a coordinated manner on one side of the body.

IN MY TRAINING SOLUTIONS

In my training sessions I apply working solutions that deal with this lack of collaboration. As I have said before, many will admit to the fact that the ability to use both feet (two-footedness) is better than depending exclusively on one foot (one-footedness), but they do nothing about it because it is an ability which is not easily trained, especially using the training methods which have been in vogue for years, training which by the way caters to the development of less skilful, more direct play oriented players. If a training session ignores the implications of a lack of bilaterality, it does a disservice to the players' development, first on the physical side and then naturally on the technical side of the game.

THE NOT SO OBVIOUS

The forward moving interpretation of life which is transferred into the coaching and playing domain results in a one footedness reality and the players do suffer all kinds of problems on the field of play as a result. Make no mistake about it, it is the lack of lateral input into the player's development program right from the word go that makes the player a one footed player. The forward moving reality creates its own consequences and if the counter to that reality is not in place in the form of lateral training formats, then the player will endeavour to play the game of soccer under imposed conditions that are restrictive, non-progressive and functional. A two footed player will always solve more problems on the field of play than any one footed player. But there is more to the lateral formats than just the quest to create a two footedness capability. The lateral formats also help the player to develop a better balanced physique, with both sides of the body able to perform the movements that are specific to the skills of the first ball game.

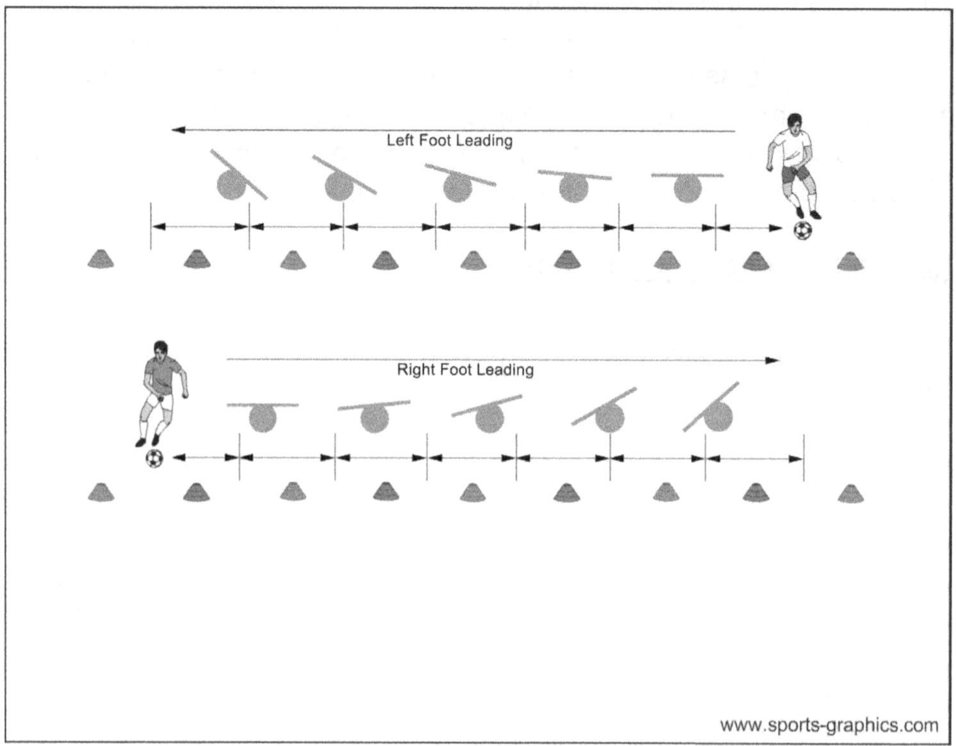

Most training session solutions simply do not question the forward moving reality. Indeed, through training regimens such as small sided games and conditioned touches (one-touch only, two-touch only etc.), coaches have for years been locking their players into the forward moving mind set. This in turn has led to the development of players without the lateral ability to play the first ball game. The diagram explains the result of coaching methods that keep the player locked into the forward moving reality.

Strange as it sounds, the counter to the forward moving reality and therefore to the habits that come from the forward moving world is the lateral dimension. The development of the 'Two footedness' of the player, therefore, is achieved by employing a counter working solution to the forward moving reality in the shape of the lateral dimension formats.

EXAMINE THE EFFECT OF THE LATERAL DIMENSION FORMAT

In (1) - In this first example of a lateral dimension format, the leading foot in the action is the left foot. The simple task of staying square on and parallel to the line of cones while moving the ball with either foot laterally with short touches to the ball (the arrow heads depict the points where the ball should stop on each of the two footed touches of the ball) can actually be almost impossible for any player who is right footed.

The same difficulty is found for left footers in the second example (2) with the right foot being the leading foot.

THE FAILURE TO KEEP SQUARE ON

The above example shows the reality when we place a forward moving, one footed player into a lateral format. What the coach can discover by using this training solution is the actual ability of the player. What we are seeing is the inability of the player to keep his weak side held in place against his strong side, which can either be the left or the right because there are those who do have a strong left side. In practice, when the player is weak on one side of his body he will not be able to maintain a square-on body position as he moves the ball down the lateral line of cones. This lack of lateral ability has a tremendous impact on the overall ability of the player to be the best he can be.

ADDRESSING THE ISSUES

Sometimes, the lack of physical balance is extreme. In other words, the player is completely useless on his weak side, in which case it is necessary to work the player to his weaker direction until the weakness is eradicated. If, for example, the weak side is the left side then the player would have to spend a lot more time in example 2 where the leading foot is the right foot.

AT THE BEGINNING

If the damage from the forward moving reality is not too great and the player is physically able on both sides then the work should be balanced out between the right and left side in equal measure.

GAUGE THE PROGRESS

The best way to determine a player's progress in terms of balance and lateral ability is again using the lateral line of cones. The player's ability to stay square on while moving the ball along the line is a great indicator of where he is in his balance and lateral movement development.

LAYING DOWN FOUNDATIONS

Staying square on and moving the ball to the lateral angle with the inside instep as described by the above arrow formations is actually a foundational soccer skill which not only develops the strength on both sides of the body, but is a skill and therefore a physical movement reality that lays down the foundations for all first ball game skill options.

SOCCER SKILLS FOR THE FIRST BALL GAME

When the player masters the above format and has the strength to move the ball with both feet to the lateral angle and length of touch, which by the way is approximately three feet, it is then possible to begin to introduce the first ball game skills and even create working formats that are specific to a particular first ball game skill. My first example of a single first ball game skill is called 'Moving the ball off the line'. This has become a controversial skill in the game of soccer, in some quarters of the game at least, because it is a skill option that does not suit the second ball game agenda. Why? Because this skill can slow the game down and is not in tune with the forward moving mentality of the second ball game. Anyway, in my opinion the off the line touch should be part of any player's playing repertoire and if it isn't then it is not a skilful game of soccer.

MOVING THE BALL OFF THE LINE

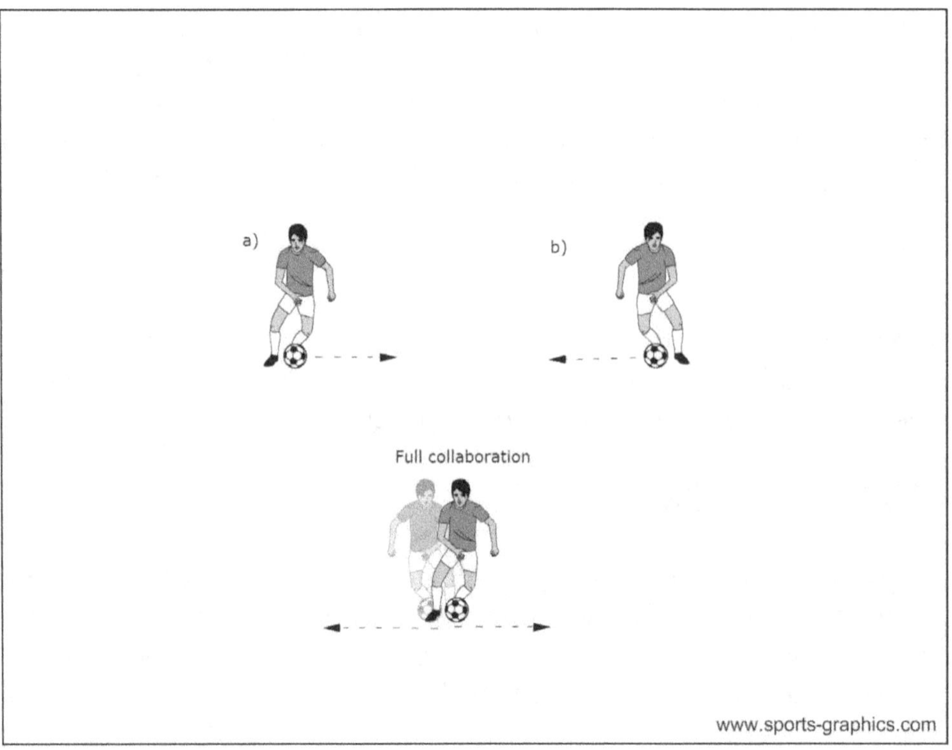

Player A1 moves the ball off the line by touching the ball on with the inside instep of the right foot (a) or with the inside instep of the left foot (b). The foot always follows through on the touch across the player's body and to the direction of the touch. The follow through on the touch keeps the player in contact with the ball.

The field of vision! For one thing, it is not convenient to the second ball game if the player slows the game down by moving the ball off the line, but to many of us who love to see the more skilful game of soccer, the above skill option is actually essential to the first ball game, because it enables the player to create the time to look up and see more of the field of play. To those who think that such a touch would slow the game down, consider that the pass of the ball off most first touch options will certainly travel faster than any man.

VOLUME OF TOUCHES

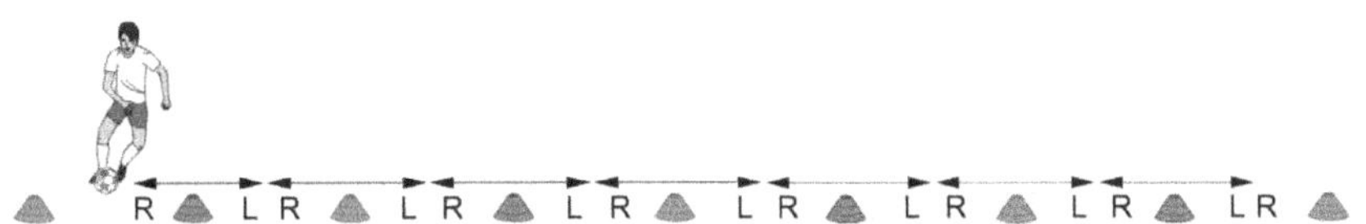

THE PRACTICAL REALITY

It is quite commonplace for the coach to accommodate at least fifteen players in his training session. In the above format, the player has the opportunity to touch the ball many times, as many as seven or eight touches on each foot, in a short space of time. Imagine how many touches to the ball the player could have if he worked in this format for ten attempts of moving the ball down this line of cones with the inside instep of either foot. It can take 10,000 hours of work to be the master of the ball in any conventional method. My method cuts to the chase so to speak, and ensures the 'Mastery of the ball' in half that time. It's not just about the volume of work here, it is also about what the lateral development does from a player development point of view. 'Moving the ball off the line' is important to the first ball game because it is a skill that opens up the angle of play to the full 180° in front of the player (also to the back of the player if he turns around!). It is the physical ability of the player that dictates what he can do with the ball and of course some would argue that it is possible for a one footed player to improvise and contort his body shape to play the game of soccer but that is not the point of any development program. Moving the ball to the 180° angle (right or left of the player) in an instant during the game of soccer will only be possible for a two footed player.

DEVELOPING TWO FOOTEDNESS
THE OFF THE LINE TOUCH

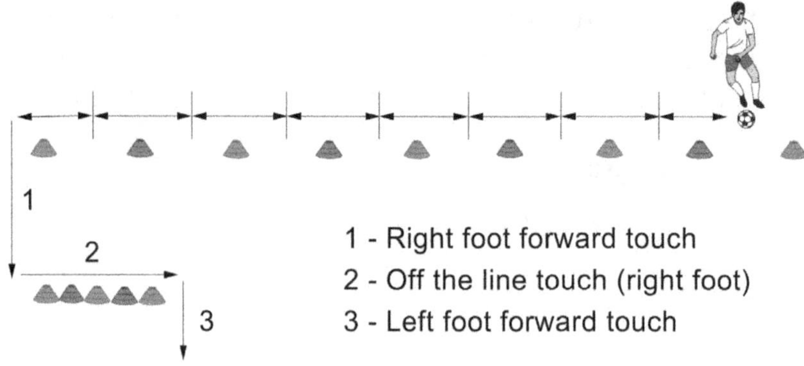

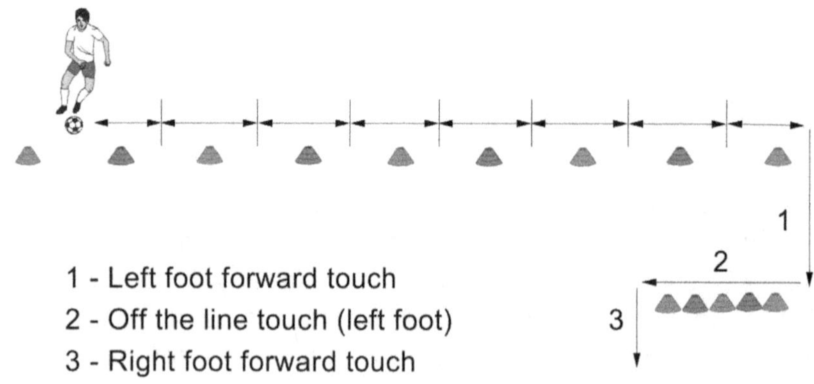

The above examples are aerobic. These exercises, working the inside instep to the lateral angle, develop strength in the leg/foot and the inside of the upper leg known as the groin.

FOUNDATIONAL

In this next example, the player works on moving the ball with such skills as the drag backs, the inside instep two footed lateral touches and the sweep overs with the underside of the boot to the ball.

ANAEROBIC - FAST TWITCH = FAST FEET

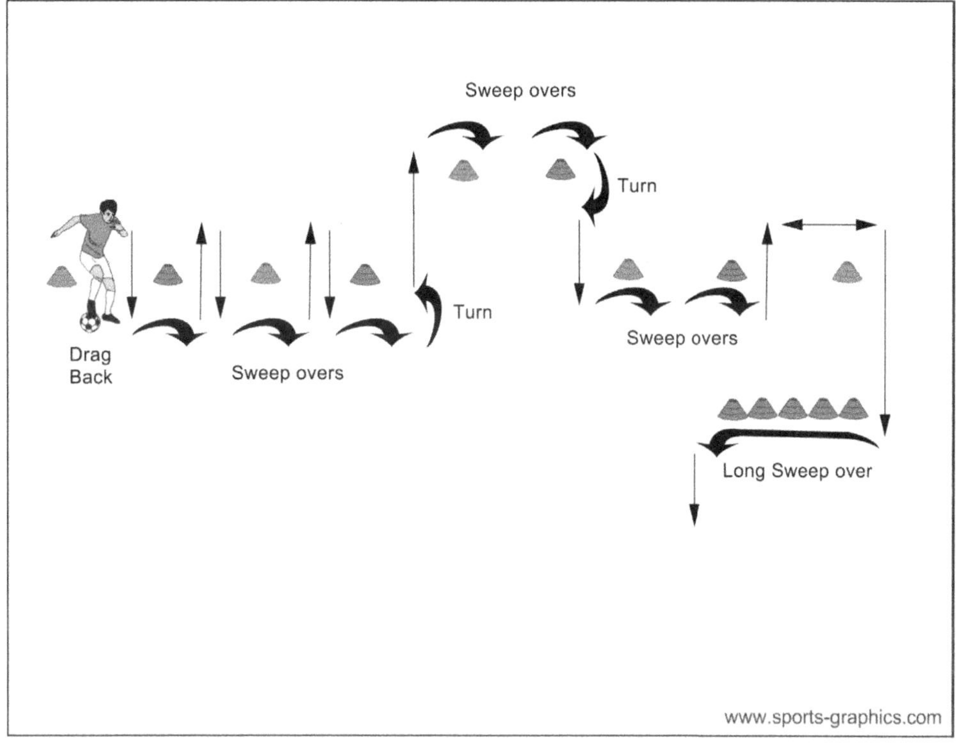

CLOSE BALL CONTROL

Stage four of the training session. The above formats represent the basic physical movement patterns required for all first ball game skills. The mastery of the lateral inside instep work is essential to the performance of many first touch skills. In the above example, player A1 uses his feet to work the ball to the forward touch and drag back of the ball, in combination with the sweep overs. The sweep overs are performed with the underside of the boot, moving the ball across the top of the cone placements. On reaching the middle section the player practices turning with the ball dragged back under his body to now do the sweep overs over the two cone placement, then turns again with the ball to continue the task set, finishing with a forward touch to the ball and the single longer sweep over across the back of the five cone placements. The short sweeps are approx 3 ft across and the longer sweep is approx 1.3 yds.

DESCRIBING THE FIRST BALL GAME SKILLS

The above formats underpin the development of the following first ball game skills.

1 - Taking the ball off the line - Taking the ball off the line is taking a touch to the ball with the inside instep, moving the ball under control across the body. If the player is two footed then he can obviously move the ball to the right or left of his body position and of course his body position can face to any direction on the field of play.

2 - Setting the ball up - This is a touch on the ball that is played with the inside instep to make the ball sit up nicely for a long pass option. The set up angle is approx 45 degrees.

3 - The Extended foot touch - This is an incredibly useful touch because it allows the player to take the ball through a 180 degree option of angle of play to the right or the left. The inside instep of the foot is applied but instead of playing the ball across the body the player moves the ball away from his body. If the player is two footed he can cover a 360 degree angle in play.

4 - The Dink Touch - The dink touch is taken to the ball with the laces of the boot - toe down. This touch is useful in a tight situation where the opponent almost arrives at the feet of the receiving player as the pass comes in. The ball is simply lifted over the opponent's challenging foot and out of his reach.

5 - The Forward Touch - The forward touch simply takes the ball to the front of the player. The most common use of this forward touch to the ball takes place when the player is moving the ball forward on a run.

6 - The Roll Touch - The roll touch is usually used by a player receiving a pass with a tight marker behind. With the outside of the boot, he sends the ball around and behind his close marker, turns and moves past the marker and after the ball.

7 - The Stop Touch - The stop touch is self explanatory- It is a touch that simply stops the ball at the player's feet.

8 - The Reverse Touch - The sister touch to the extended foot touch. The reverse touch is also very useful because it enables the player to take the inside instep of the foot to the ball and to turn on that touch.

TWO FOOTED WITH FIRST TOUCH OPTIONS

The above are bread and butter skills for the first ball game, which can be considered as standard first touch solutions. It is easy to figure out where such a touch solution would come in handy during a game of soccer. When you think about the possibilities and understand the implications of two footedness, you can imagine that in the right hands the above 8 touches become 16, become 36 and so on. By in the right hands I mean a two footed player. In addition to that reality, if you take a talented player like the great Maestro Lionel Messi of Barcelona fame, then there is no limit to what this player can do with such a skill as 'The Extended Foot Touch' that can send the ball to almost any angle on the field of play.

A PRINCIPLE OF THE PRACTICE SESSION
THE FUNCTIONAL REALITY - NO COLLABORATION

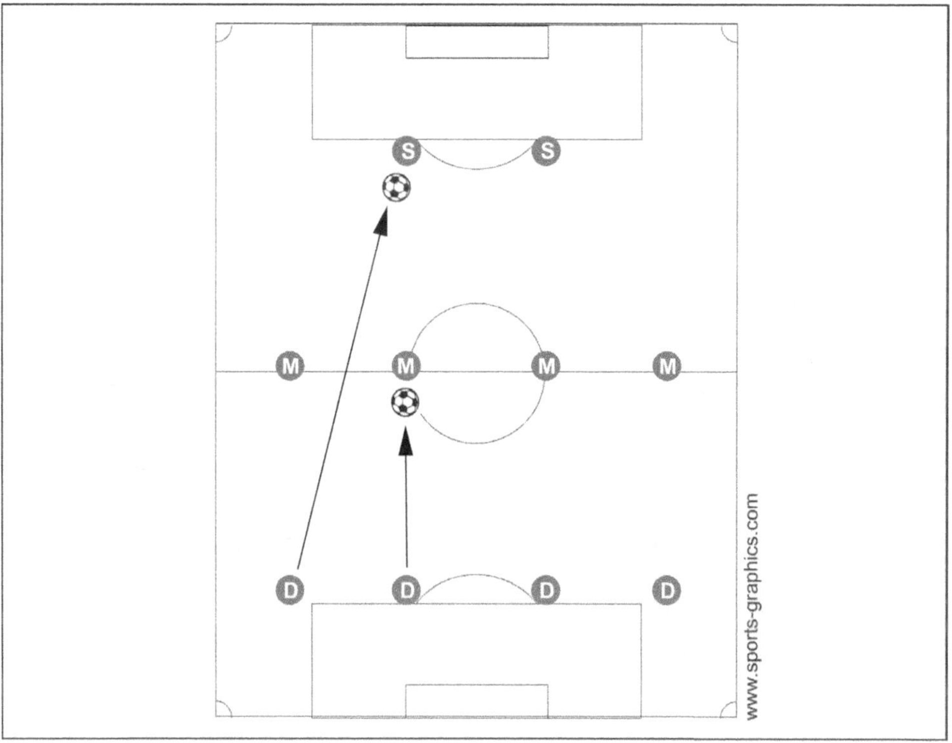

THE BARCELONA REALITY - WITH COLLABORATION

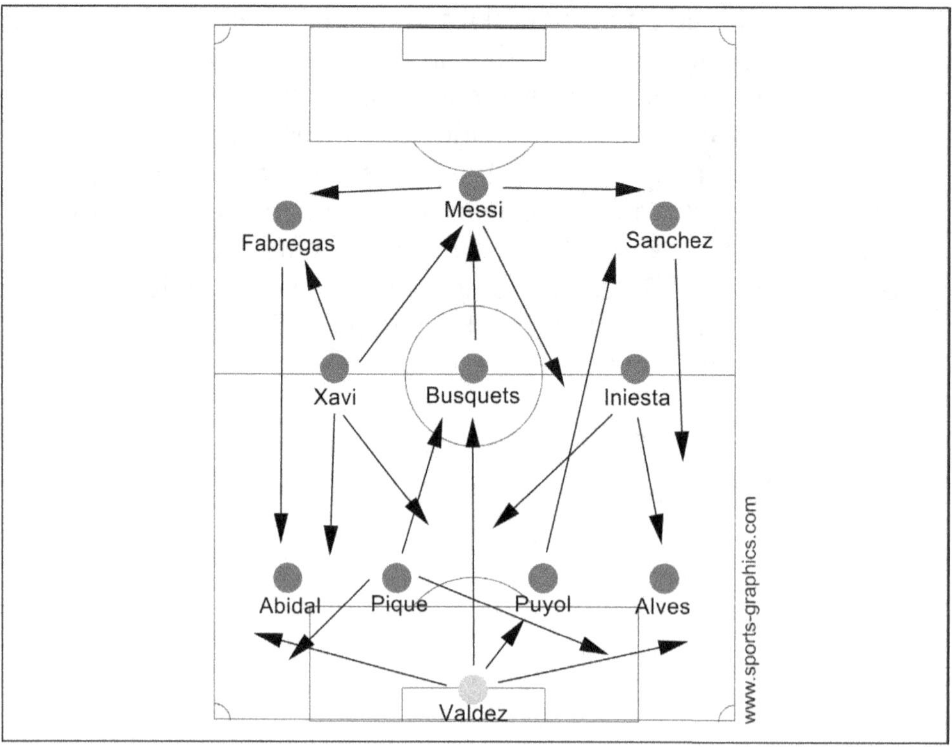

THE FIRST BALL GAME

Of course, the names change year to year but this is an example using one recent iteration of the FC Barcelona team. The examples here allow me to explain something which is key to the development of the player. In the functional game of soccer the pass of the ball is usually forward and much longer than in any first ball game team like Barcelona. One criticism of my formats is that the length of the passes is too short. In fact, I have some very serious concerns about the length of pass when it comes to working with young players that I want to share with you here.

THE LENGTH OF PASS

I don't wish to see my young players kicking the long ball to each other, for different reasons. My number one concern is the possible injury to the lining of the stomach (Hernia) which is a real concern over time. Another reason for my way of thinking is that it takes up too much time and because of it the volume of work is not good. Another concern is the effect of the long pass on the development of the touch on the ball. The long pass creates a reality which is aerobic in nature and doesn't really allow for any delicate feel and touch for the ball.

THE CORRECT WORKING ENVIRONMENT

I don't have the players kicking the long ball when it comes to working on the first touch to the ball, for two important reasons:

1. It is important to enable the player to have lots of touches to the ball in order to master the skills of soccer.
2. The working environment should not pose a risk of injury to the player.

WITH COLLABORATION - THE PRACTICE FORMAT EXAMPLES

THE PRACTICE FORMAT FOR SKILL 1 - THE SKILL OF MOVING THE BALL OFF THE LINE (ANAEROBIC)

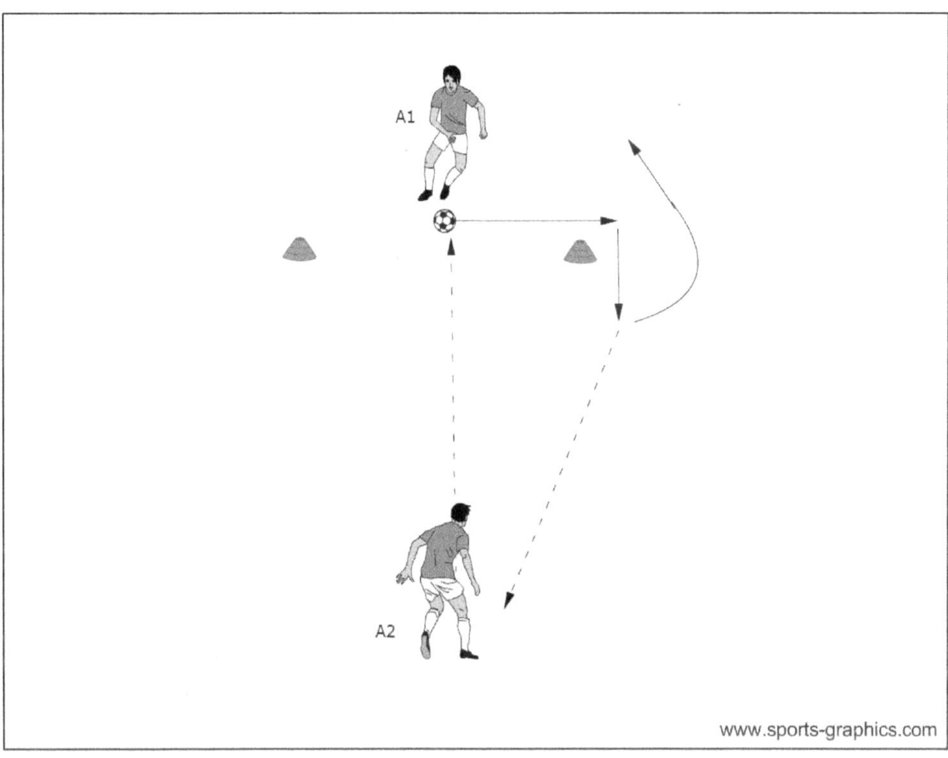

TWO FOOTEDNESS - THE RIGHT & LEFT FOOT LEADING

RFL - A2 passes the ball to the right foot of A1. A1 moves the ball off the line with the right foot, the right foot follows the ball to a touch distance of 1.3 yards. This touch just about moves the ball past the cone on his left shoulder, at which point he uses his left foot to move the ball forward and past the cone placement. At a couple of yards past the cone placement, A1 passes the ball back to player A2 with his left foot, turns and goes back into the starting position again. Players can swap places after moving the ball off the line five times. After each player has had five goes with the right foot leading, they do it again with the left foot leading.

THE PRACTICE FORMAT FOR SKILL 2 - SETTING THE BALL UP FOR A PASS

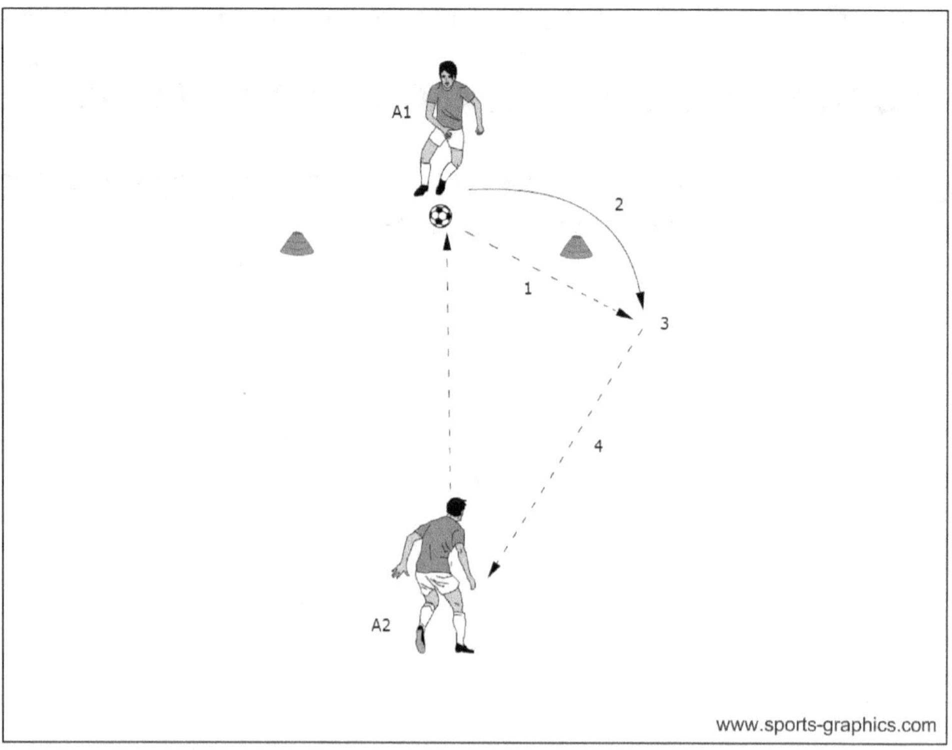

The pass to player A2 is 5 yds in length. A2 takes up the ball with a set up touch angle of 45 degrees to the cone (#3) and passes the ball back to the player A1. In the left diagram the right foot begins the working sequence and on the right diagram it is the left foot. As with all techniques, the follow through on the touch is important. Regarding the inside instep touch, sometimes it is made with the foot completely turned out to a 90 degree angle and sometimes to a 45 degree angle and sometimes anything in - between. In the above format the players concentrate on the practice of taking a 45 degree angle touch to the ball. The set up touch is a touch option on the ball that enables the player to play a 30 or so yard pass, but in this exercise we don't play the long pass off this touch. Instead, ask for the short pass to feet in keeping with the main theme of the practice. Please note that the set up touch can be played when the player is already in possession of the ball. We will look at the long pass in stage five of the training session examples.

THE PRACTICE FORMAT FOR SKILL 3 - THE EXTENDED TOUCH

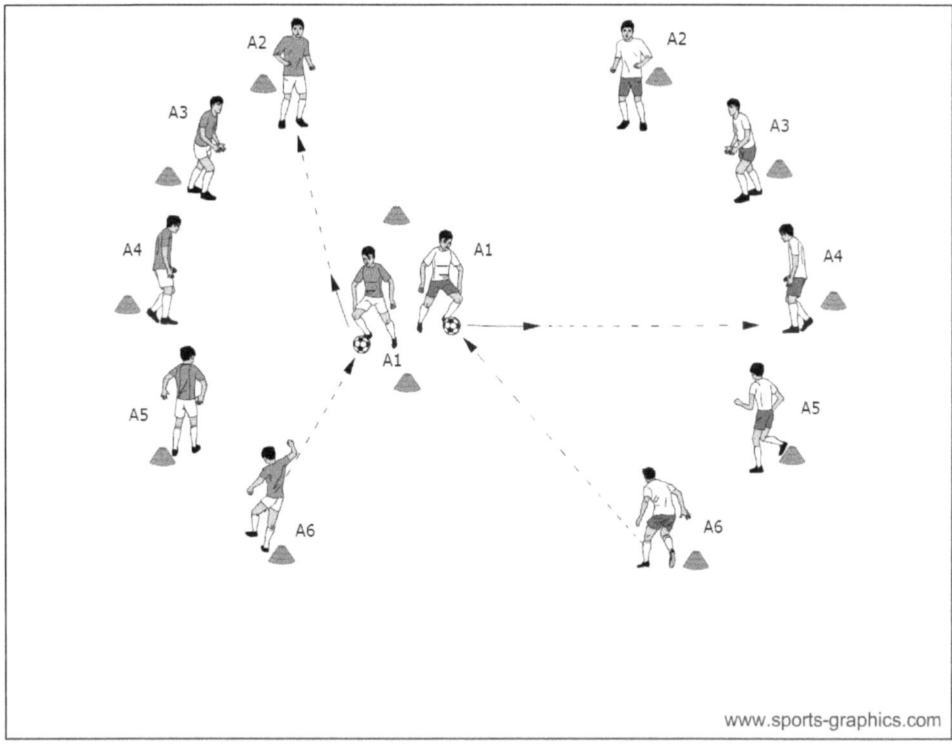

The above format looks a bit lopsided but that is because one side has the 20 yard pass and on the other side the pass is 10 to 15 yards. It is possible to speed the work up by reducing the length of the pass even more. In this case, the players can work not only on the extended foot touch (the foot moves away from the body on contact with the ball) but also on the short pass, in which case they can work on which foot they pass the ball to. The short work is more beneficial than the long ball from a touch development point of view, which is important. The extended foot touch is taken at the center of the above format off the pass by player A6. On the RFL side of the format, player A1 presents the inside instep of the right foot to the ball, taking a touch to any angle of his choice. For example, he takes the extended foot touch to approximately 1.3 yds and passes the ball off that touch to player A2. The original passer of the ball, player A6, moves up to position A1 - A1 moves to position A2 - A2 moves to position A3 - A3 to position A4 - A4 to position A5 and A5 to position A6, with each player taking turns in the middle. The same format applies to the LFL side of the format.

THE PRACTICE FORMAT FOR SKILL 4 - THE DINK TOUCH OPTION

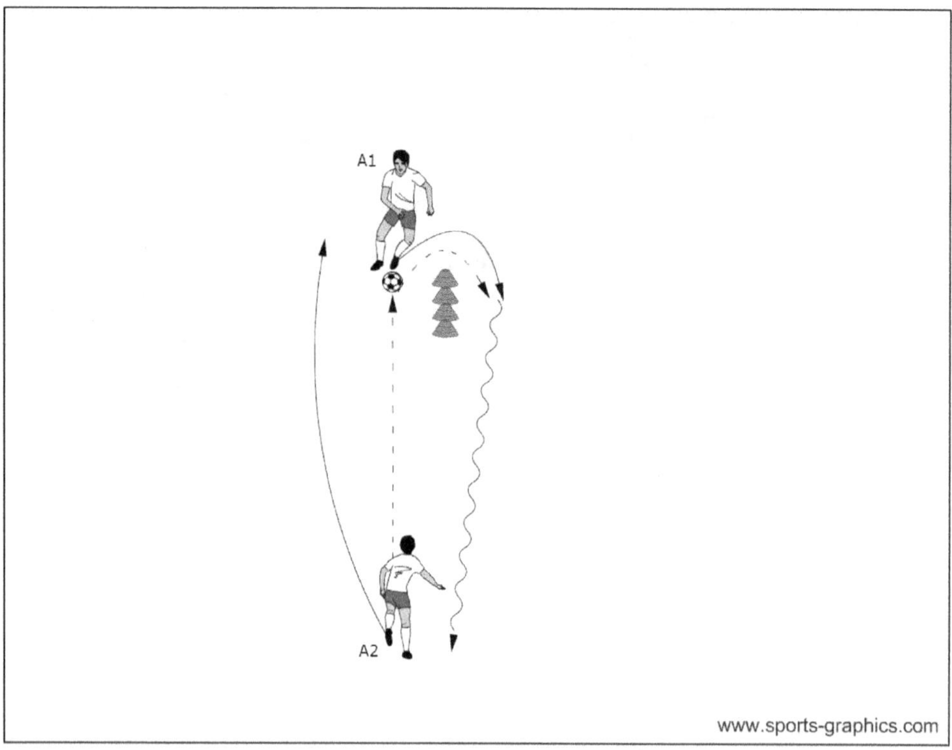

The ball is played in by player A2 to the right foot of player A1. Player A1 takes up the ball with the boot toe down to the ball and lifts it over the cones, then moves to the ball in one movement and takes it up again and moves to position A2. Player A2 at this point moves to position A1. Each player plays the ball and each player works on the dink touch. The working sequence is repeated five times for each player. In this format the players can swap positions or simply stay as they are and practice working the dink touch with the other foot. It is also possible to work with more than 2 - 4 players using a rotation, which is also good from a movement development point of view.

THE PRACTICE FORMAT FOR SKILL 5 - THE FORWARD TOUCH

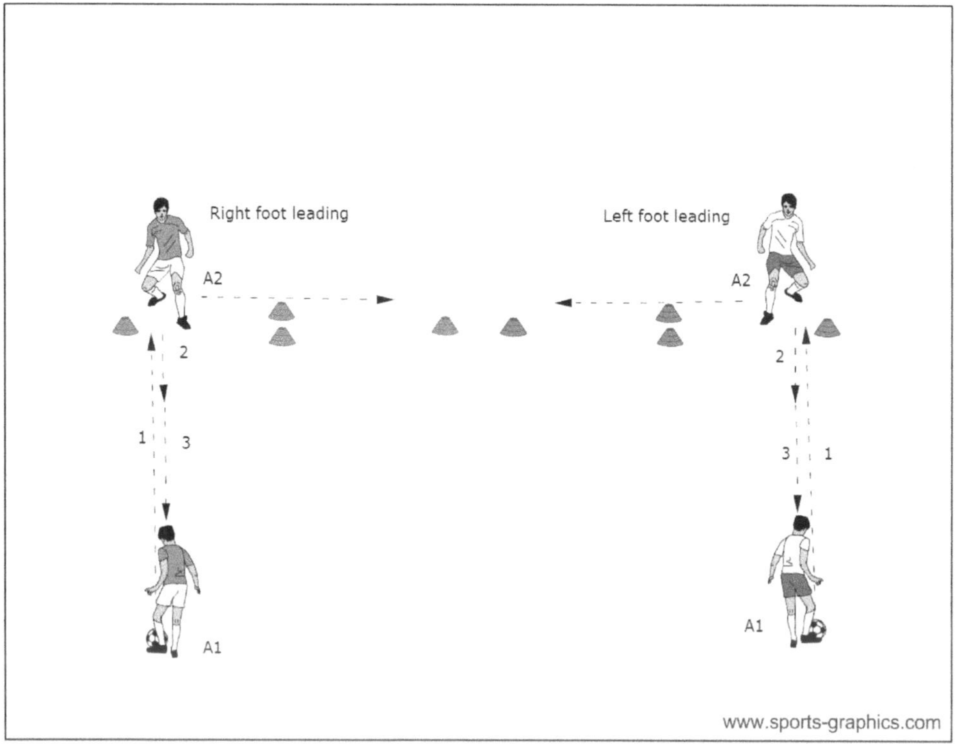

Note - The practical application of the skills here will be shown in stage five of the first ball game training session.

THE PSYCHOLOGY OF ORGANIZATION

If you look at the cone placements, it is just as easy to instruct the players to work the ball in the format to either foot. Sometimes though, breaking the practice up by having the players rotate (move to a different position) takes the monotony away because moving to another spot relaxes them, which is always a good strategy. Starting fresh at another point in the formats is a good way to get the player to think about the task at hand. The two cones at the center point of each of the above formats creates the thought of accuracy and touch direction. The ball is played in to the right or left foot. For example, player A1 takes the inside instep of the foot to the ball with the foot at almost a 90 degree angle and touches it forward of his position (approx 1.3 yds). Then with his second contact passes the ball to player A1. Work to repetitions of 5 on each foot touch. The players take turns.

THE PRACTICE FORMAT FOR SKILL 6 - THE ROLL TOUCH

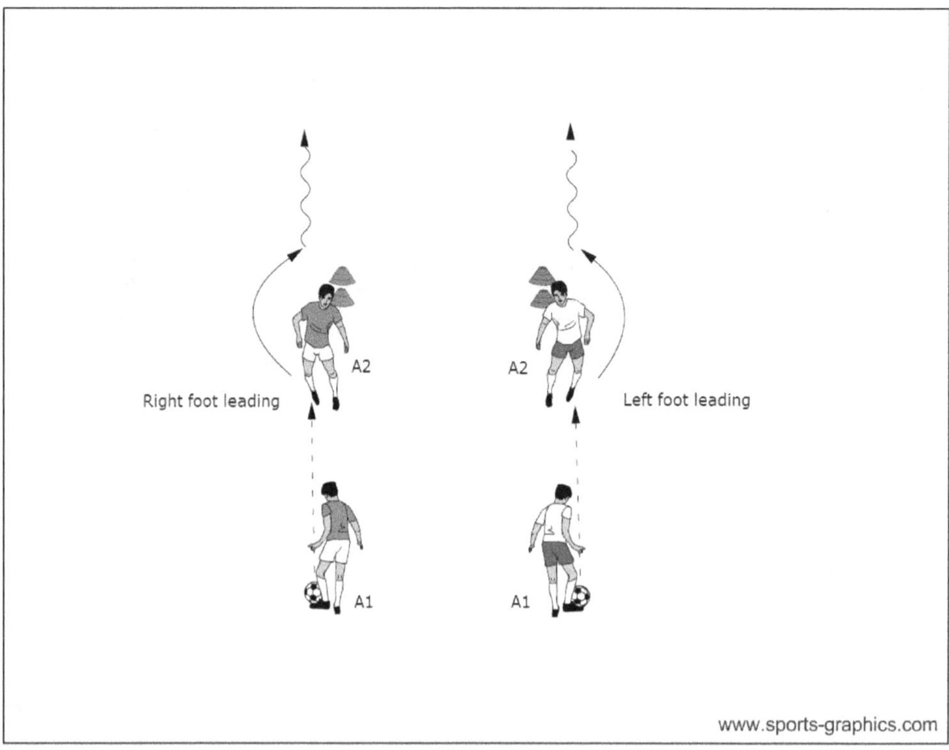

In this example, the skill is based on taking the outside of the boot to the ball and roll touching the ball past the marker. You can use a live defender but to begin have the two cones on the ground to simulate the position of the marker/defender. The technique of rolling the ball around the corner is useful when the opponent is marking tightly. The ball is taken up with the outside of the boot toe down and the player flicks the ball around the corner. In the same motion, he uses his hand to turn against the body of the opponent, in effect moving past the opponent after the ball.

THE PRACTICE FORMAT FOR SKILL OPTION 7 - THE STOP TOUCH

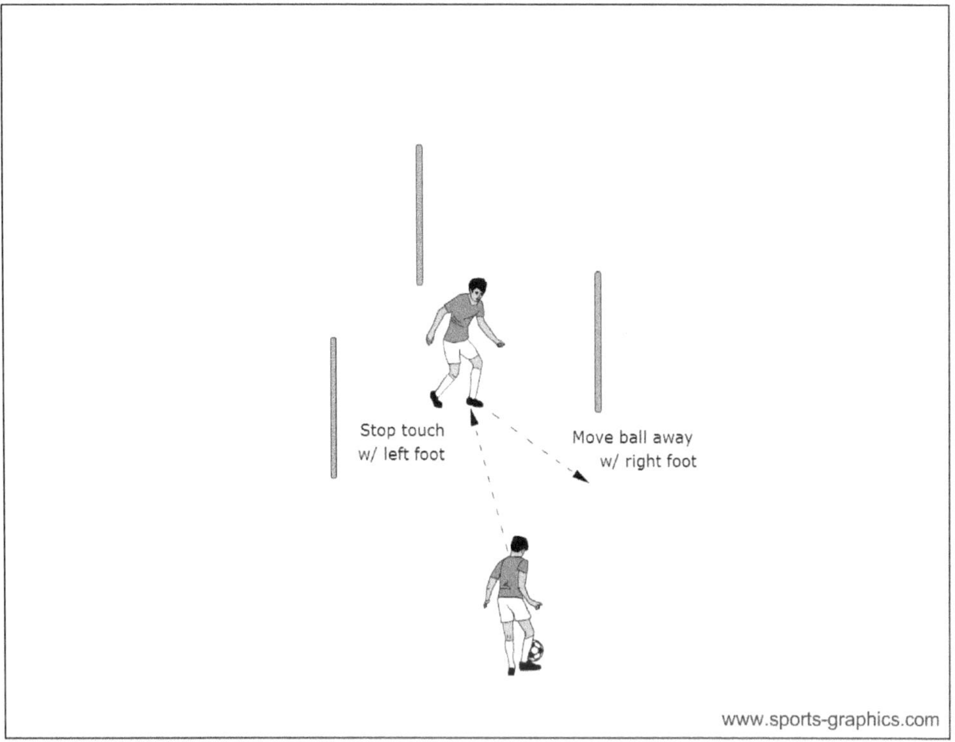

This practice can involve live markers, but to start place some stick markers for the player to practice receiving the ball, first to take a stop dead touch with the one foot and then move the ball to a safe escape point and out of the marker zone with the other foot. For example, right foot stops the ball, the left foot moves it. The left foot stops the ball, the right foot moves it, to the safe out direction.

THE PRACTICE FORMAT FOR SKILL OPTION 8 - THE REVERSE TOUCH

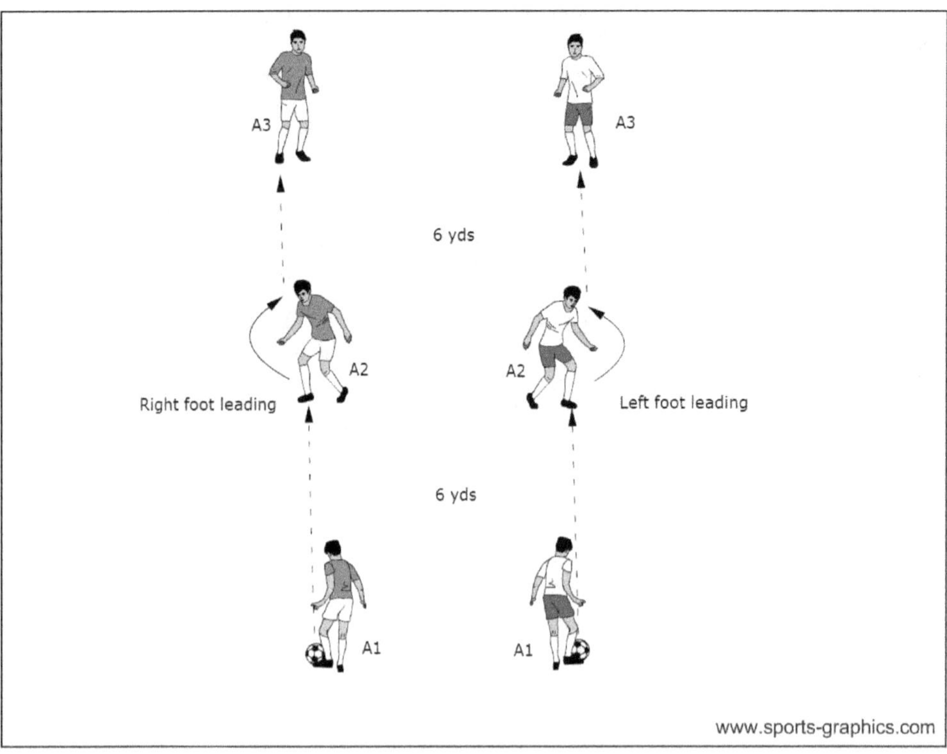

One of the finest practitioners of the reverse touch option in the world of soccer that I have ever seen is Andres Iniesta of Barcelona. Once again, just like the stop touch, in order to be able to do this skill the player must be two footed. Otherwise, any turn he makes will be predictable.

RFL - Player A1 passes the ball with his left foot with a fair amount of pace to player A2. Player A2 takes up the ball on the inside instep of the left foot, cushions the pace out of the pass and turns around on this touch. On turning he passes the ball with his left foot to player A3.

LFL - Player A1 passes the ball with his right foot with a fair amount of pace to player A2. Player A2 takes up the ball on the inside instep of the right foot, cushions the pace out of the pass and turns around on this touch. On turning he passes the ball with his right foot to player A3.

Note - The layout of the practice format focuses on the task at hand but it is up to the coach also to think of ways to organise the format if he has more than two players to work with, which is not obviously unusual. One way is to rotate the players through the format. Another would be to construct more than one format. Yet another way would be to organise a rotational circuit. In any case it is always a question of using logical solutions to any problem.

THE ADDITIONAL WORK FOR STAGE FOUR

In a functional game of soccer, the players can be spread out over a greater distance, with the players keeping to their designated positions on the field of play which adhere to a strict structure such the 4 - 4 - 2 for example. The distance between the players can be much greater than even 30 yards and this has its implications to the type of skills that come to the forefront. The players generally play with their backs to the opponents or run with the ball. They don't get caught in possession of the ball, not in general terms. The main reason for this is that they don't play the short passing game.

In the first ball game reality (as seen in the previous diagram of the Barcelona team) the players play the short passing game and because of that can find themselves working in situations where the game is a lot tighter in terms of space. In these situations, players need to be able to work both feet and use skills that can get them out of trouble.

The additional work in stage four, therefore, includes examples of formats that enable the players to practice either keeping the ball off the first touch or getting themselves out of tight situations. The first example practice formats are called 'Playing off the first touch'

THE ABILITY TO PLAY OFF THE FIRST TOUCH

Once the players have mastered the above first touch options we can then work with formats that enable them to develop the ability not only to get out of trouble in tight situations but to solve any problem off the first touch.

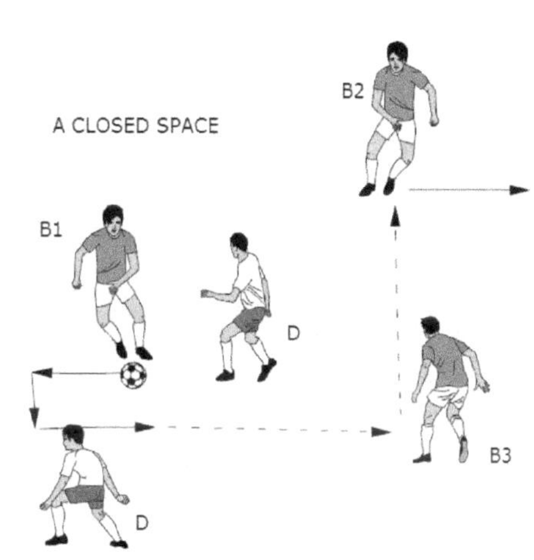

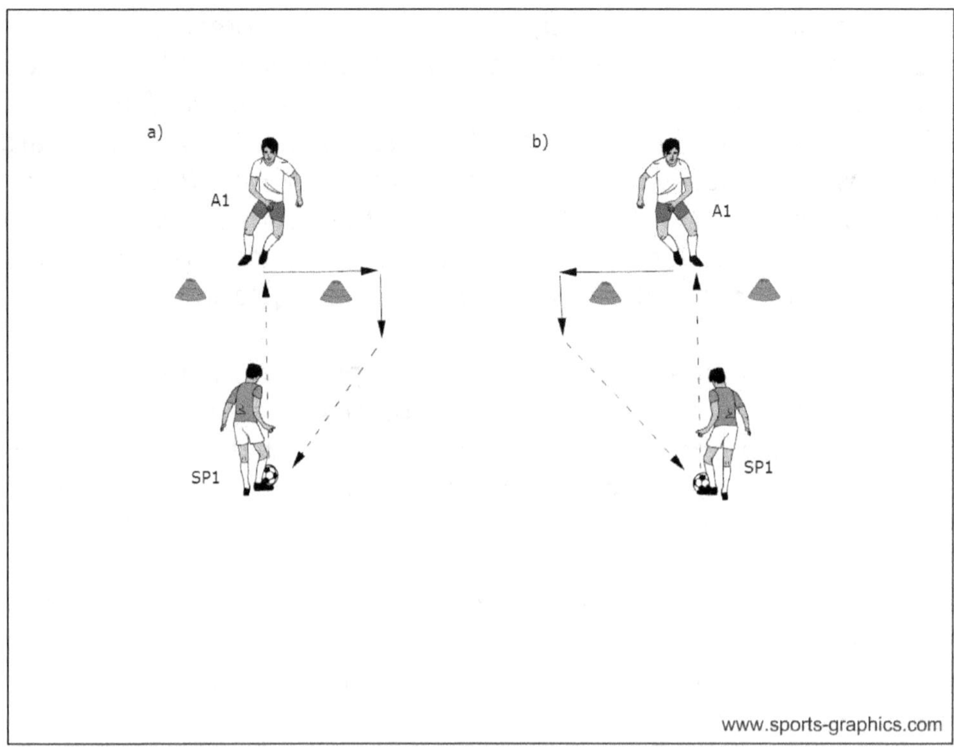
a)
A1
SP1
b)
A1
SP1
www.sports-graphics.com

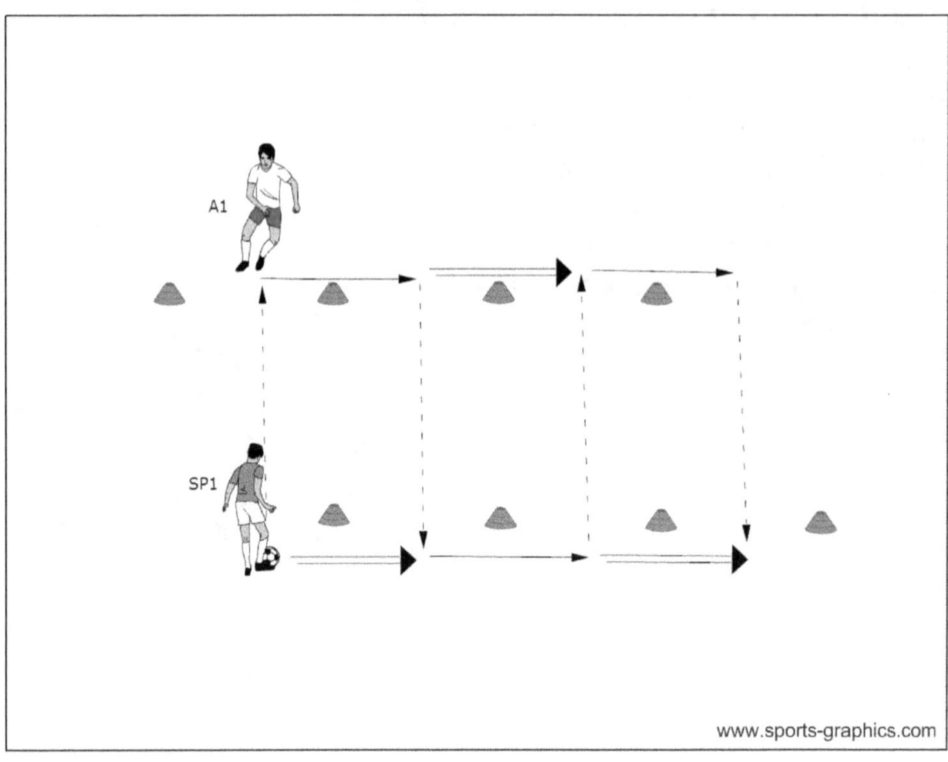
A1
SP1
www.sports-graphics.com

TOUCH PASS & MOVE - LOOKS SIMPLE ENOUGH

'Moving the ball off the line' is easy to do and a great format for teaching the players to work together. In so many ways working together is the most important skill any player can have. In the above format the players work the off the line touch and pass the ball off the touch to each other across the format.

MOVING THE BALL OFF THE LINE - SQUARE ON - ANGLED

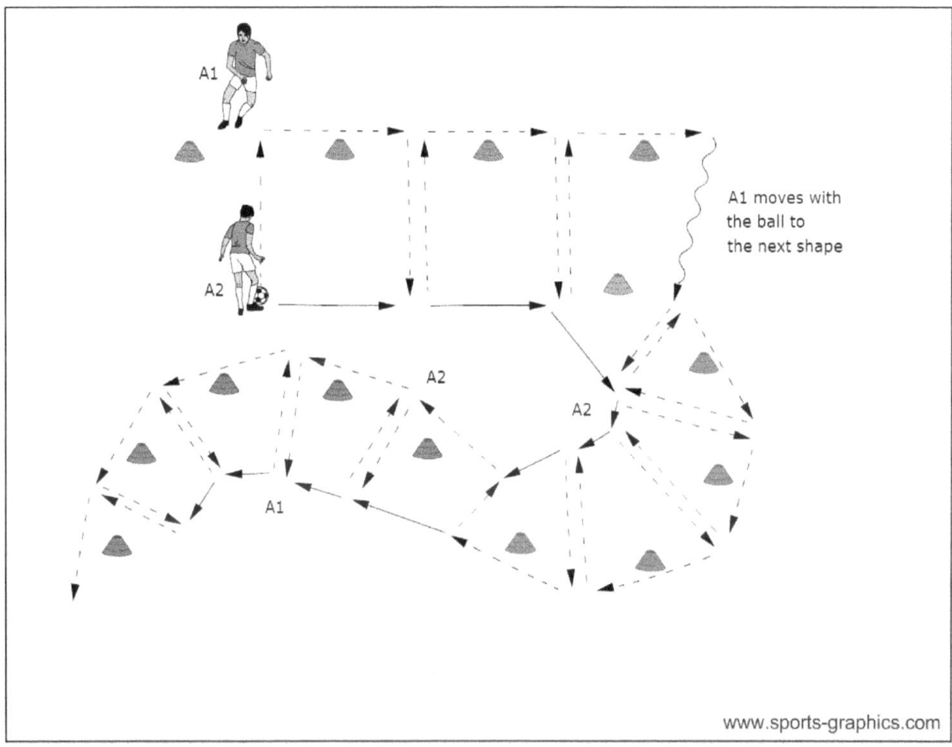

Touch pass and move, working in twos. Taking a square on touch and the touch that pulls the ball back, working clockwise, player A1 receives the pass from A2 and works the ball off the line then through the single line of cones using the sequence of touches on that side of the format. He then moves up to the next shape, where he again receives the ball from A2 and works around the shape as shown. At the end of the working sequence, players swap roles.

My next format is called 'The Inverted Steps' - The off the line touch moves the ball with either the right or left foot. In this next example, the player moves the ball off the line with one foot then quickly moves the fall forward with the other foot. I call this the inverted step. I bring it into focus at this point because I want to highlight a two footed skill that can get the player out of a tight situation.

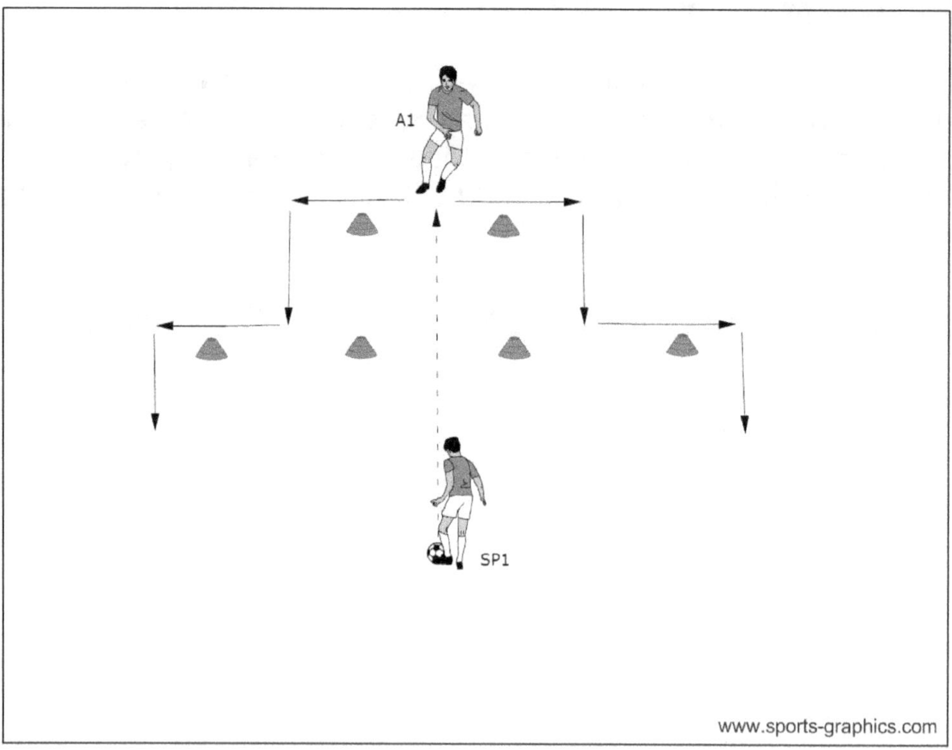

FAST FEET DEVELOPMENT

The most important feature of the working formats is the reality that these are neutral when it comes to which foot the player applies to the movement patterns, which when broken down to the detailed components are actually each representative of a single first ball game skill. The reason for the bigger shapes in the training equation is because only a repetition of the movements gives the player the adequate time on the ball that can create the correct effect on the physical development of the player.

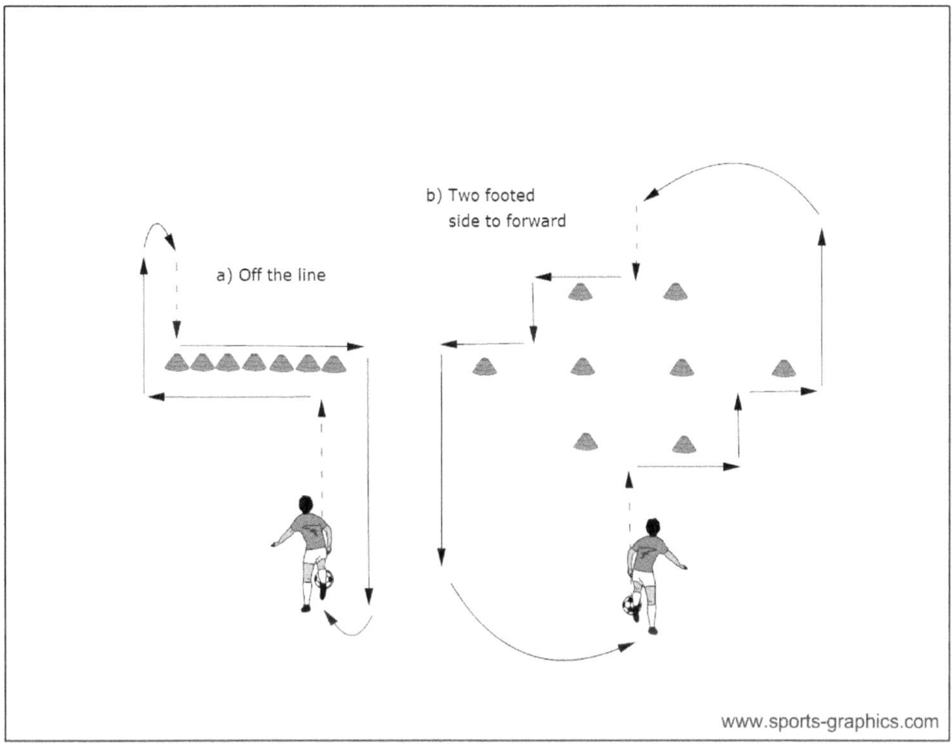

In this example, we combine the practice of moving the ball off the line with the inverted steps skill - a one foot or a two foot combination. Players rotate around the two formats.

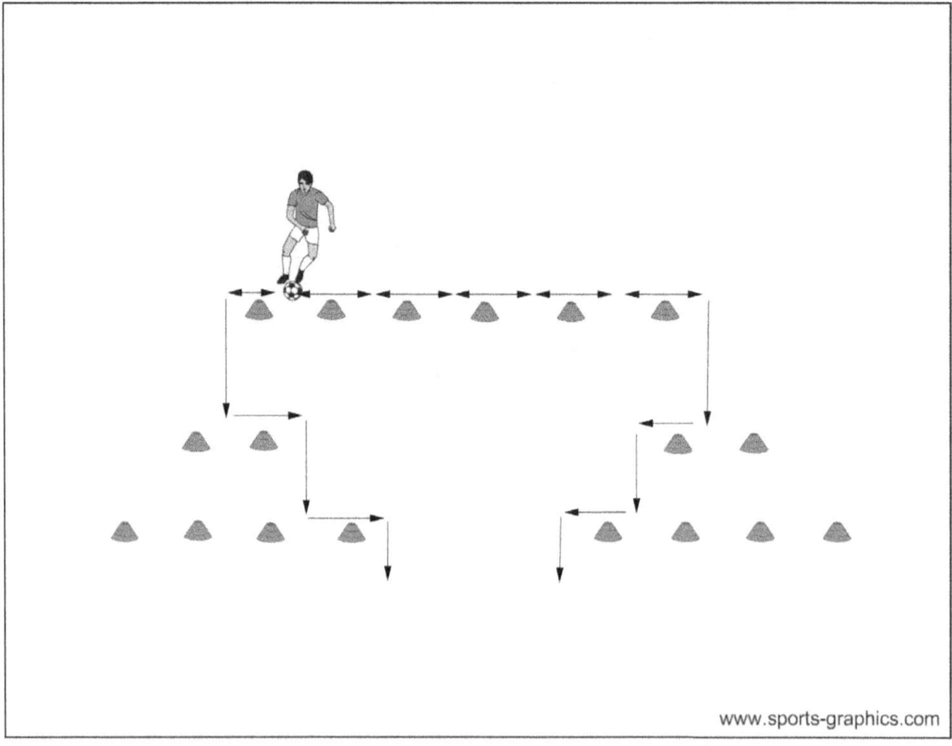

Developing both sides of the physical being (effective collaboration) is achieved by implementing a development program based on the lateral formats. The development of fast feet, which includes the forward touch and the two footed side to forward touch combinations are excellent movement forms for strengthening the muscle groups responsible for the physical ability to work the ball effectively to a first ball game standard.

Without this skill it would simply be impossible to play the ball to the lateral angle or use a combination of touch options via the two footedness combinations that we have on show here.

THIS EXAMPLE IS AEROBIC

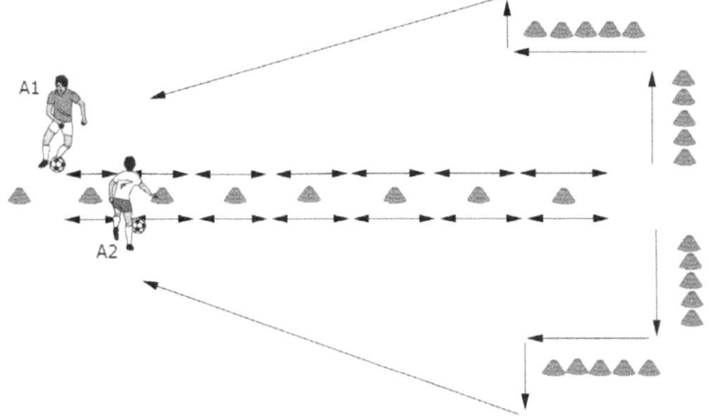

DEVELOPING STAMINA

A working sequence can end for each player with an additional request that can be performed on the outside of the format, in which case the complete working sequence can easily involve players to the outside of the format and the player can finish his turn with a pass and move objective. The objective can end therefore, with a keep possession game, where the player and his partners try to string at least five passes together. That could look something like this:

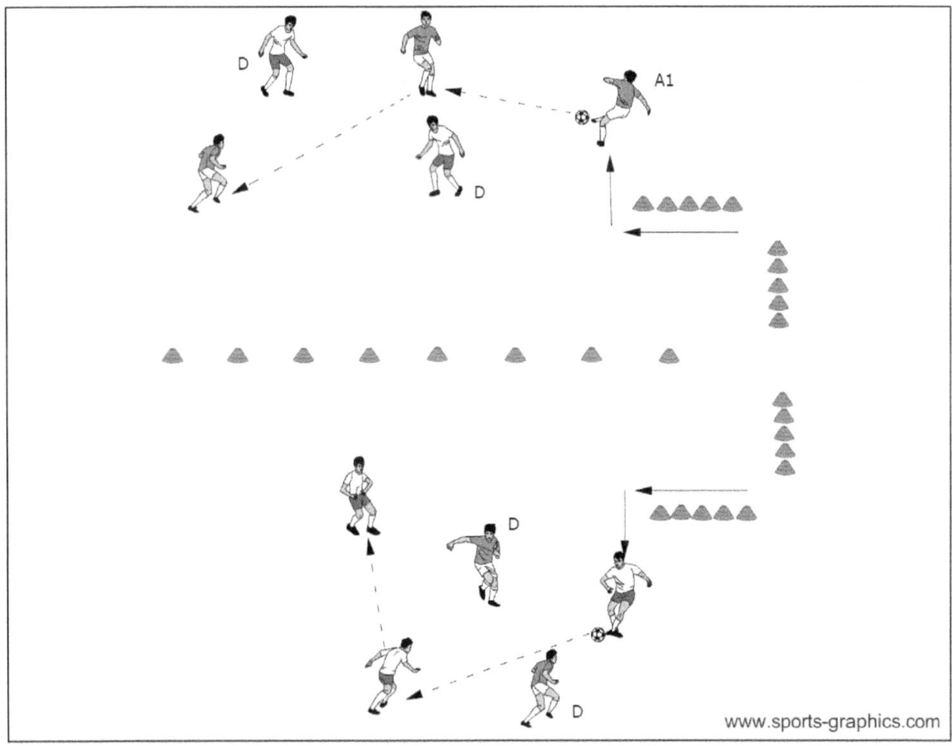

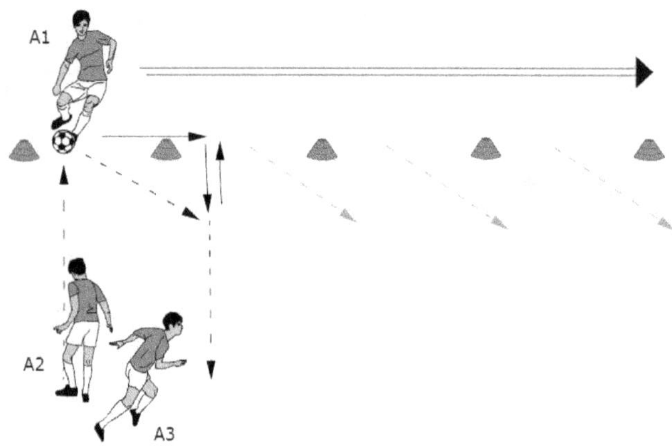

In the setup touch format, A2 passes the ball to A1 who makes a setup touch and plays the ball to the third man who is making a run. This third man option can also be incorporated using other touch options, such as the off the line touch.

8 - CHANGING THE PRACTICE FORMAT

THE FOUR CONE PLACEMENT

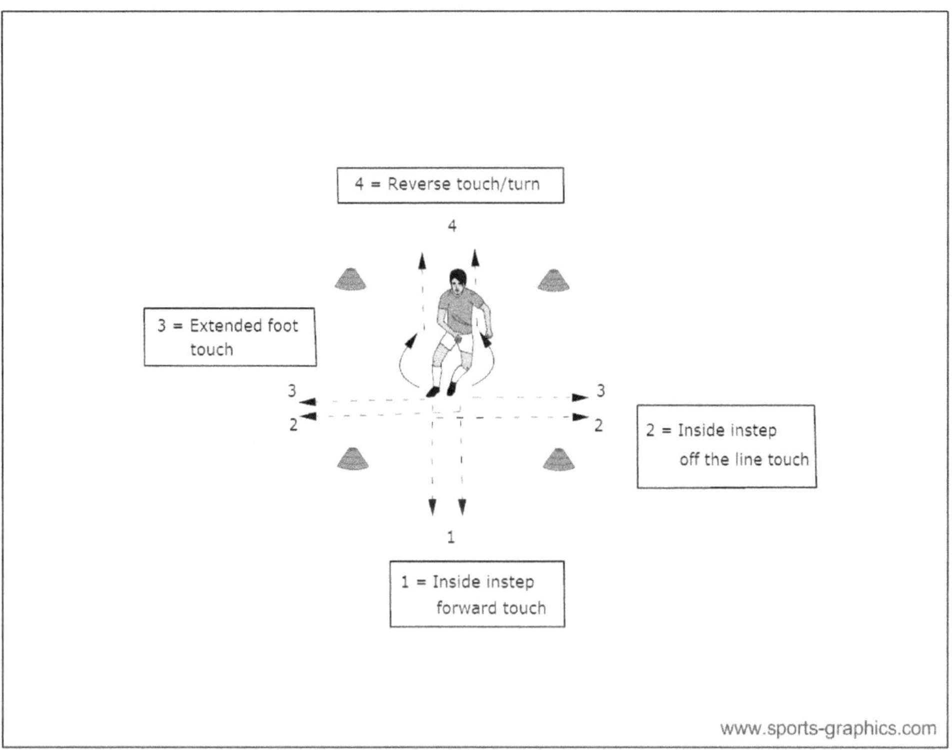

THE ORGANIZED STRUCTURE OF THE FOUR CONE PLACEMENTS

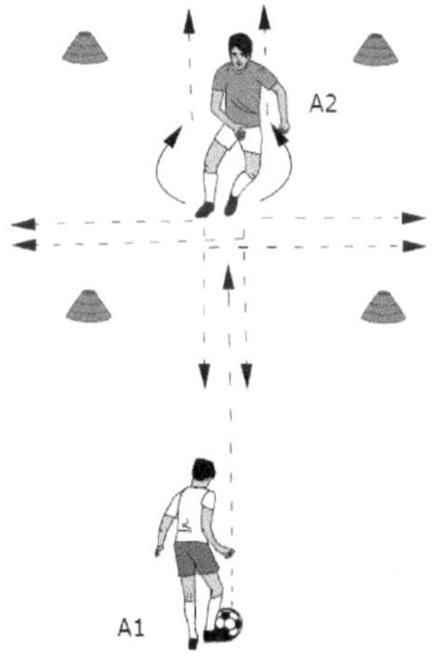

- **2.6 yds cone to cone square**
- **Length of touch 1.3 yds to any direction**
- **Entry pass approximately 8 yds**
- **360° playing possibilities**

THE FIRST TOUCH OPTIONS PRACTICE

We have seen how to work on the development of the 'Two footedness' of the player based on the lateral formats which promote the foundational skills for the first ball game. The next level of practice examples is called 'Playing off the first touch'. During a game of soccer, the player in possession of the ball may have to deal with an opponent that is close enough to challenge for the ball. In that situation the player needs a fast feet skill solution to take on the first challenger. This is possible when the player has the skills I have highlighted thus far.

There are times when the player will already be in possession of the ball and his next playing solution or choice of action will take place off that reality and there are times when the player will receive the ball and take control of the ball on his first touch and then work out a playing solution. In either case, the choice of what the player wants to do with the ball can begin off one of the first touch options that I have described thus far. In the above four cone placement format, the player practices taking the first touch options to the directions shown, with no opponent in sight.

PLAYING OFF THE FIRST TOUCH

In this next example, player A2 will practice taking the first touch and playing off the first touch solution known as moving the ball off the line.

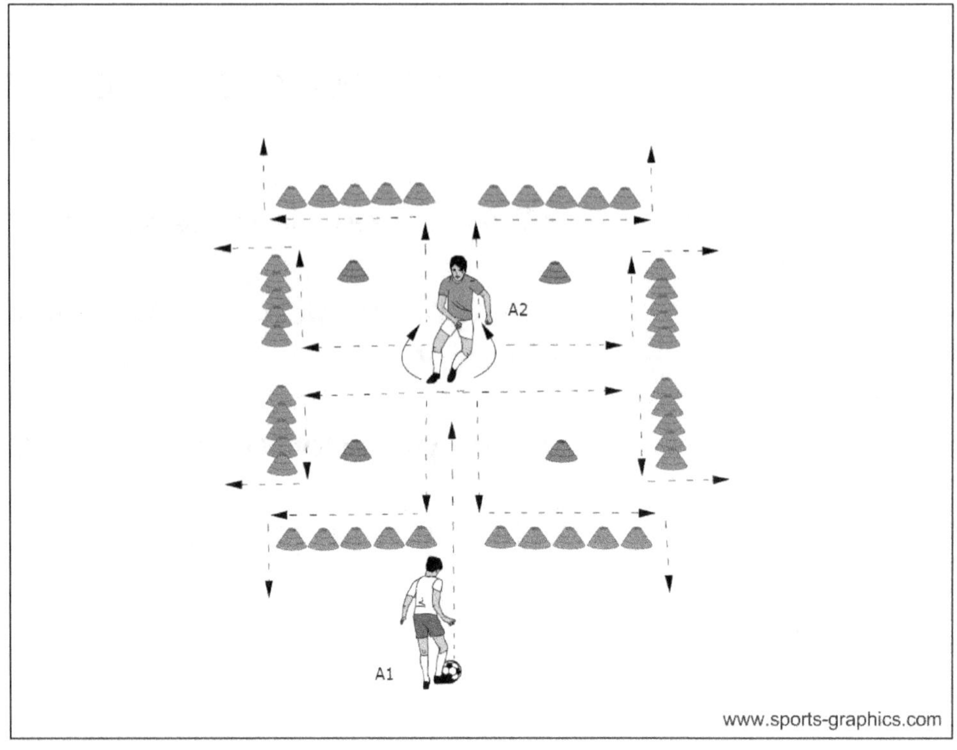

EXPLANATION OF THE ABOVE WORKING FORMAT

I have split the above format into four sections in order to explain what's involved.

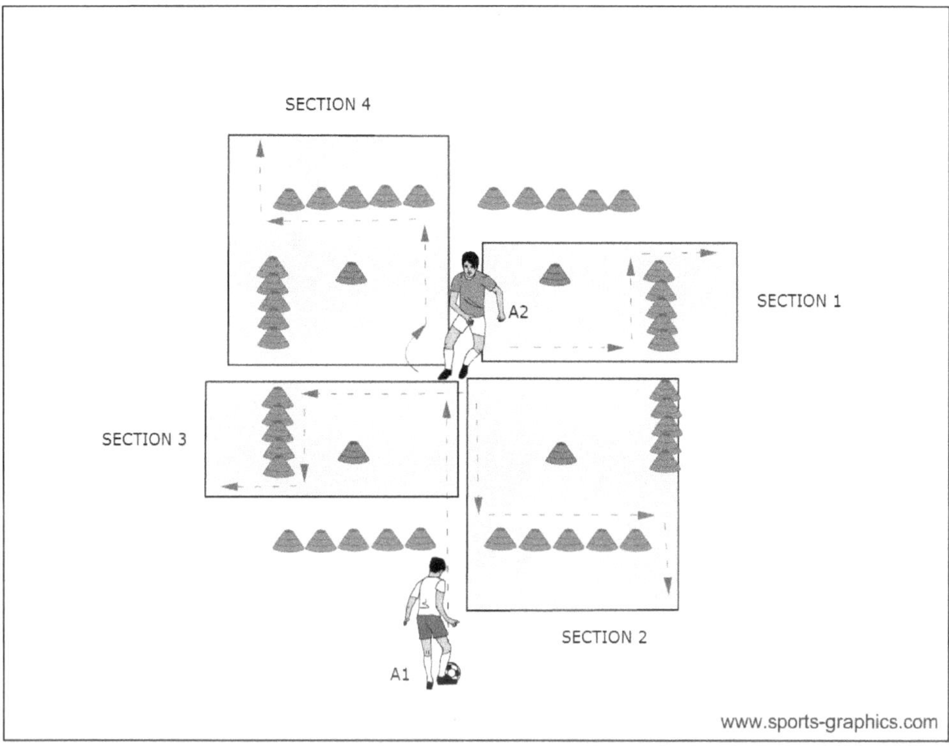

Section 1 : A2 receives the ball on his left foot, moves it out of his body on his left shoulder, turns on this touch to face the cone placements and moves the ball off the line again. Then a forward touch out of the format.

Section 2 : A2 receives the ball on his left foot, using the inside instep to move the ball forward, staying square on to the cone placement in front of him. He then uses his right foot inside instep to move the ball off the line and moves the ball out of the format with another forward touch with the left foot.

Section 3 : A2 receives the ball on his right foot and uses the out turned inside instep to the ball to make an extended foot touch to the cone placements to his right, then uses the inside instep of his right foot to move the ball off the line, finally moving out of the format with a forward touch with his left foot.

Section 4 : A2 receives the ball on his right foot, makes a reverse touch turn on his right shoulder and moves the ball off the line at the cone placements using his right foot. Then out of the format with a left foot forward touch.

THE INVERTED STEPS FORMAT

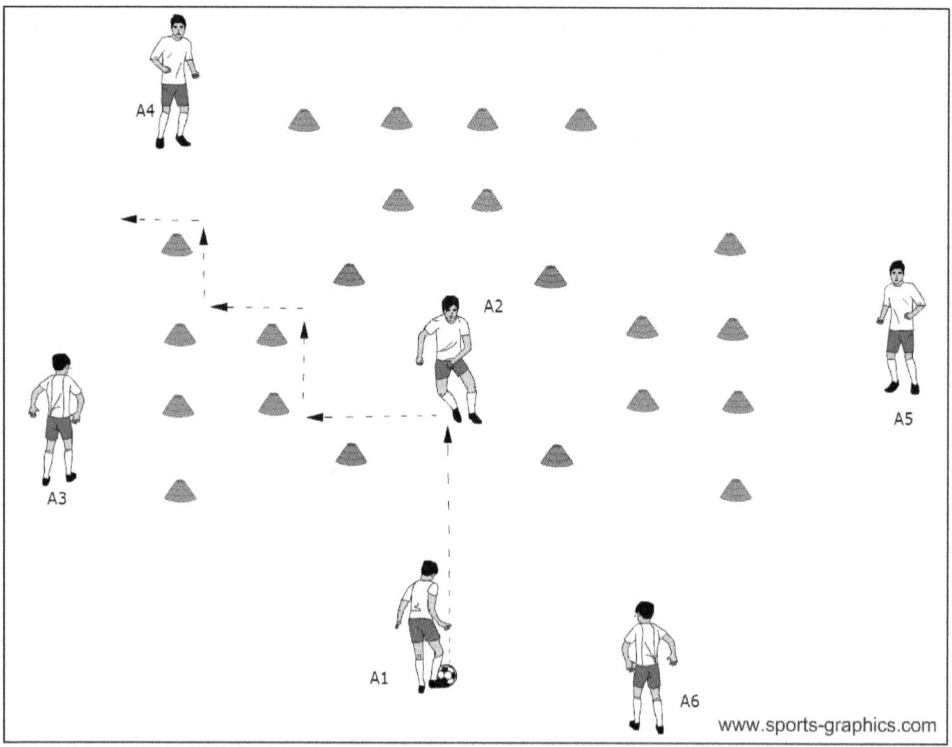

Once again, the four cone placement is the heart of this practice format. This 2.6 yd square (the four cones at the center point) is special when it comes to the needs of taking a meaningful touch to the ball. In this format the player works on taking his first touch to a length which gives him the ability to control the field of play to the 360 degree angle. In the above format, the practice is based on the player working the ball off the first touch to the cone placements where he performs a two footed combination skill called the inverted steps.

THE ADDITION TO THE FOUR CONE PLACEMENT - INVERTED STEPS

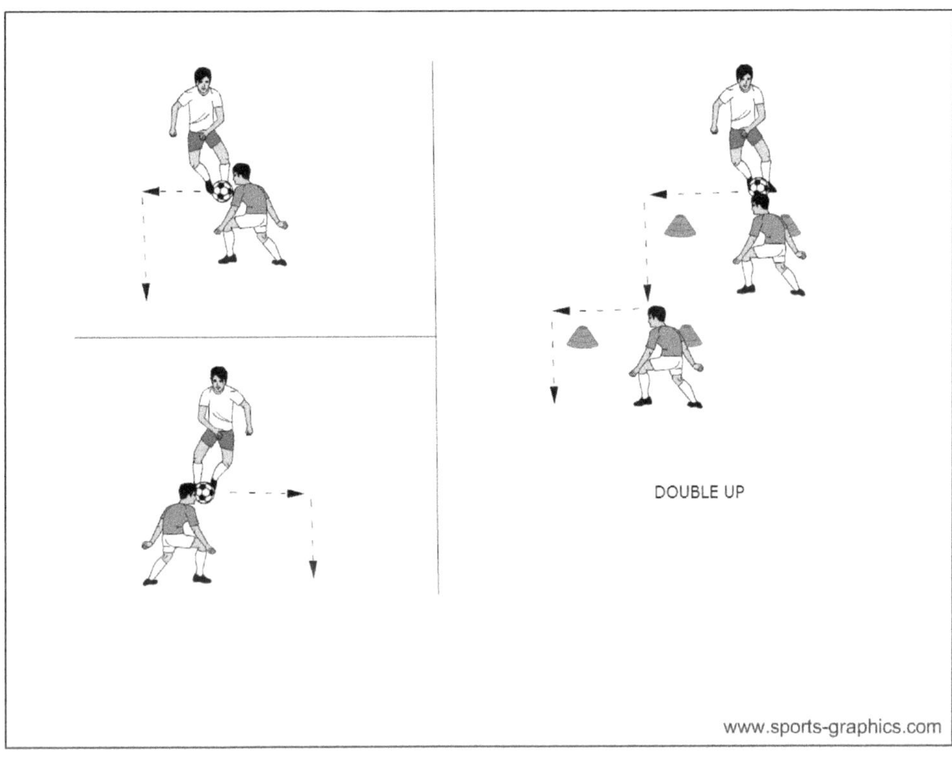

WHAT IS AN INVERTED STEPS SKILL?
FAST FEET - TWO FOOTED COMBINATIONS

The above diagrams describe what 'The Inverted Steps' is all about. It is a two footed combination, moving the ball to a short touch, first to the side, then to the forward direction. The ball is moved with the inside instep of either foot. On the left of the diagram, the side to forward movement is against the one defender, and on the right side of the diagram the side to forward fast feet movement is doubled up, moving the player away from the second challenger in the form of cover. LF Indicates the start of the movement with the left foot leading - RF indicates the start of the movement with the right foot leading.

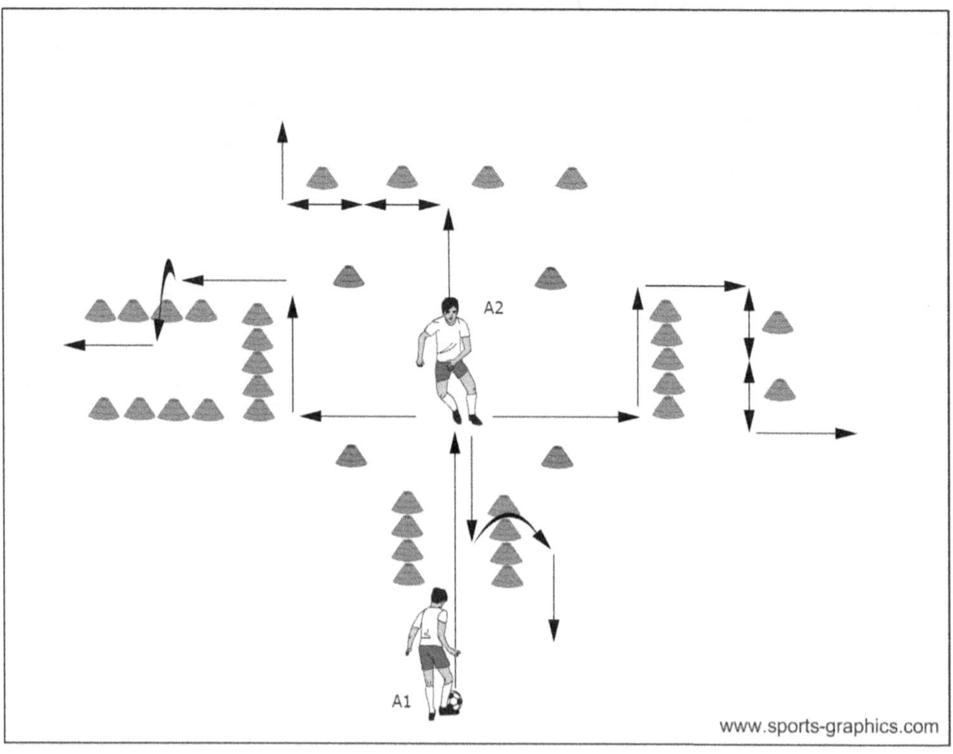

Developing the fast feet ability begins with the simple inside instep work in the lateral format. That work is foundational to all the skills of soccer, the first touch to the ball as well as all the short fast feet action. All movement forms here are related, everything is relevant. When it comes to the practice of the first ball game soccer skills we can link the work up between the first touch and the individual skills. The four cone placement and the position of the player at the center is as shown. What can be changed is the shape of the cone placements to the outside of the format. A working sequence can be as follows - Player A1 plays the ball to player A2 - Player A2 moves the ball off the line on his left shoulder and moves the ball against the shape known as the 'Inverted Steps'

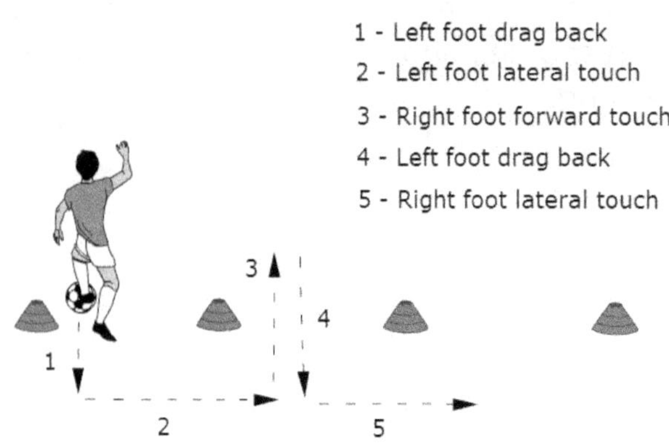

DOING THE DRAG BACKS
INSIDE INSTEP & OFF THE LINE COMBINATION

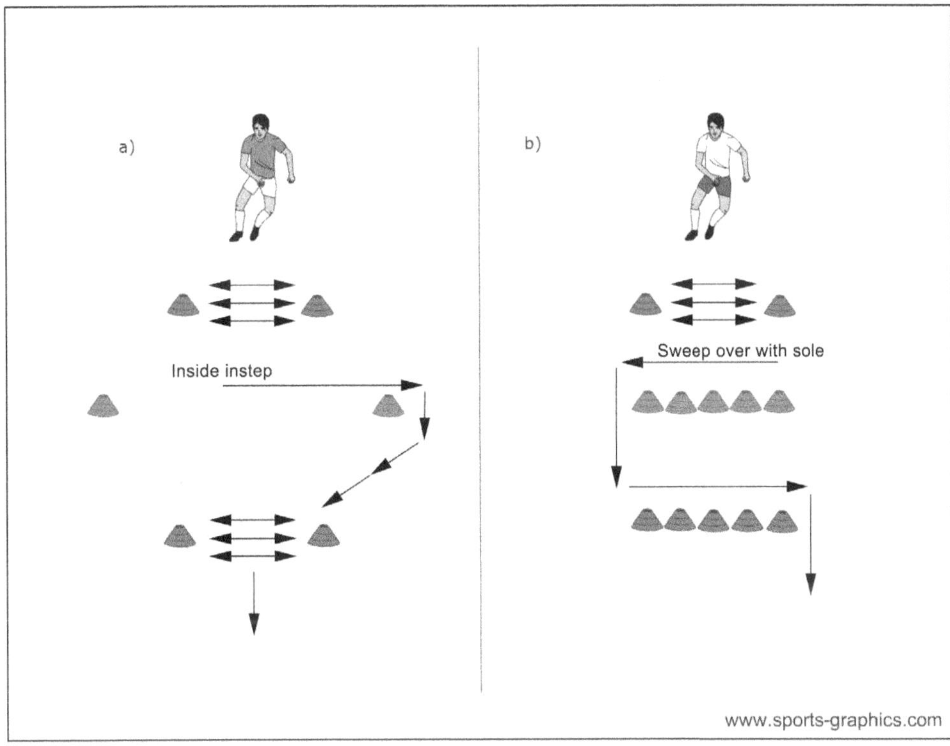

The short lateral touches to the ball are only about 3 ft in length. The off the line touch is 1.3 yds in length. There are two methods of moving the ball off the line, one is with the inside instep and the other is the underside of the foot as shown by example (b). Study the formats - look at the feet and follow the ball.

Note - What happens to the outside of the four cone placements can be changed to enable the player to link up and practice the different movement patterns that make a first ball game skill possible. In addition to the cone shapes in the structure of the format, the coach can also place players to the outside, in which case the working sequence can end with a pass and move game.

LAYING DOWN THE FOUNDATIONAL TOUCHES FOR ONE ON ONE SKILLS

The working shapes here can be used to the outside of the four cone placement. These are specific to the development of two footedness which has a specific aim, one that not only gives the player the chance to develop fast feet but also to develop skilful feet.

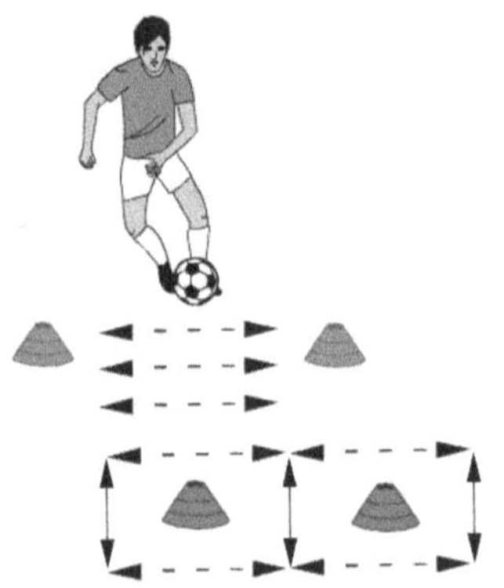

Inside instep to inside instep (tap taps) through the gateway, then the lateral short touches to the ball, work the ball around the two cone placements - turn and go back to starting position, repeat the working sequence.

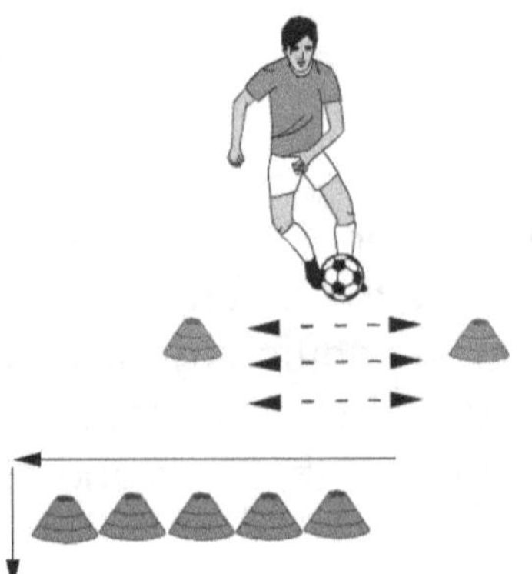

The ball is at the player's feet. He moves the ball forward by tap-tapping the ball from foot to foot through the gateway. Once through the gateway he moves the ball off the line, moving the ball on to the next objective.

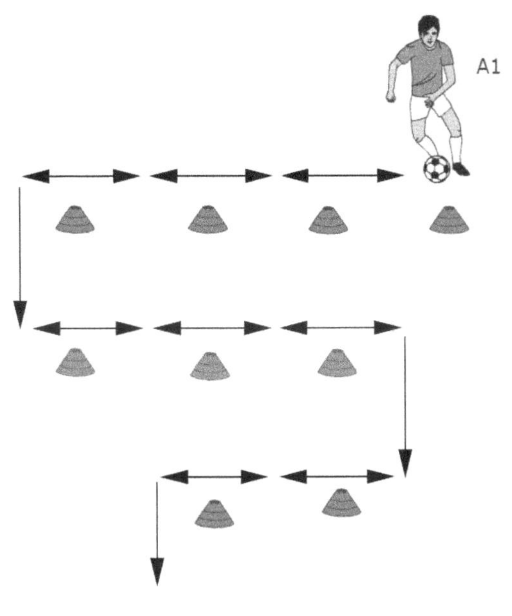

Changing directions - A1 moves the ball along the lateral line of cones using the inside instep of both feet to move and stop the ball. He then makes a forward touch up to the next line of cones and proceeds in the opposite direction.

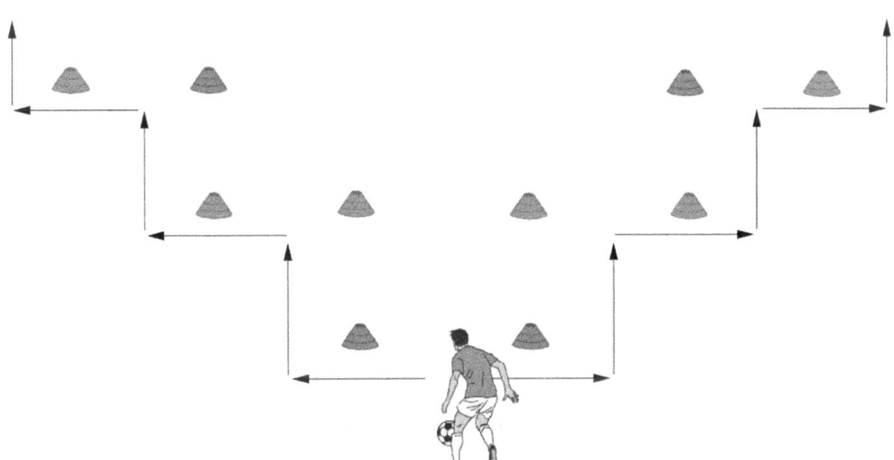

ALWAYS NEUTRAL

It is always important to work both feet in equal measure. The balance of the player depends on making sure he leads the action with both the left and right foot. The essential ability to go past several defensive positions is dependent on the player's ability to implement a quick change of skill for a particular moment. A good skill that can deal with the first and even consequential challenges is the 'Inverted Steps' solution, but of course there are other skills that also can make anything possible.

STAGE FIVE - WORKING ON THE SKILL OF DRIBBLING

THE DRIBBLING SKILL FORMATS

In stage four, the players worked on the individual skills that empower them to be skilful with the ball. In stage five of the training session the players will work with formats that enable them to develop the ability to link up and change the skill options at will.

FOUNDATIONAL

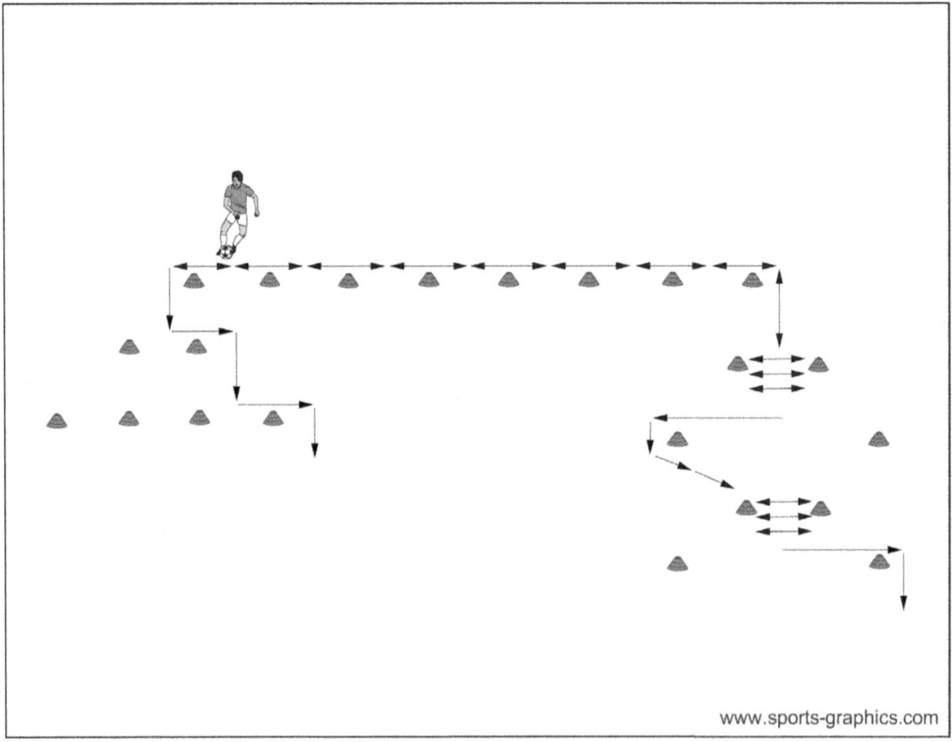

A REMINDER - A flat movement is typical within the game of soccer - it is a question of what is meant by a flat movement. A walking gait can be said to be a flat movement. In soccer the term 'flat' mostly has to do with having the ball close to your feet and playing the ball with the inside instep of the boot. The natural tendency is to keep the ball close to the feet because you don't want the opponent to get the ball and so the feet stay fairly close to the ground, hence the name flat movements. We change the reality of any downside to a flat movement in soccer by working with formats that ensure flexibility, mobility and most importantly the capability of the player to be balanced and physically skilful with and without the ball.

IN THE ABOVE FORMAT

The inside instep work in the single line of cones keeps the legs fairly close to the ground and the lateral movements are for the benefit of developing strength in the inner core. We build on the lateral inside instep work with the ball by introducing other skills into the working equation. You can see how we do that by observing the shapes to the front of the player and the lateral line of cones. On the left as we look we have the 'Inverted Steps' cone placement and to the right the 'Tap Taps' cone placement shape. The (a) and (b) positions show the application of the off the line touch.

Flat Movements - The off the line touch on the right hand side of this format can be played to a flat movement (a) or to a sweep of the foot over the top of the ball (b).

THE PRACTICE SOLUTIONS

The working solutions here are not just about the straight forward inside instep work, which is always described by the two headed arrow sideways on to the action. In the next example the skills on offer are the drag backs, the sweeps, the double sweeps, the forward touch, the fast feet movements and so on. These are foundational formats, part of the motor learning process also known as formal development.

FOUNDATIONAL

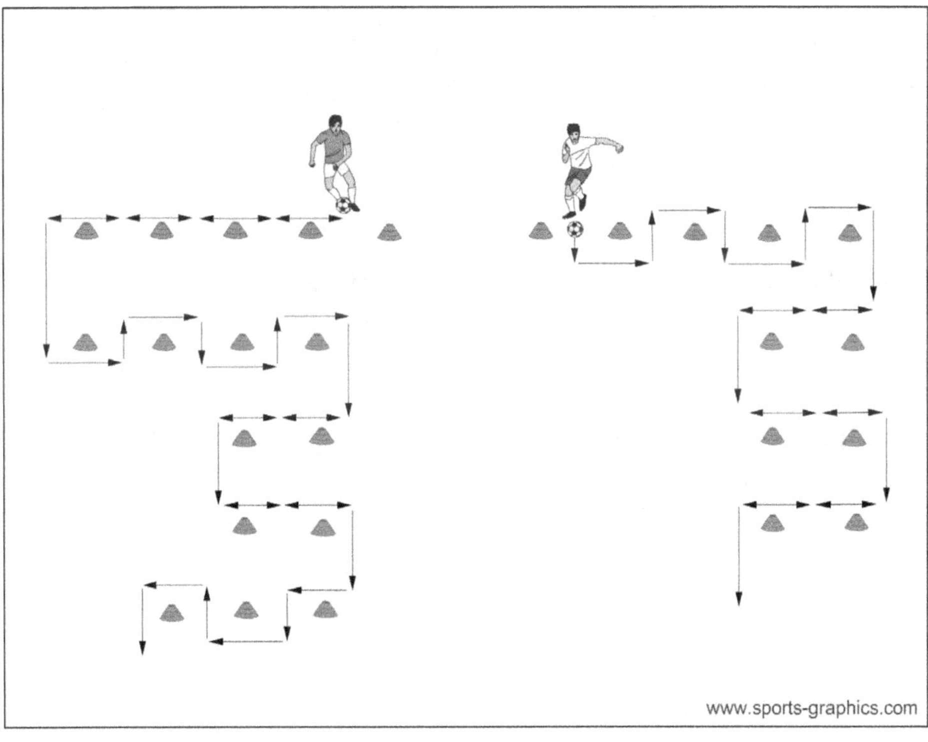

A DRIBBLING SKILLS FORMAT

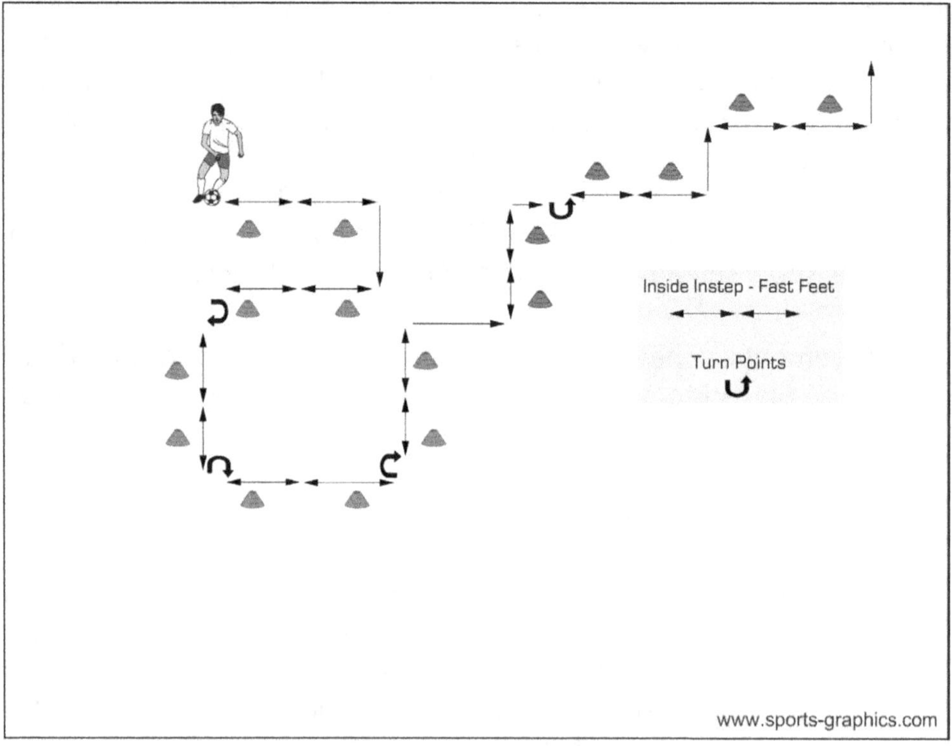

MAINTAIN THE MOMENTUM

In some formats we can bring in the turn to the working sequence. Dribbling skills involve all sorts of movements, formats of this nature are foundational to the skill of dribbling with the ball (the development of close to feet ball control) and this means that we target the development of the player's ability to use the ball effectively and therefore keep possession of the ball in tight areas.

Note -All of my format examples come from my personal archive collection. I have worked on the formats for a number of years with my players and have put them together on the practice ground. It took a lot of time to put a format together and so it would be a shame not to bring them into the public domain and use them in training sessions, everywhere, at least that is what I would love to see happen, naturally!

ANOTHER DRIBBLING SKILLS FORMAT

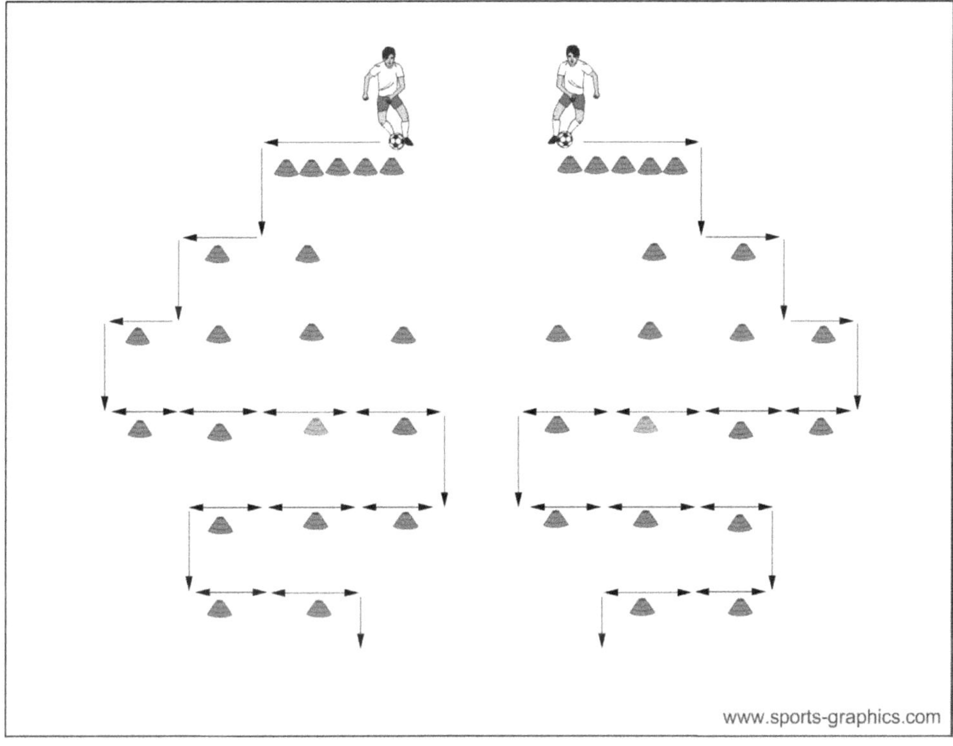

TWO FOOTEDNESS

In this example, the start of the working sequence sees the players working the ball off the line. If you care to go back and look at the movement shapes I showed earlier, you will understand how this dribbling skills format is put together.

THE DINK TOUCH FORMAT

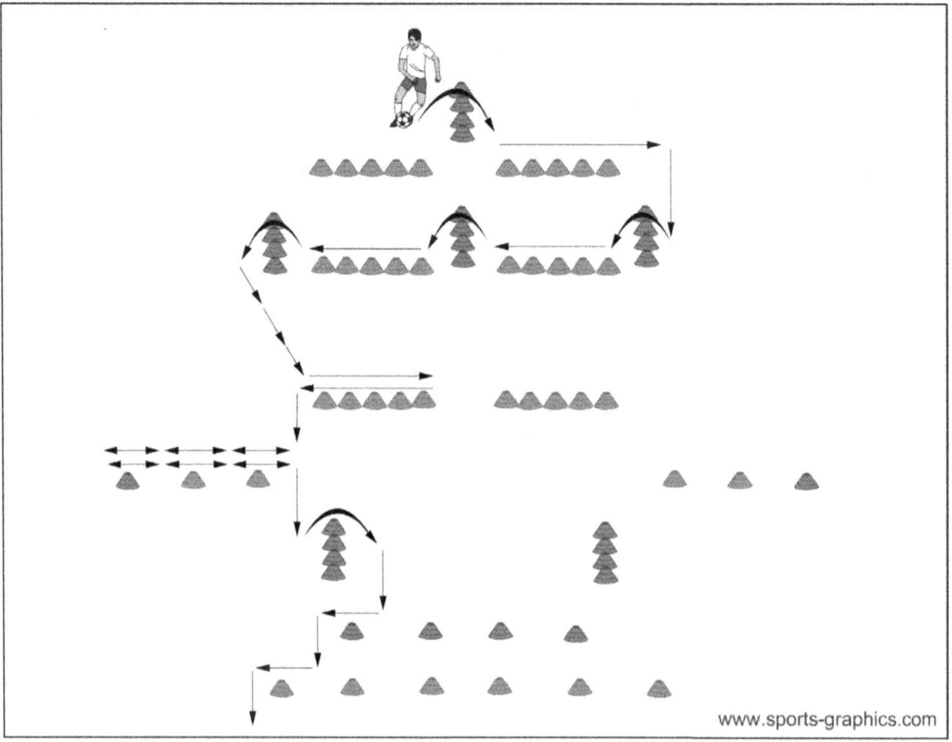

SKILLFUL FEET

The great maestro of the game, Lionel Messi, is no stranger to the dink touch. Lifting the ball over the foot of the opponent is one way of making sure the challenge for the ball is neutralized. In the above format the player implements the dink (lift over) touch, the off the line touch with both the inside instep and the sweep of the foot over the top of the ball, the double up on the short inside instep to the ball lateral touches etc. What is possible? I haven't filled in some sections of this format in order to highlight the reality that the movement forms throughout, on the left and right hand side, are the same from a design point of view. But when it comes to the practice reality, what changes is the leading foot. In the above example, the players start off the movements with the right foot dinking the ball over the cone placement. Once the ball is over the dink cone placement shape, the player moves the ball off the line with the outside of the left boot and forward to the dink overs. The dink touches are performed with the left foot. Understanding what is going on here is simply a matter of getting to know the cone placement shapes and their skill function.

Sometimes, it is a question of waiting for the challenger's foot to come into action before reacting to the challenge at the last second. The Dink is useful because when the challenger's foot comes in, lifting the ball off the ground at that point can leave the opponent on the wrong foot with his weight moving in the wrong direction. The same applies to the double inside instep touches. The short fast feet inside instep touches to the ball, combined with the longer touch can also come in handy when confronted by the opponent's challenge for possession.

IN COMPETITION MODE - FAST FEET

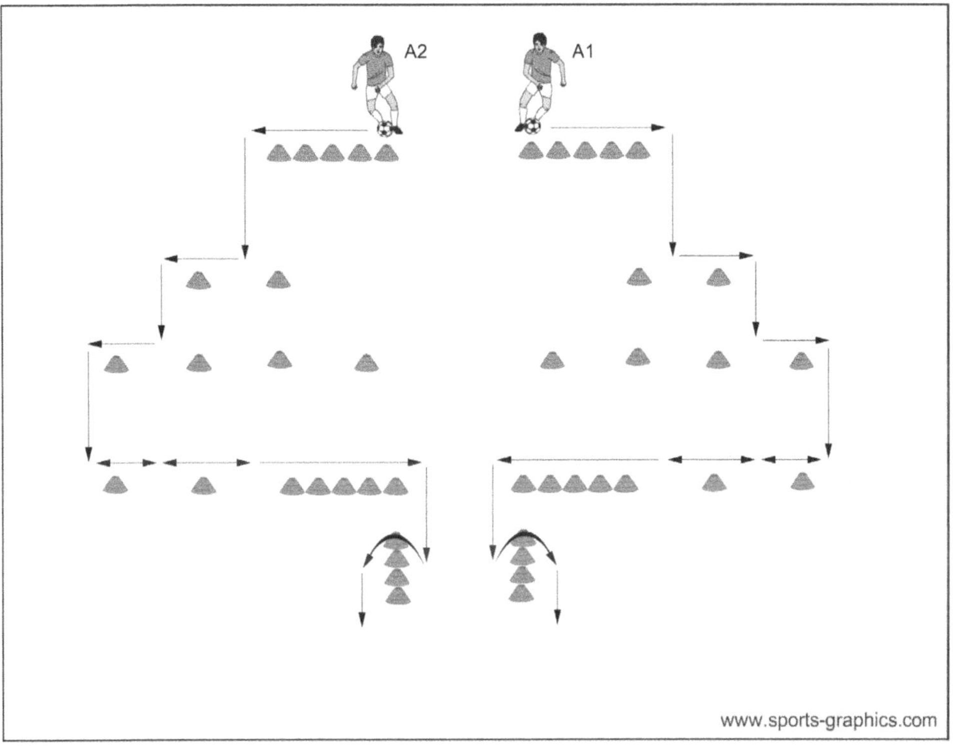

It is possible to set the format up in a way that can move the players into a competitive mode. In the above format we have two players lined up to compete against each other to see who has the fastest feet. Both players have the same task. The players start the working sequence by taking the off the line touch, then they move the ball forward to the section that requires the use of the side to forward touch sequence. Once through the side to forward section, both players take a forward touch to the lateral inside instep touches that link up with the off the line touch before moving forward again up to the dink touch cone placements, playing the dink touch, and finally out of the format. First man to finish proves the point.

Note - I don't use a competitive type of format when it comes to the development of two footedness and specific skills for playing soccer on a regular basis because the players in a competitive mode tend to cut corners and the quality of the work becomes improvisational, rather than specific, so from a development point of view I prefer to see quality rather than quantity.

Please Note - Although the ball is not placed at every arrow head point, the coach can safely assume that every arrow point points to the position of the ball and therefore the foot contact to the ball and the player moving through the working sequence.

CHANGING THE SHAPE OF THE DRIBBLING FORMAT

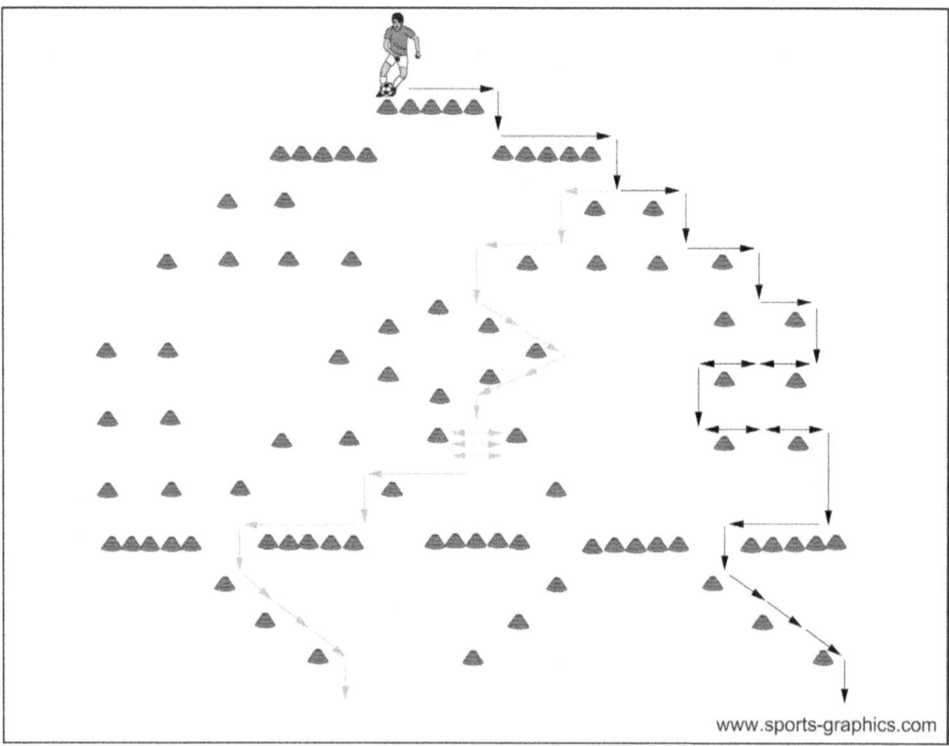

THE SUPER FORMAT - AEROBIC

Knowing the movement shapes that work the feet to a skill option is fundamental to the creation of a working format. If you know the choreography of the first ball game you can create your own dribbling sequence format.

THE UNFAMILIAR SHAPE - At the base of the above format we have the diagonal angled cone placements. The single headed arrows show a one footed touch. This is a useful skill to have when dealing with a defensive position on the edge of the penalty box.

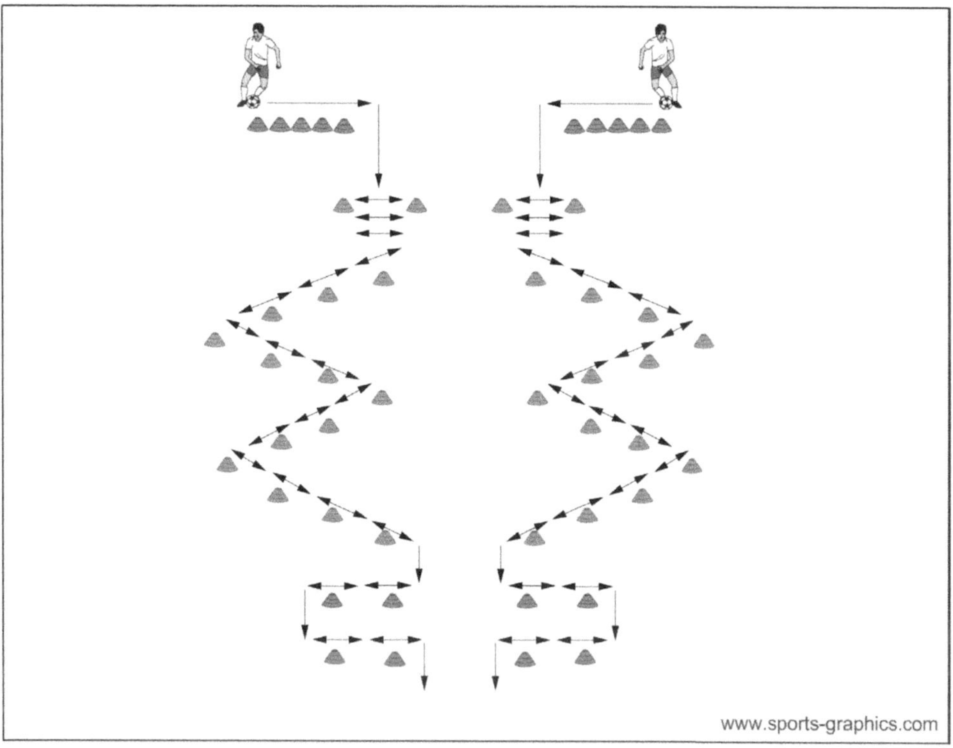

I can break down the format to create a different working sequence in order to enable the player to practice linking up a number of touch options, in sequence or out of sequence. The ability to implement any skill option depends on having the skill options in the first place and that requires practice. In the above example, the player begins the working sequence with the off the line touch, which is a slower action than what takes place next. In the next section he takes a number of touches moving the ball through the gateway, then up to the angled touches. The leading foot changes on the change of shape angle (LF - RF - LF - RF). These diagonal touches finish up with a forward touch up to the inside instep lateral two footedness action (double cone placements). Finally, finish by taking a forward touch out of the format. Players rotate - Take turns.

EXAMPLES OF THE ANGLED TOUCHES

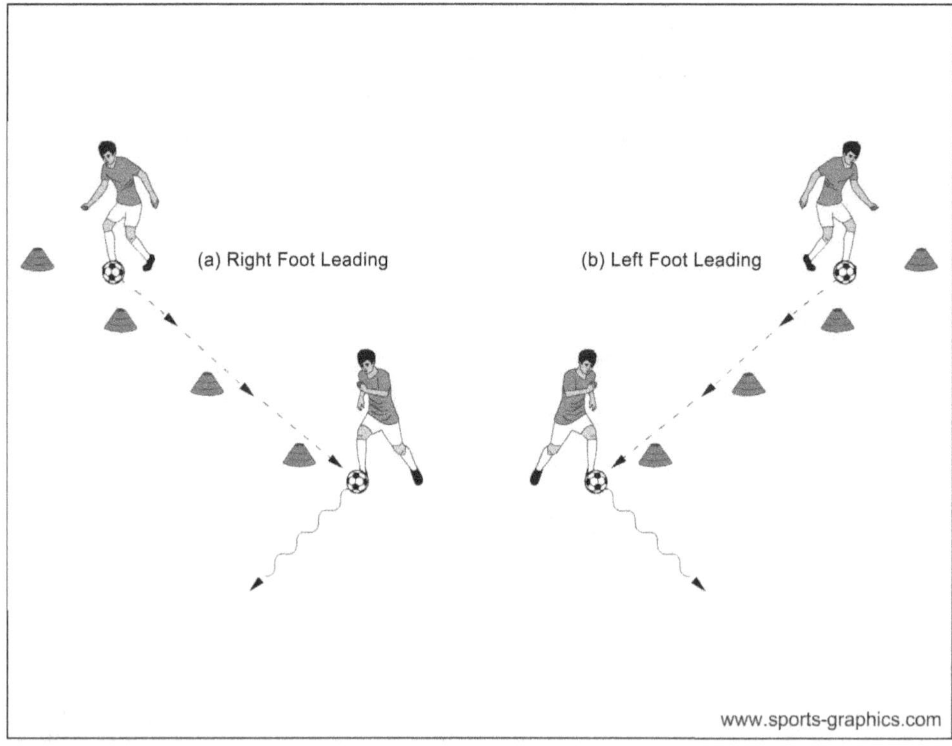

One of the most difficult skills in the game of soccer is the ability to change the skill option on the run up to more than one defensive position.

Many famous goals have resulted from a dribbling sequence past more than one defender. The great Diego Maradona of Argentina made a habit of scoring goals after leaving several defenders in his dribbling wake. Taking on more than one defender (dribbling with the ball) is less seen nowadays, perhaps because the effects of functional realities are different and the players simply don't have the skills to create such a goal scoring solution. Whatever the problems, it is my belief that with the right development we could see such a dribbling run making a comeback.

CHANGE THE SKILL OPTION - ON THE MOVE ANAEROBIC AND AEROBIC

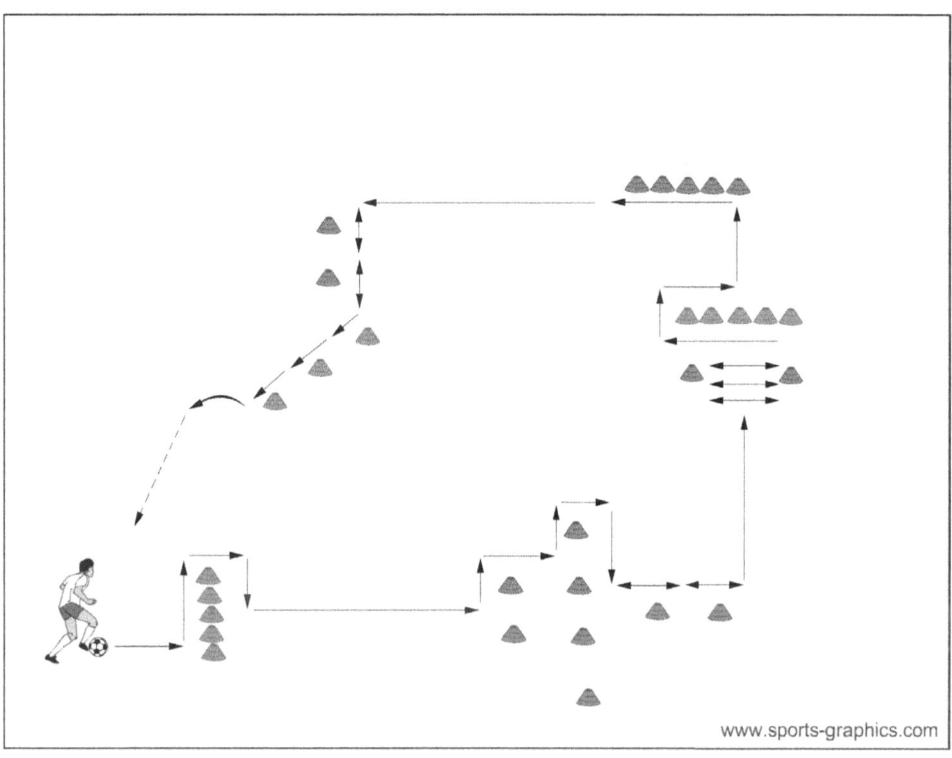

STAGE SIX OF THE TRAINING SESSION THE APPLICATION OF SOCCER SKILLS - INTO GAME TYPE FORMATS

In stage six of the training session, the endeavour is to practice playing the game of soccer. But before we do that, let us first visit what is arguably the most important skill of all, the skill of passing the ball. All the skills in the world will be of little use if the players can't pass the ball to a very good standard. The good news here is that the development of the ability to pass the ball, from a physical development point of view, has already been worked on through many of the previous format solutions. How and why is interesting. For example, the work on the lateral inside instep movements within the nine cone placement format has the effect of developing the Sartorius muscle of the upper leg, a muscle which among many other actions is involved in kicking a ball to any distance.

THE TECHNIQUE OF PASSING THE BALL

Basically, the pass is made to the player's feet/chest/head or into free space, to the side, back or forward. The length of pass can vary, anything from one circumference of the ball to one of any length managed by the most competent of kickers. What makes a good pass successful is measured by the ability to keep possession of the ball. It is interesting to note that the strike on goal can be based on either a strong kick or one that can be described as a touch finish. The latter is not a contradiction because the art of actually scoring a goal can be based on placing the ball into a specific area which does require a different type of skill to that of simply slamming the foot through the ball in the hope of hitting the target.

THE WORKING FORMATS

EXAMPLE ONE (ANAEROBIC)
THE STRAIGHT FORWARD PASS OPTION

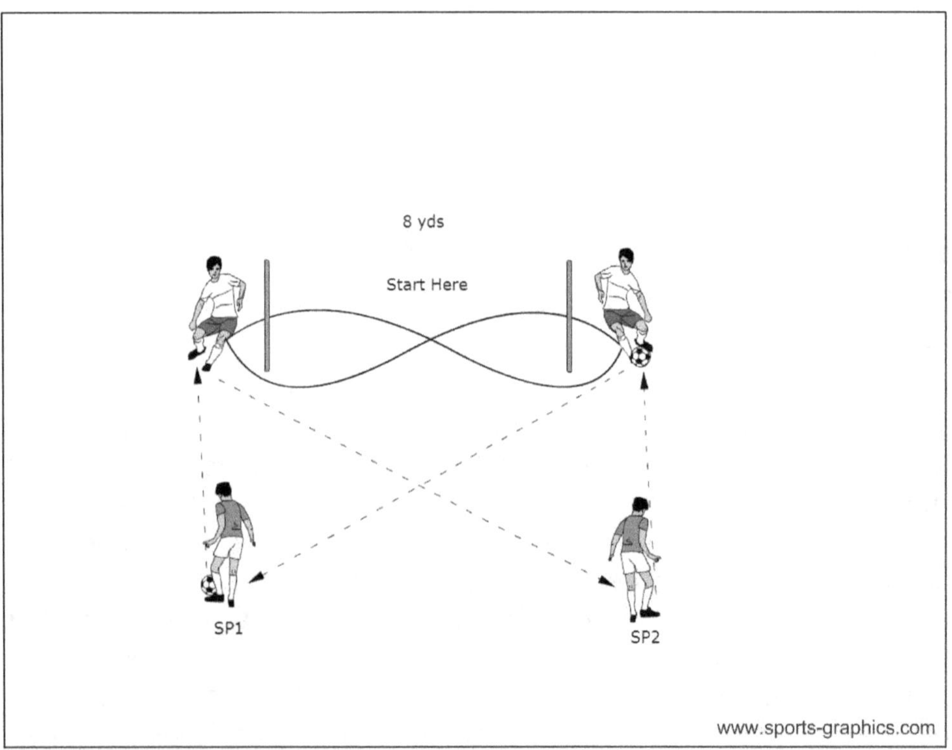

The figure eight run through the two gates is not just for show. There are important points of reference here regarding the pass of the ball. From a development point of view, I want the player to acquire the right passing attitude, which means never standing still when making the pass. Coming out of the figure eight run, make sure that the foot and body position is relevant to the type of pass made. In the above practice format, the players move through the gateways in order to work on keeping the body shape more upright, while presenting the out - turned foot position and therefore the inside instep to the ball. The pass is approximately 10 yards, with the left and the right foot respectively. As for the service players, please note that their job is also specific. SP1 and SP2 practice playing the ball to the correct foot of the figure eight runner. SP1 passes the ball with the left foot to the right foot of the runner and player SP2 passes the ball with the right foot to the left foot of the runner.

EXAMPLE TWO - PASS & MOVE (ANAEROBIC) LACES TO THE BALL - THE DIAGONAL PASS OPTION

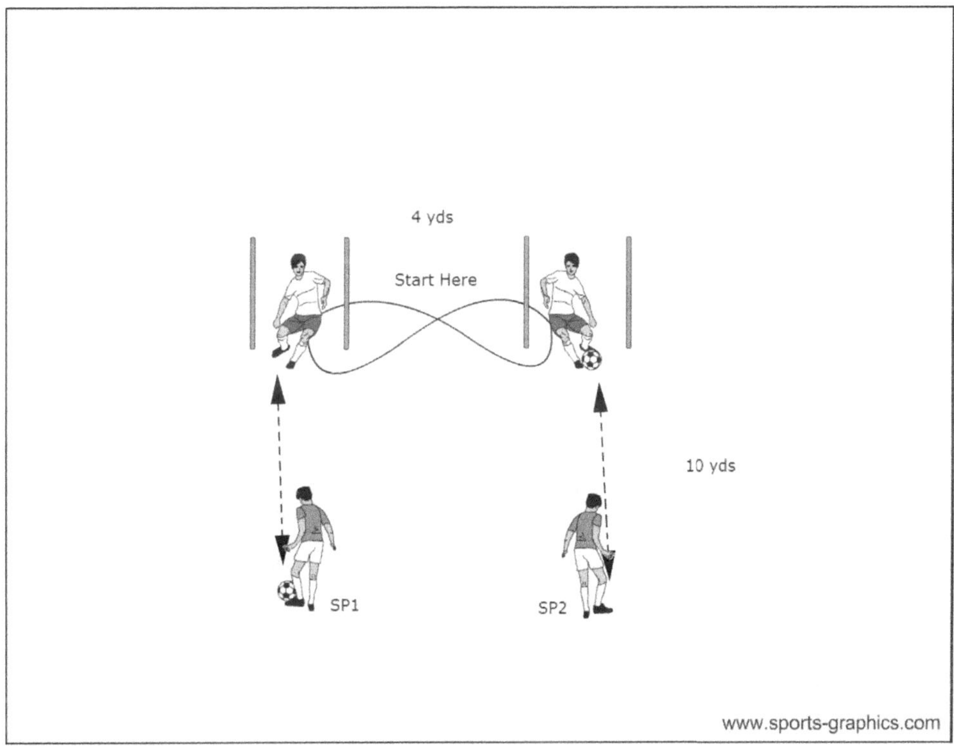

The same format, only this time the runner plays the ball back to the service player with the laces part of the boot, making a diagonal pass. When the runner receives the ball from the service player SP1 on his right foot (left side of the above format as we look) he plays the right foot pass to the diagonal angle to the service player SP2 and on receiving the ball from SP2 he plays the diagonal pass with his left foot up to SP1. The distance between the passer of the ball and the runner is about 10 yards. The diagonal pass distance is approximately 20 yards. The figure eight run helps the player to understand and implement the correct angled approach to play the right and left foot diagonal pass. Moving off the pass to the diagonal angle also ensures that the player gets into the habit of following through on contact with the ball, thus making the pass more accurate.

DEVELOPING THE STRENGTH OF PASS (ANAEROBIC)

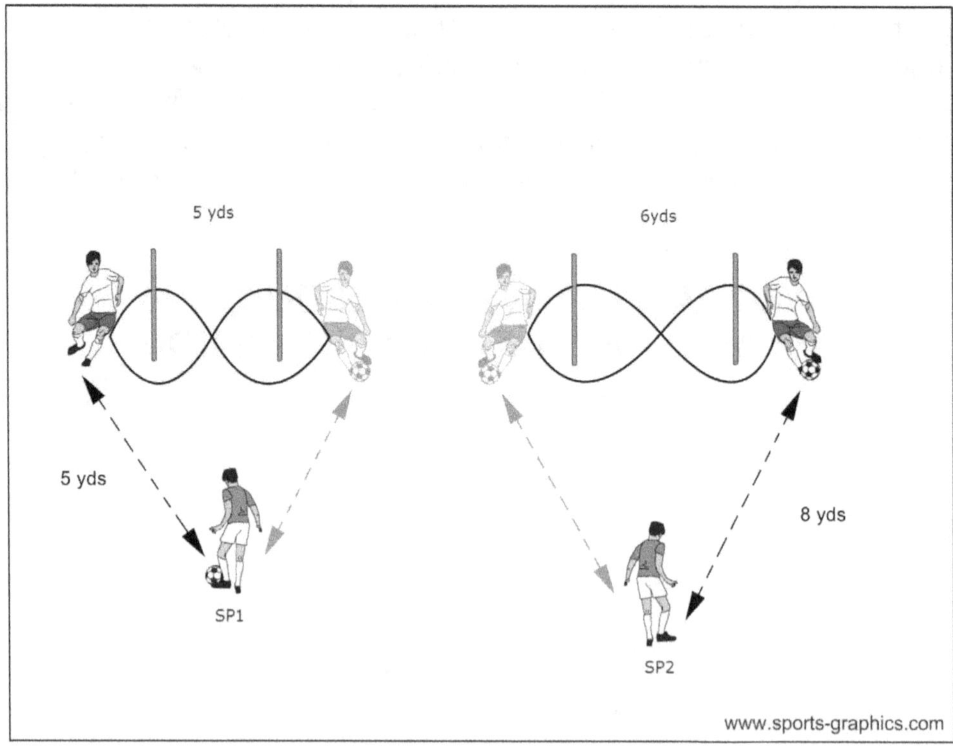

The same figure eight run configuration. The different length of pass and the different length of run has its physical effect. The short runs create the anaerobic state, so this has to be a repetition based format. In this format the pass is made to a semi diagonal angle over a short distance. When the distance between the passer and the receiver of the ball is variable, the player's ability to judge the strength of pass is developed. It is also the intention here to give rise to the skill of making the pass not only in the right direction but also to the correct foot of the receiver. You should not be surprised that my next coaching example keeps the player in touch with the continued development of his two footedness, because the decision as to which foot the ball should be played to is of concern. The standard in terms of what level the game is played at depends on it. If you care to go back and examine the first touch options, these are proper first touch options that, combined with the ability to pass the ball to the correct foot, make all the difference in keeping possession of the ball.

PASS THE BALL - THE FOOT TO FOOT PRACTICE FORMAT

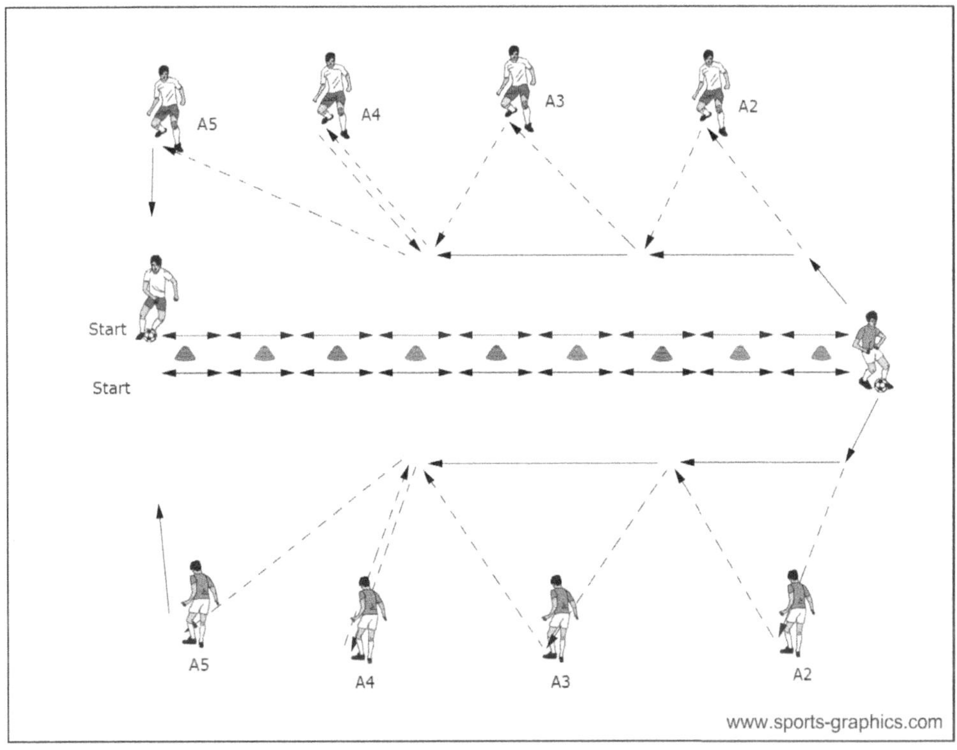

THE PASS TO THE LEFT AND RIGHT FOOT

The players rotate around the lateral format. The inside instep work with the ball through the lateral line of cones enforces the use of both feet. In higher standards of the game, the pass to the correct foot makes a difference. The following few examples will prove this to be the correct approach to teaching the skill of passing the ball.

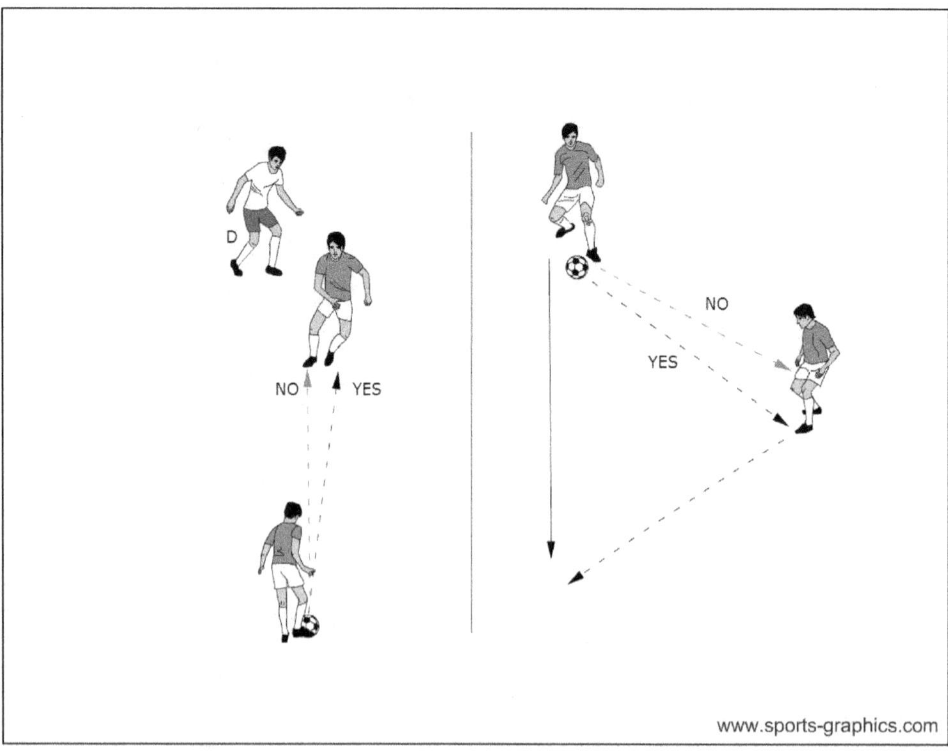

Player A1 passes the ball to the left foot of player A2. Keeping the playing direction in mind, there would be little or no sense at all for A1 to pass the ball to A2's right foot.

These are some of the more obvious problems for the players to solve on the passing side of the game. All the more reason for developing a two footed capability.

PLAYING OFF THE FIRST TOUCH

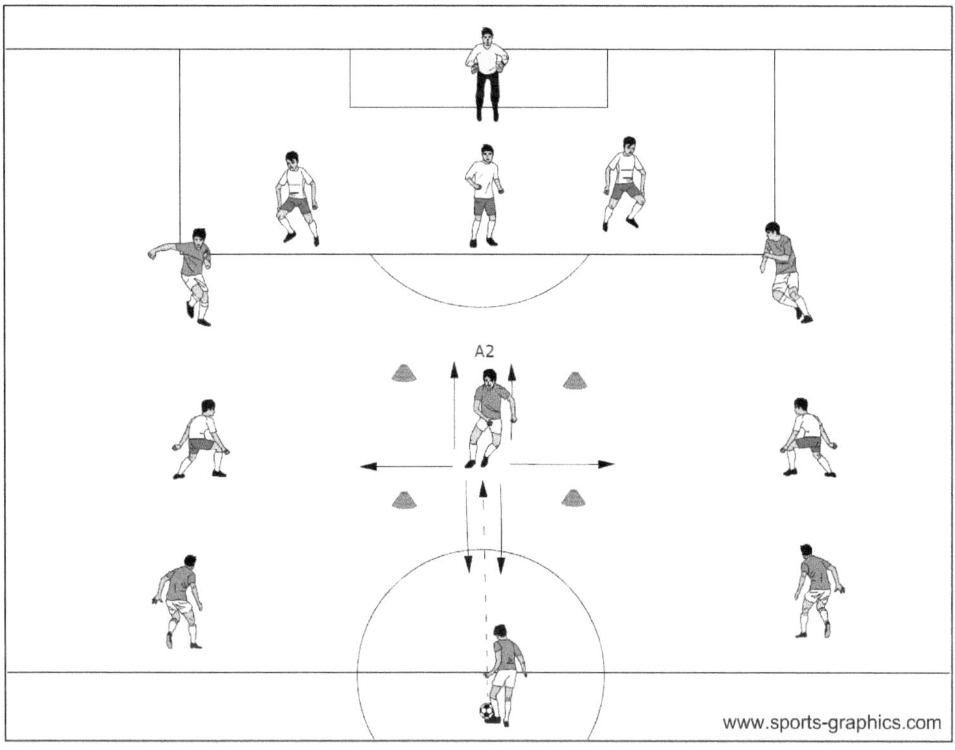

PASS AND MOVE - MAKE TRIANGLES

THE FIRST TOUCH OPTIONS : THE FORWARD TOUCH - THE CHANGE OF ANGLE TOUCH - THE EXTENDED TOUCH - THE REVERSE TOUCH - In this example, player A2 has the above first touch options available to him. Upon taking any of the touches to the designated zones shown by the above arrows, his teammates react and move to that side in order to build up attacking play. The name of the game is to support the player on the ball by staying close to create effective movement patterns against the defense. There is no such thing as a bad goal, but the best goals are created with imagination and skilful play.

THE 20 BY 30 YDS FORMAT - 2 V 1

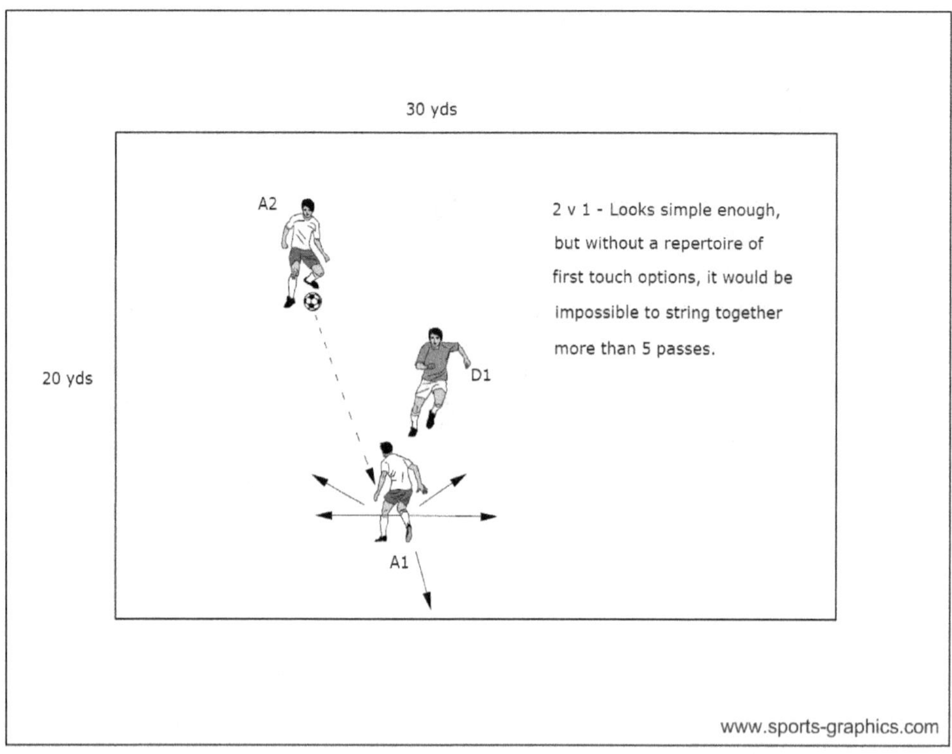

This is a 2v1 format. The first pass is free. The defensive player D1 moves in on the two players to try to win the ball after the first pass has arrived at the feet of A1. It may not look like much but I can assure you this format would test any player's ability to keep possession of the ball for any meaningful length of time. If the players involved implement the off the line touch and the extended foot position touch and move off the pass into good supporting positions where the ball can reach them, then and only then do they stand a chance of stringing five passes together.

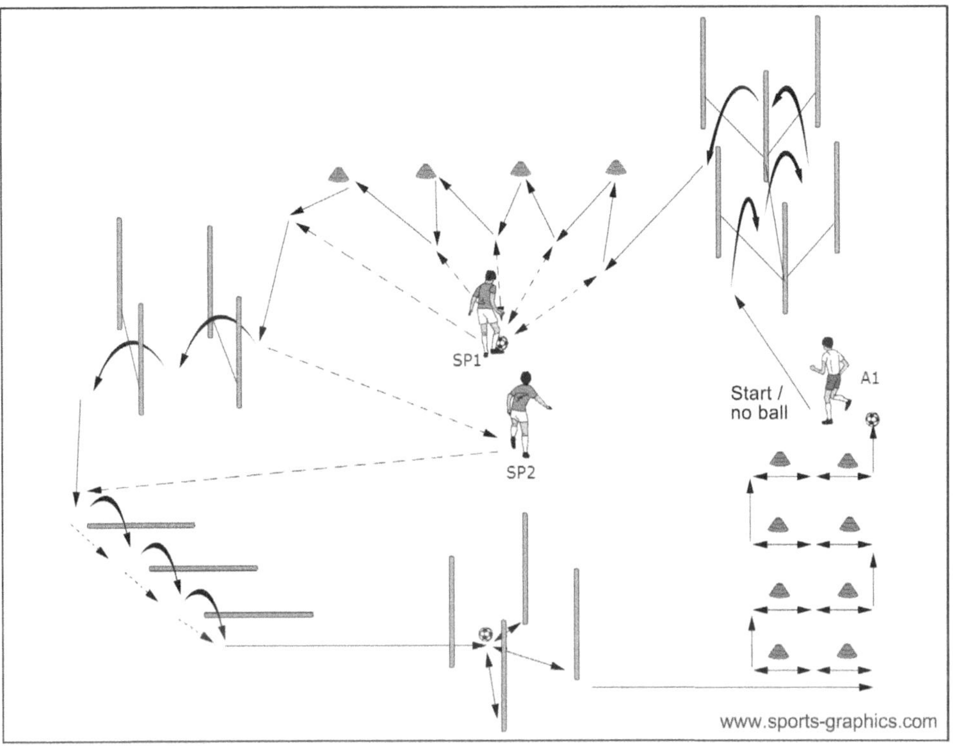

One major concern for any player is the lack of match fitness. The problems associated with a lack of match fitness could include the risk of injury, which is something that can be avoided. In this next example, the player can practice playing soccer by experiencing lots of soccer movements, more than he could ever do in any 90 minute game of soccer. I call this way of training 'Smart Movement Circuits'. This type of work reduces the risk of injury because the player can reach higher fitness levels in a much shorter time than would be the case if he simply relied on playing the game. The choice of formats can create an anaerobic or aerobic effect. This example is most certainly one that is difficult from a physical effort point of view and is therefore anaerobic in nature. This a reps format, which means that the player does 7 reps of the full circuit, working 2 minutes in each station. This is the equivalent to a game of soccer. I use this type of work to help players with their 'Match Fitness'.

TEAM WORK - WORKING IN PARTNERSHIP

The game of soccer is a team game and, as such, it should not be about the promotion of one player. In fact, it is true to say that a team like Barcelona would not be the team it is today if it had even one egotistical player in its make up. The only way to be a successful team is to play the game in a manner that spreads the effort and the glory of winning, or even losing, equally between all the players. There are important reasons for the implementation of these formats. One is so that every player gets to work on every aspect of his game, without being left out of any situation. In some sections of the above format, the ball can be a part of the practice where players SP1 & SP2 pass the ball to the practicing player who can then choose to either use the ball through a particular section or return the ball on each pass played to him.

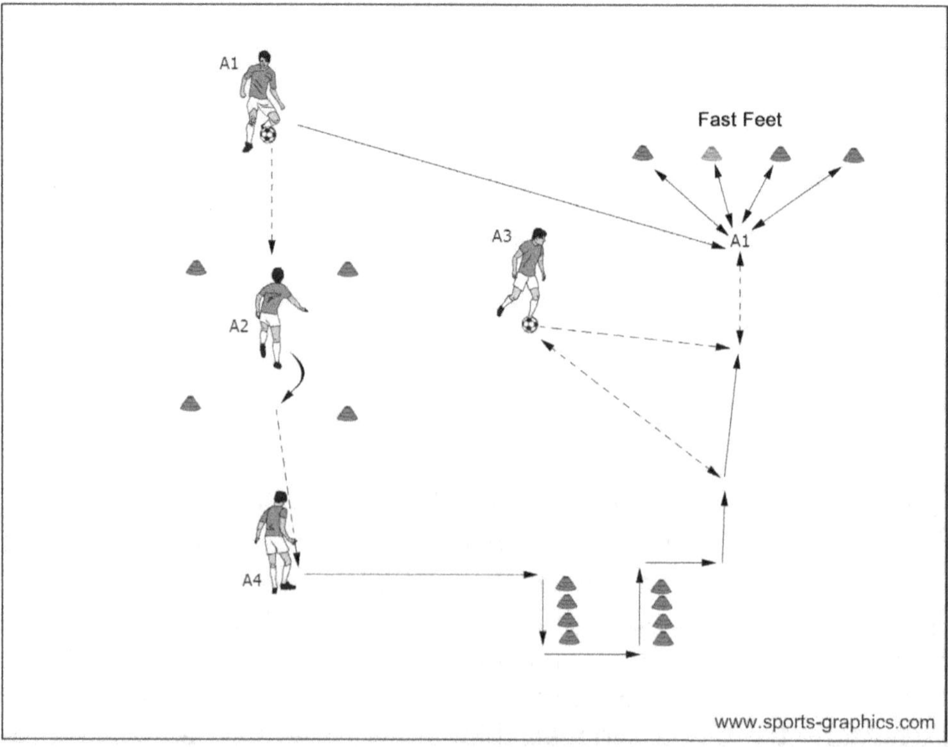

In this format we have three stations and four players which means that there is always one player free. The start to the above working sequence is the point when the ball is played from player A1 to player A2. Once A2 performs the 'Reverse touch' and plays the ball to player A4, A1 is then free to move to the fast feet shape. The practice is then continued by all the players re-positioning all the time in a way that makes sure that each of the sections of the format is worked on and serviced with a pass of the ball. This way of working with players helps them to be a team because they have to help each other through the work. By helping each other, the players acquire the ability to see the next move, the next pass, the next best solution etc.

IN PARTNERSHIP

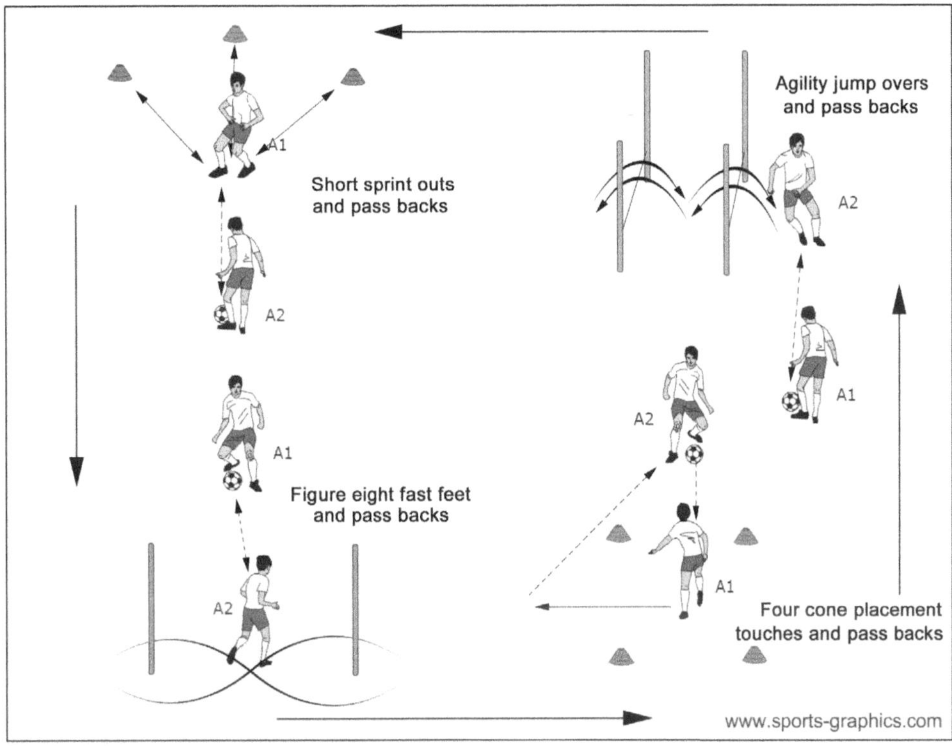

Just because there are only the four stations doesn't mean it is easy! Two minutes per player in each station is enough. The players can swap on each station or work the four stations and then swap places. The fitness formats help the players to play effective soccer. There is just one more thing that we need to look at here, winning possession.

WINNING POSSESSION OF THE BALL

There are three parts to winning back possession of the ball. When the ball is given away for whatever reason (bad touch, bad pass, mistakes, etc.), winning the ball back is a priority, but one that requires a special skill set to accomplish. Here is the first of the formats that work towards the skill of winning the ball back.

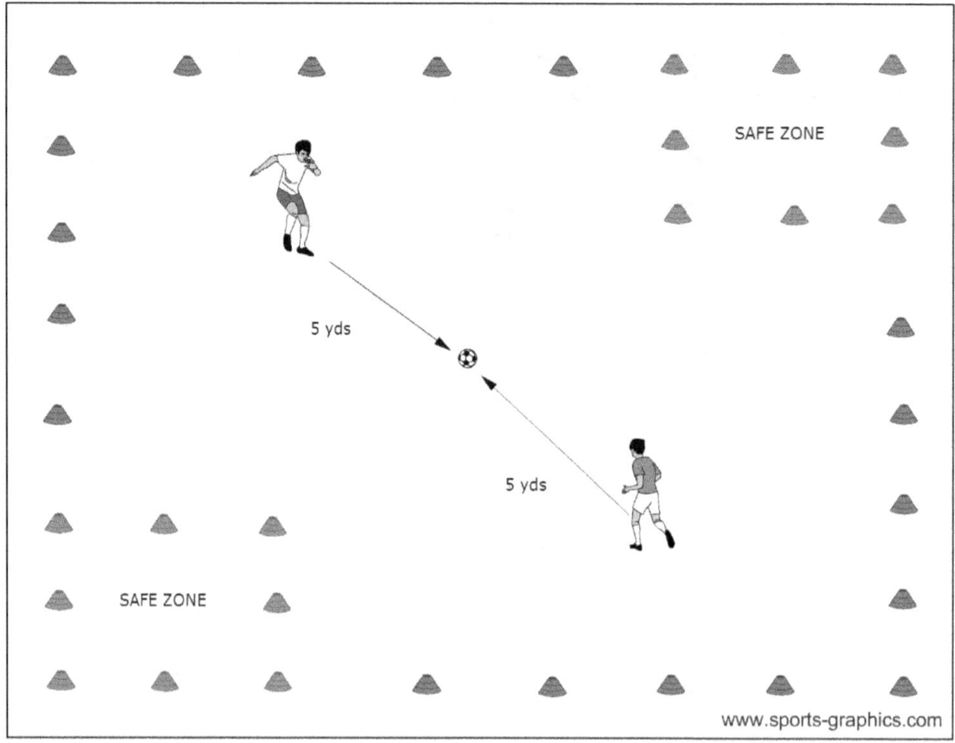

NO TACKLES ALLOWED

In this one both players are positioned about five yards from the ball. On the word "Go!", the players race to reach the ball first. As strange as it sounds, this is not about tackling for the ball, but in fact is about letting the opponent have the ball, to then control the actions of the opponent and try to stop him from reaching the safe zone. This is a one minute format, meaning that once a player is in possession of the ball, he has one minute to get it into any of the safe zones. If the player can't manage to get the ball into the safe zone in the allocated time, that is a success for the player not in possession.

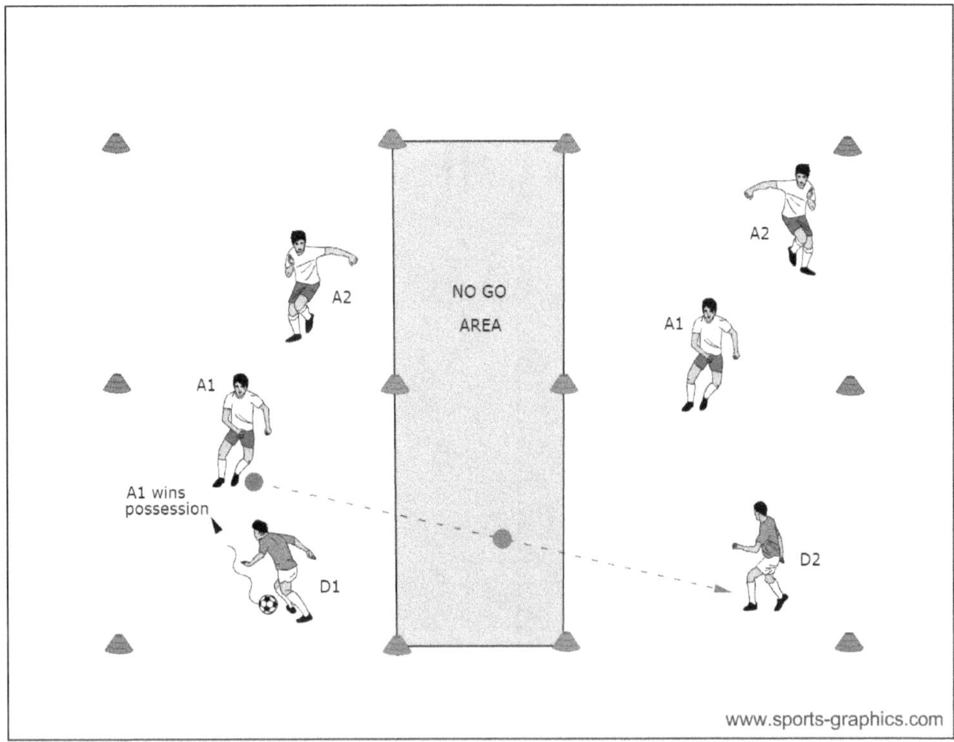

This is a 2v1 format. The theme of the practice is winning possession of the ball. The start of the practice is not the usual attack v defense because in effect the defense has the ball. This format is in recognition that nowadays it is just as important to win the ball back as it is to keep it. Tackling for possession of the ball is not allowed. What is called for is a much more clever approach to winning possession of the ball.

The start of the practice to win the ball back is on the left side of the above diagram. The ball is at the feet of player D1 (the opponent). The nearest man to player D1 is player A1 whose job it is to close D1 down and attempt to win the ball. The attempt to win the ball must be done without fouling. A1 also has his teammate A2 and both of them can try to take possession of the ball from D1. Once in possession of the ball, the A players must pass the ball across the neutral zone to the other side to D2, giving the ball back to the defensive team on the opposite side of the format. The practice is then repeated on that side to the same expectation. The above is part two of the winning formula. In part three, after winning possession, the A players play the ball across the neutral zone to the A Team. The A team's job will be to not only keep possession of the ball, but to create a goal scoring opportunity.

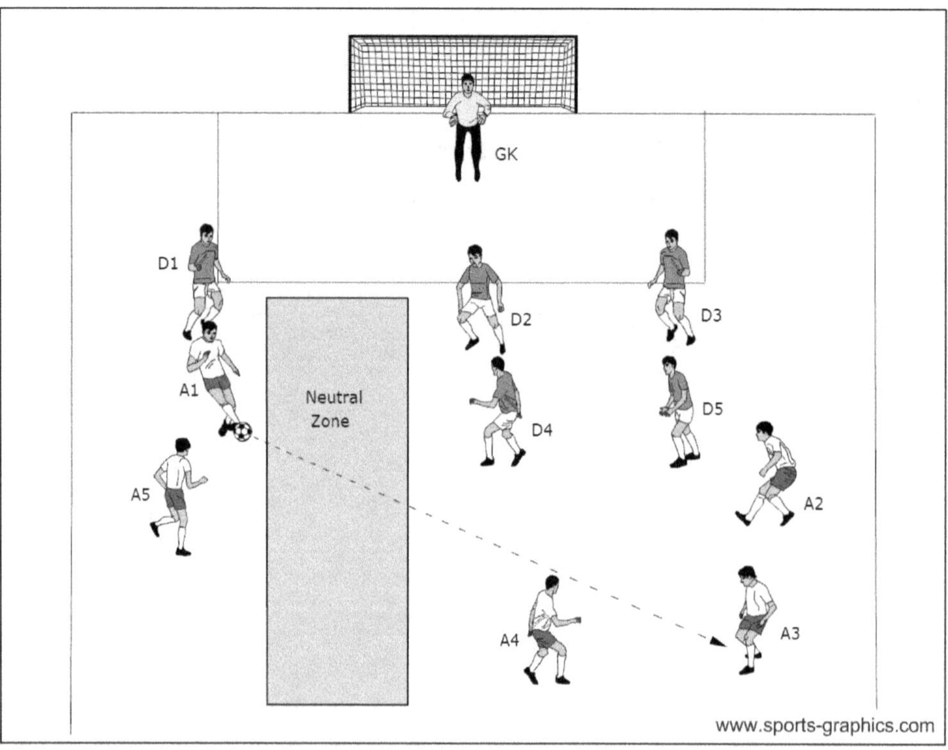

SCORING OPPORTUNITY

When all of the above is taking place, the A team moves the players to the one side and in effect creates a neutral zone in order to establish the ability, once in possession of the ball, to find free space or switch the ball back to players A1 & A5. Moving on, the players can return to the normal reality of attack v defense, in which case it is the attacking team that will start the practice from the back with player A3 in possession of the ball.

9 - THE DETAILED WORKING PHILOSOPHY

THE FIRST BALL GAME

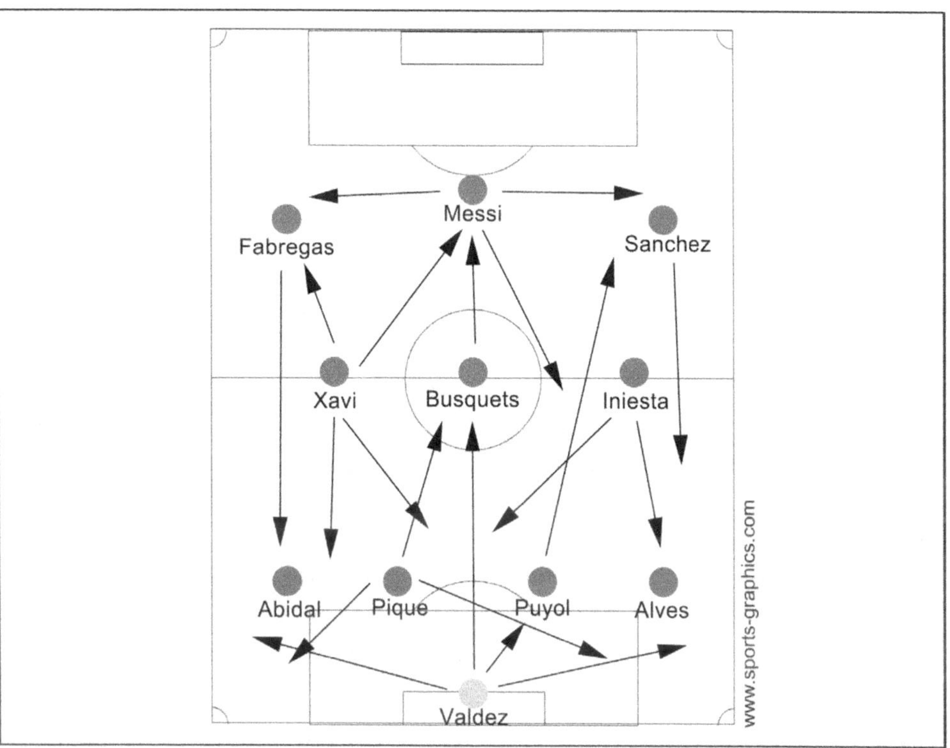

Some of the players I have highlighted in the above diagram are no longer with the team, but Barcelona still plays the game to a high standard because the players that come into the side have the right qualities and fit right in. There are lots of teams in Europe which bring in players on deals that don't fit in, business is business, right? FC Barcelona is one of the finest examples of the first ball game I have ever seen. As coaches of the game we can set up all sorts of playing examples, but when all is said and done a team like Barcelona would not be able to play the game of soccer the way they do if the coaches didn't put a great deal of effort into the players' personal development. The point of the above diagram is that it doesn't show a clinical forward moving functional game of soccer, but rather a very imaginative one that requires many of the skills that I have highlighted in this book. It is the style of play that I most certainly support, especially at youth level.

One of the most harmful realities I have witnessed at the youth Academy level is the imposition of the 'Get rid of it!' mentality. Both the parents standing on the sidelines and the coaches in charge of the youth teams were more interested in results than on anything to do with what is or is not right from a development point of view. I watched many games where the baying crowd, as well as the coaches in charge, shouted to the players at the back of the team when they had the ball to 'Get rid of it!'. This could only be interpreted by the player as 'Kick the ball!', preferably either long and out of danger or out of play. This is the year 2016 and you would think that our sport has progressed beyond the 'kick it out of the park' mentality. A game of soccer which is busy and devoid of skills is not sustainable in the long run.

And why is this mentality to get rid of the ball as soon as you have it seemingly unique to youth soccer? Do we encourage youth basketball players to throw the ball as far down court as they can as soon as they secure a rebound? Of course not!

HARD WORK

What I find astonishing is the idea that anyone can rely solely on their talent, that without hard work things will drop out of the air like manna from heaven. If a player is not prepared to work hard and put the effort in, then the result is always the same, a low standard. All of my coaching examples here strive to create the type of coaching forum that helps the players to develop the skills for the top drawer, because as far as I can see, playing the ball from the back, right though the team, using creative and imaginative movement patterns is the name of the game. FC Barcelona scores goals but it is the way they score goals that should be an inspiration to coaches in the game today. I don't support the imposition of the long ball game on any young player. That type of thinking is not for me. There is only the one honest way of coaching young players and that way is the first ball game way and not the way of the parents and the coaches who are more interested in the results than on development.

AN EXAMPLE OF MY TRAINING SESSION

Playing the game of soccer is no different from any sporting endeavour, it is not easy and it does require training. A training session should touch the base of the anaerobic and aerobic state of being and the methods used should therefore be all about the movement forms that develop the player's potential to be a first ball game player. The structure of the training session should reach all aspects of physical and technical development. Here is my example of my everyday approach to working with players on their personal development.

BEGIN WITH - 1 THE WARM UP

Sitting down, straight leg - pull on the toe - get up - stretch the back of the leg (Gastrocnemius) - stretch the lower back of the leg (Soleus) - Next - face down, alternative leg - keeping the leg straight, lift and stretch as high as you can without forcing the movement (stretching gluteus medius - minimus - maximus - back of the leg (biceps femoris) Next - get up and loosen up with a gentle jog for a hundred yards or so - stop - Next do the hand circles - full body lateral stretches (latissimus dorsi) - forward stretches (rectus abdominis) - After stretching, finish off with fast feet jump rope agility work (1 minute) -

NEXT - DYNAMIC - AGILITY - FORWARD AND LATERAL MOVEMENTS

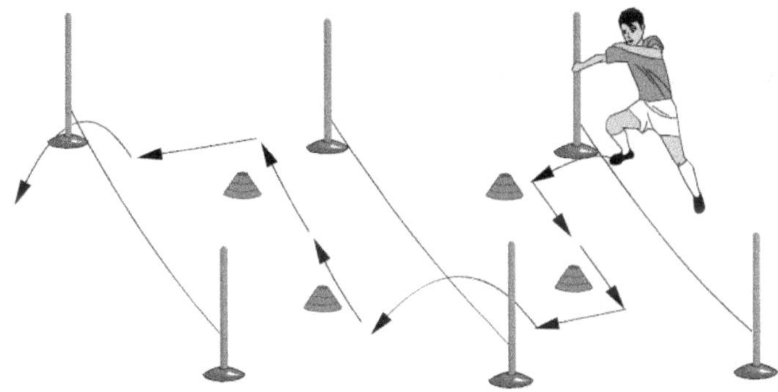

ROTATIONAL - THE ANAEROBIC FORM

LATERAL TO FORWARD - FAST FOOT WORK

NEXT - ANAEROBIC - FAST TWITCH = FAST FEET

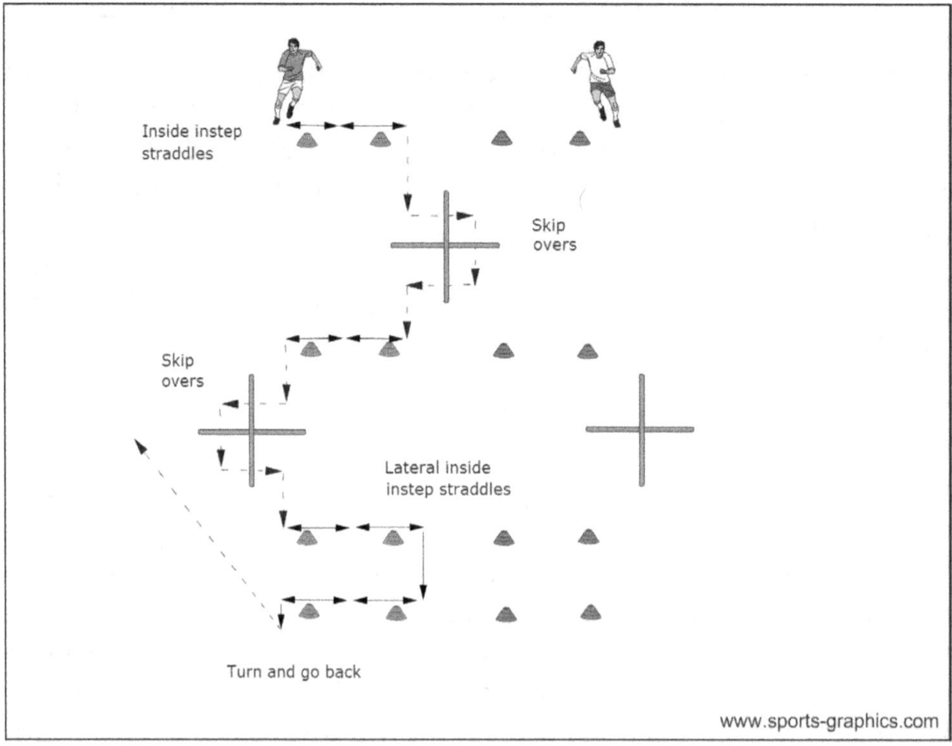

My next choice is all about developing the 'Two footedness' of the player and therefore applying the type of movement forms that are foundational to the individual skills that underpin all activities with the ball at the player's feet. The ability to work the ball with both feet enables the player to perform a combination of soccer skill movements without which no player could play effective soccer to any worthwhile standard.

WORK ON THE FIRST TOUCH OPTIONS

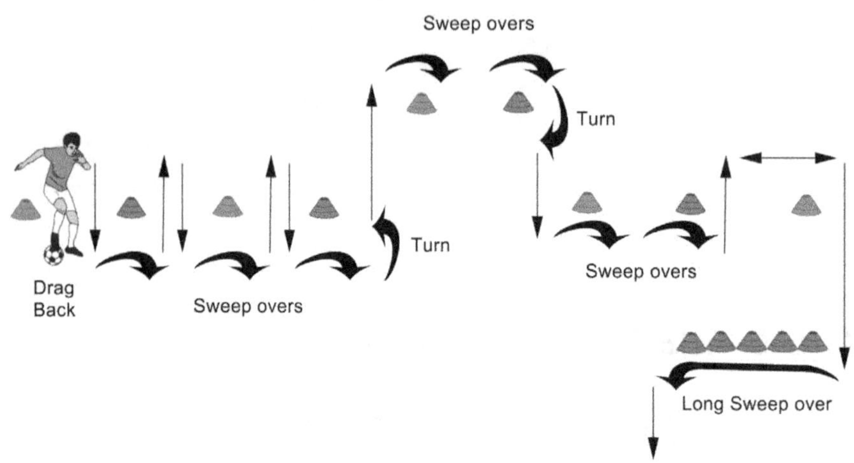

THE FOUR CONE PLACEMENT FORMAT

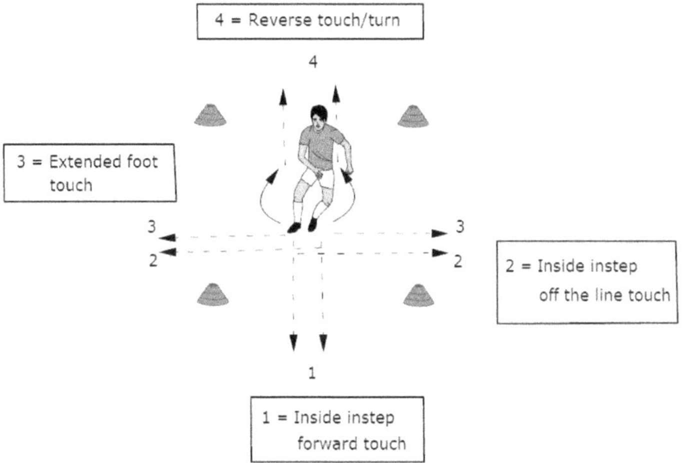

NEXT - PRACTICE & PLAY THE FIRST BALL GAME

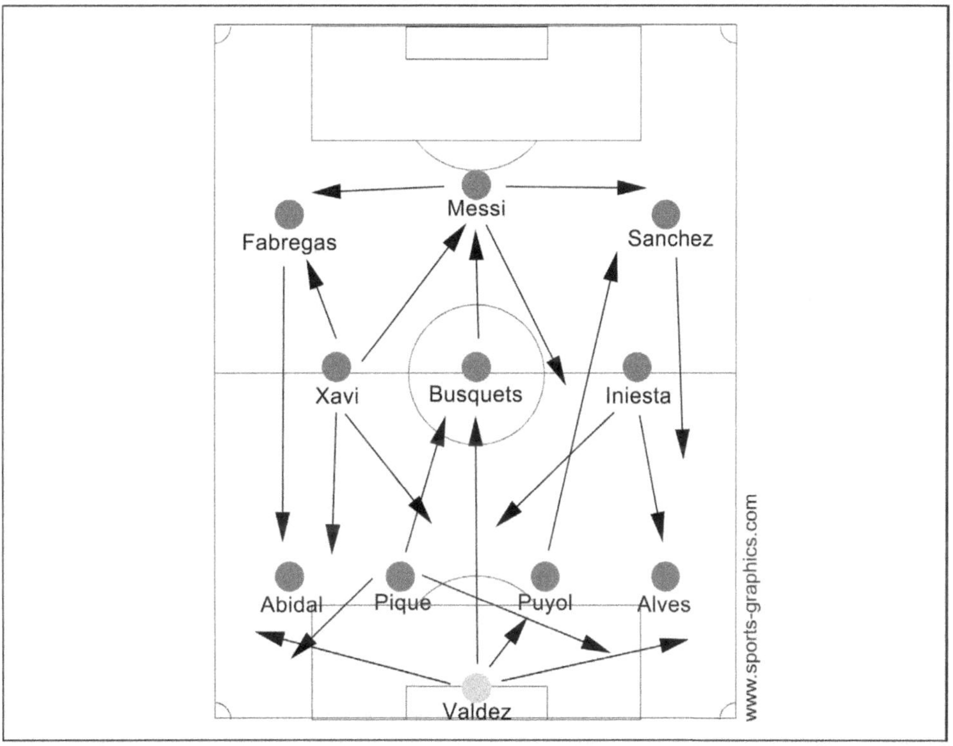

Ambitious? Not really! The ultimate part of the training session is all about playing the game of soccer. If the coach implements a skills based training session then he also has to go down the path of trusting his players to play the game of soccer from the goalkeeper right though the team. It is no rocket science as they say, a game of soccer in stage six doesn't start with the long ball from the goalkeeper, it starts with the ball being played from the back to the front of the team, with the ball on the ground for 90% of the game.

SUMMING UP

Coaches should not worry about what the parents or spectators and the like think when it comes to the development of young players. After all, what future has the game got if the young people coming into it fail to reach their potential and their dream of playing professional soccer for a top club? Without the right coaching, the answer is just that, 'A Dream'. In finishing my account of the coaching side of the game I want to pay tribute to one of the British game's great players, Kenny Dalglish. When Kenny managed Blackburn Rovers, he loved showing his ability to hit the cross bar from outside of the penalty box. He represented a game of soccer that anyone would be proud of back then and appreciated the skills side of the game, having been one of the best midfield players and representing Scotland many times. It may not have been noticed at the time but I appreciated my time in the presence of such people because some of them inspired me to think about the coaching side of the game.

JUST A BIT OF FUN - PERHAPS

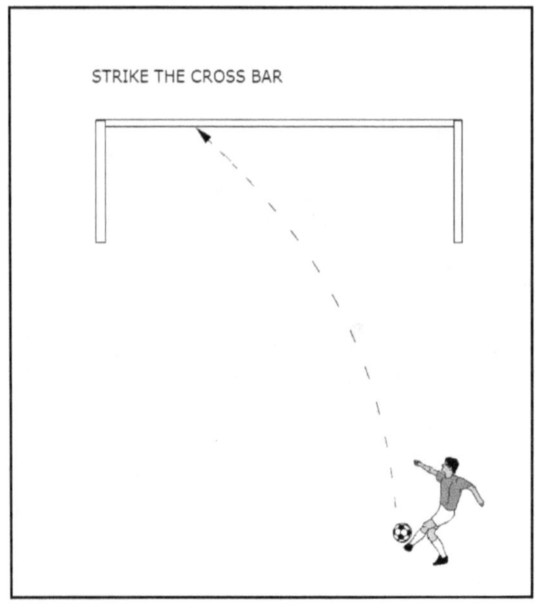

PLAY GOLF

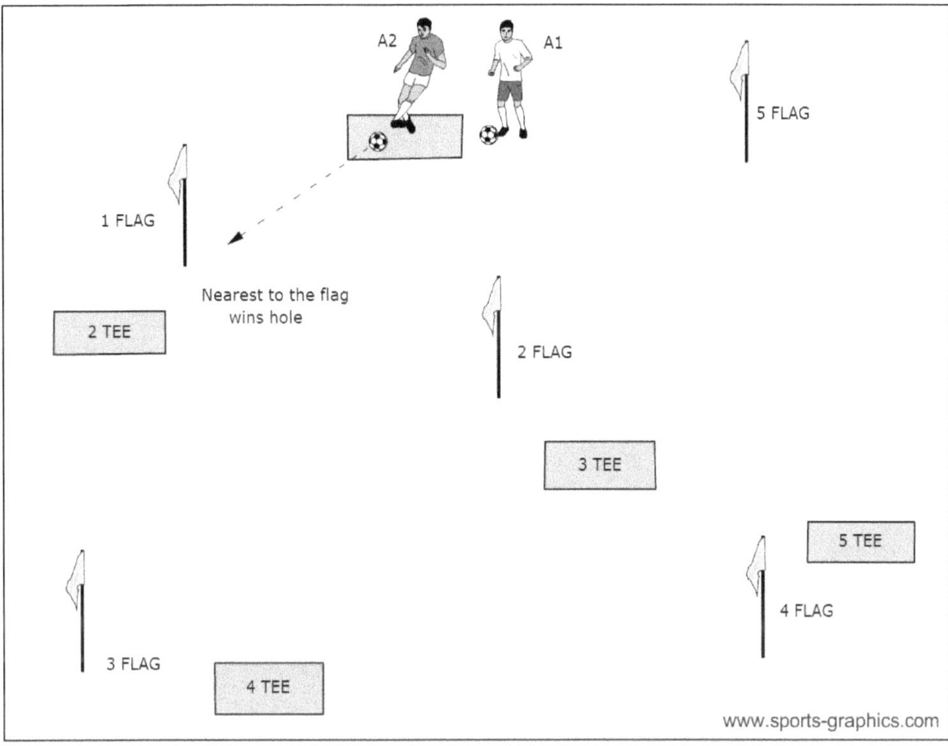

The game of soccer will always be a game based on passing the ball. In the last thirty or so years we have seen the implementation of ideas aimed to create a way of playing soccer that relied, not on the pass or the first touch to the ball, but on the kick of the ball. Football ended up with the long ball at its heart, making the game look busy but failing to promote the proper game of soccer. Sadly, this is still the case in some quarters to this very day. One of the biggest mistakes made is the media's willingness to hire ex- soccer players as commentators on the game. The fact is that the ex-players won't rock the boat and in fact promote the game in a way that doesn't question seriously anything that might be wrong with it. For them, whatever happens on the field of play is fantastic, no matter what the reality, especially when the game ends up 5 goals to 4. We should have live games on television only and the comments made about the game, honest ones, simply tell it like it is without fear, in which case it would be down to everyone in the game to make an effort to improve the quality of the product! My personal hope in writing this book is that whosoever reads it takes it in the right spirit. This is a coaching book, with some hard truths thrown into the mix. It is not meant to offend anyone but to give food for thought to coaches of aspiring professional and amateur players alike.

Support the first ball game

COACHING VS PLAYER DEVELOPMENT

THE FORWARD MOVING WORLD

When it comes to the game of soccer, there was a time in my early development years as a player that I accepted how things were done, without question. Now, of course, with time and a greater understanding of the game of soccer, I do not accept the old ways of doing things. The old ways of 'Coaching' the game of soccer adheres to the reality that all human beings perform every physical movement to the front and forward of the physical position. Walking or using our hands to pick something up can be an example of this forward moving reality. I now know that most coaching solutions from the past are product of the forward moving reality. This is what lies behind the soccer coaching evolution and its consequences on how the game is played.

THE SOCCER COACHING IMPLICATIONS A SECOND BALL GAME REALITY

A standard practice of typical soccer 'Coaching' methods is a forward moving game format known as the 'Drill'. The term drill describes work that can be repeated.

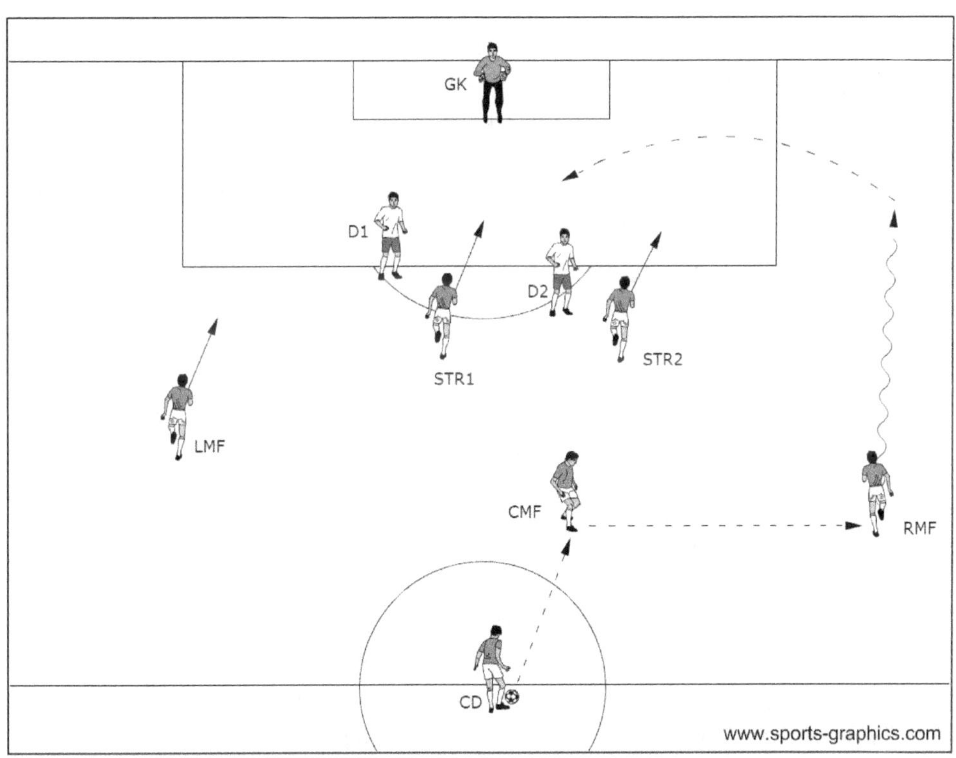

This type of functional drill solution is actually not beneficial to the overall development of the individual player. When the players' work consists of functional drills, most coaches will simply ignore the lack of quality in the individual performance. The forward moving functional example here does little to promote a wide range of skill options, but rather keeps the player limited mainly to the forward touch to the ball and to the 'One Footedness' reality.

In the above drill example, the downside from a player development point of view comes from the functional reality. In other words, in this training type solution, where the players keep to their designated role, they do not have the natural freedom to do anything other than play the game to a set plan of action. For example, In the above example of a drill, the plan of action may be as follows: The ball is played to the midfield player, the midfield player in turn passes the ball to the wide right side midfield player. The job of the wide right sided midfield player is to cross the ball into the penalty box, where the strikers are located. The striker's role is to try to score a goal off the cross.

This work is functional, but in truth it is not really focussed on the personal development of the player. The drill is therefore a 'Coaching' solution, but not a player development solution as such.

During the last twenty or so years, coaches have applied coaching solutions that have secured a forward moving mentality on the game. But again, from a player development point of view, these forward moving solutions did little more than simply further enforce an anti-skill mentality in favor of other attributes such as physical strength and height. Asking young players to run forward with the ball in the final attacking third on the pitch is a typical solution that supports the forward moving mentality and, in effect, the anti-skilful reality. Running with the ball looks good and is exciting from a punter's point of view, but in truth the player running with the ball at his feet has a limited experience because he uses very few skills to move the ball forward and will often only see to the front of his position, thus promoting what is known as a 'Head down' position. Running with the ball has become an integral part of the game, but when it comes to the development of the player it has the effect of creating a lack of vision, a kind of tunnel vision state, where the player does not see the 180° angle to the front of his position, but has a much narrower angle of view, one that can be described as a 90° playing angle, with all it's implications.

Running with the ball does little to encourage the development of the mentality of sharing possession of the ball during the attacking phase of the game. Running with the ball actually creates the opposite effect, as the players tend to become selfish and not share the ball. This is of little value to the development of the playing skills that enable all the players to interact with one another in order to create the movement patterns that can end up with a goal scoring opportunity.

SMALL SIDED GAMES - ANOTHER FORWARD MOVING ENDEAVOR

In my research of the game in the last thirty or so years I have found that from a player development point of view, most of the functional solutions have been 'Coaching' solutions, not player development solutions. Ideas such as running with the ball or working the players in a functional reality did little to actually promote the development of the individual. Another example which served the second ball game mentality is the 'Small Sided Game'. The truth from a player development point of view is that small pitches, with very little width, also lock the players into a forward moving mindset. The forward moving mindset in turn locks the players into a 'One Footedness' reality, which in effect further enforces the lack of development and when it comes to playing the full sided game, creates limitations. The true result of a solution such as a small sided game is simply overlooked. In a small area, most of the players will enforce the use of the one good foot to the ball and will continue to be weak on the other side. The small sided game is in fact a functional solution, rather than a player development solution.

THE CHANGING MENTALITY

Functional coaching is the norm here in England/Europe with the exception of some countries, notably Spain and France. Certainly when it came to England everyone simply ignored the issues regarding the lack of individual development. It is true to say that the lack of input into the individual development and the support for the collective (not in the interpretation of the first ball game sense and therefore not in terms of the individual development) was translated into the way some managers in the game had their team playing football.

Thankfully, the game here in England is evolving as a result of the new owners of the big clubs bringing in managers who have implemented the proper way of playing. Times have changed and we are seeing more and more the proper way of playing soccer here in England under managers like Pep Guardiola at Manchester City. Under Guardiola, the goalkeeper does not simply launch the long ball and hope for the best, but has to have the ability to pass the ball out of the defense and work with his teammates using effective skilful play. This is the foundational building block for what we now know to be the 'First Ball Game'.

THE FIRST BALL GAME

In a skilful game of soccer, the goalkeeper is considered another outfield player, one who most certainly has to have the ability to control the ball, see the correct pass out of the defense and of course make the pass that will secure the safe passage of the ball out of the defence and beyond. The goalkeeper will be involved at every opportunity and will use either a throw or a pass of the ball with his feet to a player that is in free space and in a position to receive the ball. Looking to pass the ball to a player in free space ensures possession of the ball, which is of course a priority for a first ball game team.

THE DEVELOPMENT IMPLICATIONS

The development of the player's ability to play the game to any worthwhile standard, which is the first ball game style, is actually dependent on a different approach to that of any forward moving functional expectation. If the coach wants to see player development, then he needs to dismiss the idea that in order to develop the full potential of the player he needs to employ a forward moving mentality into the coaching philosophy. If any manager wants his players to play the game more skilfully, then it is important to implement training solutions that are actually player development solutions.

THE TYPE OF SKILLS REQUIRED

1 – The physical ability to take control of the ball.
2 – The skills necessary for an effective keep ball strategy and counter attacking play.

CREATING A FIRST BALL GAME PLAYER DEVELOPING COLLABORATION

The serious approach to player development requires the coach to think 'outside the box' so to speak. When it comes to player development, the coach needs to get away from the forward moving mentality because it simply develops a functional player, one that will most certainly lack many of the playing attributes that can make the player a 'Top Drawer' player, one that can play to the standard that is represented nowadays by first ball game teams such as Barcelona or Arsenal at times or even Manchester City or Chelsea. The more skilful game of soccer is called 'The First Ball Game' – It is a game of soccer where the players are not shackled to a strict forward moving functional role during the attacking or defensive phase of the game, but are allowed to be creative throughout the team formation.

MOVING AWAY FROM THE FORWARD MOVING MENTALITY - THE LATERAL PLAYER DEVELOPMENT SOLUTIONS

The lateral based foundational cone placements explained in this book represent a change in the training philosophy, one that gets the players away from the forward moving mentality and targets specifics, such as the development of the player's collaboration between the left and right side of the body, ensuring the development of the player to be 'Multi Directional'. In the context of player development, the word collaboration here refers to the development of the left and right side of the brain as well as the physical side of the player so that the player can possess a greater effective control over his body. By effective control of his body I mean possess a 'Two Footedness' capability which gives the player a greater range of skills and the ability to play the game of soccer to a greater range of angle options.

THE FIRST BALL GAME VS THE SECOND BALL GAME
A STATISTICAL ANALYSIS

Call it football – Call it Soccer, the ability to play the game to the standard represented by the best teams in the world is based on development, and that development cannot take place in functional 'Coaching' type solutions. There is a serious difference between 'Coaching' and Player Development. My Coaching method is all about player development. I want to see young players given the opportunity to develop their skills to a level that will allow them to fulfil their dreams. You can't play your way to become a top drawer player! Every player needs good development solutions and it just so happens that after years of research the solution to player development has to be based on the lateral angle and not the forward moving one. The lateral angle is foundational to the quest for excellence, in developing technique and to the development of the physical ability to play the game of 'Soccer' to a first ball game standard.

UNDERSTAND THE DIFFERENCE

At this point in my explanations I would like the Coach to understand the difference between the first and second ball game. To get a better picture of what is actually happening on the field of play and, to therefore understand the difference between the long ball game which is a second ball game mentality and the skilful possession game of soccer, which is a first ball game mentality, it is what unravels during the game when the goalkeeper or the defense have the ball that matters, and it is at this point that we can observe what type of game is actually being played. In order to get a true picture of the style of play we need to examine in detail what happens to the ball when both keepers have the ball and what happens to the ball when both sets of defensive players have the ball. The conclusions allow you to understand the type of development the players require. The conclusion is upgraded following the given statistics.

We will look at the first half of a Premier League match between Bristol City and Middlesbrough followed by a real time play by play look at a full match between Barcelona and Real Madrid.

BRISTOL CITY V MIDDLESBROUGH FC
A SECOND BALL GAME EXAMPLE FROM THE ENGLISH GAME

TIME	GK	DEFENDERS
00:00:09		LONG BALL
00:03:09		LONG BALL
00:03:21		LONG BALL
00:04:24	LONG BALL	
00:05:30		LONG BALL
00:05:48		LONG BALL
00:07:10		LONG BALL
00:08:07		FREE KICK - LONG BALL
00:09:16		LONG BALL
00:09:44		LONG SHOT - NO GOAL
00:10:07	LONG BALL	
00:11:34	LONG BALL	
00:12:19		LONG BALL
00:12:57		LONG BALL
00:13:43		LONG BALL
00:14:46	LONG BALL	
00:15:10		LONG BALL
00:16:00		LONG BALL
00:18:30	LONG BALL	
00:18:50		INJURY - TIME OUT
00:19:42		LONG BALL
00:20:09		LONG BALL
00:20:39		LONG BALL
00:20:55		LONG BALL
00:21:51		FREE KICK - LONG BALL
00:22:07		LONG BALL
00:22:40		FIRST CORNER - LONG BALL
00:24:20		LONG BALL
00:24:30	LONG BALL	
00:25:29		LONG BALL
00:26:39	LONG BALL	
00:27:48		LONG BALL
00:28:17		LONG BALL
00:28:31		LONG BALL
00:28:53		LONG BALL

TIME	GK	DEFENDERS
00:29:00		INJURY - TIME OUT
00:30:11		LONG BALL
00:30:35	LONG BALL	
00:31:09	LONG BALL	
00:31:24	LONG BALL	
00:31:46		LONG BALL
00:32:16		CORNER - LONG BALL
00:32:43	LONG BALL	
00:32:57	LONG BALL	
00:33:13	LONG BALL	
00:34:00		HEADER OUT - LONG
00:34:35		FREE KICK - LONG BALL
00:35:03		LONG BALL
00:35:10		LONG BALL - CROSS INTO BOX
00:35:35	LONG BALL	
00:36:05		INJURY - TIME OUT
00:36:25		FREE KICK - LONG BALL
00:36:45		LONG BALL
00:37:31		FREE KICK - PLAYED SHORT
00:38:00		LONG BALL
00:40:00		CLEARANCE - LONG BALL
00:41:44		LONG BALL
00:42:13	LONG BALL	
00:42:53	LONG BALL	
00:43:19		LONG BALL
00:43:31	LONG BALL	
00:44:29		LONG BALL
00:45:24		LONG BALL
00:45:44		LONG BALL
00:46:07	LONG BALL	
00:46:19		LONG BALL
00:46:33		CORNER - LONG BALL
HALF	SCORE 0-0	

Summing Up The First Half

The above describes a typical second ball game mentality with all it's implications. It is simply true to say that the above type of game is not based on skillful play. In fact, the long ball game creates a physical game, one where no team was able to come out on top and be in effective control of the play. The defense and the goalkeepers have used the long ball solution at every opportunity, which had its implications for the rest of the players in both teams. The ball would often fly past the midfield, where both teams ended up playing on the defense because the long ball was almost always lost to the opposing team. **In the first half of this game there were 62 long balls played which gave the ball away**. In this type of game, the playing attributes of the individual player is based on physical rather than on technical ability. The long ball game creates a reality that can damage the player's development over time due to the lack of meaningful possession of the ball.

A DIFFERENT REALITY

The next example describes a first ball game mentality. When it comes to the first ball game, the players are selected on the basis of talent. More importantly, the players are coached in a way that develops that talent. The key to everything that a first ball game team does is based on skillful play and on a playing mentality that keeps the ball, period! It is the defense that sets the style of play and that style of play is based on keeping the ball. The following match timeline proves hands down that in keeping the ball and sharing possession of the ball, the game is based on skilful play.

REAL MADRID V BARCELONA
A FIRST BALL GAME TIMELINE FROM THE SPANISH GAME

10 seconds into the game : Barca defender Pique receives the ball from the kick off, takes a reverse touch to the ball, turns on the touch and passes the ball to his goalkeeper - The goalkeeper plays the short ball out of his area - The ball is intercepted by a Real Madrid forward player - The forward player passes the ball - the pass is not clean - the ball is almost intercepted by a Barcelona player - there is a deflection - the ball lands at the feet of Benzema - He gets lucky and scores - Barcelona are a goal down inside 20 sec of this game.

Note - This moment gives pleasure to the long ball game supporters. Yes, the goalkeeper gave the ball away. However, did the Barcelona team then play the long ball after that incident? No! Did the manager of Barcelona demand that his goalkeeper now change his style of play and play the long ball after that incident? No! Patience is a virtue! Let us see how the game evolved from here on in.

Kick off taken

1 min 14 sec : Real midfield player tackles for the ball but doesn't get it - the loose ball ends up at the feet of Pique - Pique takes control of the ball and plays the ball to his left full back. Barcelona on the attack - Corner given to Barcelona

1 min 50 sec : Pique up for the corner - Barcelona play a long ball corner (sometimes they do that) - Pique competes for the ball - Real defense clears the ball out of their area - Pique tracks back to his defensive position.

3 min 20 sec : The Barcelona goalkeeper passes the ball between two Real Madrid players to his midfield player who is just beyond the two Real players on the edge of his penalty box - the Barcelona player knocks the ball across his goal area to his left full back who in turn plays the ball to Pique to his right - Pique takes a touch to the ball that enables him to play the ball to his right full back - passing the ball across the field of play in his defensive third.

Note - Clearly, the playing patterns related to the pass of the ball are not based on the forward moving mentality but clearly on keeping possession. In a second ball game mentality the ball would have been kicked long, long ago, just as soon as the goalkeeper or anyone in the defense had the ball. NOT BARCELONA - EVIDENTLY

4 min 16 sec : The Real Madrid defense plays the long ball out of their defensive third, the ball ends up in the hands of the Barcelona goalkeeper - he in turn rolls the ball out by hand to Pique (just out of his penalty area) - Pique takes a reverse touch to the ball, turns and dink passes the ball over the opponents' heads to Iniesta, who is positioned on the left side of the pitch and close to the halfway line - The pass is accurate - Barcelona in possession.

A POINT OF REFERENCE - Some teams like Manchester United find it easy to play in the English Premiership because most of the teams in the league will give the ball away. A problem arises only when they meet up with a team that rarely gives the ball away cheaply, as is the case with a team like Barcelona.

CONTINUED OBSERVATIONS

4 min 35 sec : In this sequence the right center half of Barcelona intercepts the ball inside his defensive third, turns on the touch and passes the ball to his goalkeeper - The goalkeeper knocks the ball on to his his left full back, passing the ball across his penalty area - The left full back plays a short pass forward of his position to his midfield player - the midfield player, under pressure from his counter midfield player, plays the ball to Pique (the left center half) - Pique takes a forward touch and plays the ball forward of his position to the center midfield player.

5 min 23 sec : Real Madrid plays the long ball out of their defense - ball ends up at the other end of the field of play - Goal kick to Barcelona - The Barcelona keeper takes a short pass option to his right center half.

5 min 54 sec : Messi intercepts the ball in midfield - goes on a dribbling run - Ends the run with a shot on goal - Madrid keeper gives away a corner - Corner to Barca

6 min 26 sec : Corner to Barcelona - Pique moves into opponent's penalty area - Corner taken and cleared - Barcelona in possession - Pique takes up a center midfield position, receives the ball from Xavi and takes a touch with his right foot - He plays the ball to the wide man on his left - the wide player takes the ball on a run and is fouled by the Real right center half - free kick to Barca.

7 min 40 sec : Free kick taken by Messi near the opponent's penalty area. Messi drives the ball low into the near post - the ball is cleared.

9 min 13 sec : Free kick to Real in their own half - Long ball played - The ball reaches the front edge of the Barcelona penalty area - Inaccurate long ball gives the ball to Barcelona - Barcelona in possession.

Note - The competition in midfield is strong from both teams - mistakes happen. However, the pass and move sequence displayed by Barcelona FC is effective because they do not give the ball away by resorting to the long ball solution.

9 min 50 sec : A throw-in taken inside the Barcelona defensive third - A header moves the ball on to Pique - Pique is some 20 yards from his own penalty box and heads the ball on to his right center half - The center half heads the ball on forward and to his midfield player - He in turn plays the ball back to his left full back who in turn plays the ball out of his defensive third but gives away a throw-in to Real Madrid.

10 min 55 sec : Pique gets a block tackle in inside the midfield third - The ball is deflected to the Barcelona center midfield player who in turn passes the ball to Messi, just short of the halfway line - Barcelona in possession

11 min 5 sec : Messi is brought down - Free kick given - Free kick taken quickly with a short pass option

11 min 32 sec : Pique has the ball now on the halfway line and plays a longer pass to his striker (some forty yards) - Gives the ball away to the Real defense.

11 min 41 sec : Real Madrid defense plays the long ball - Pique watches the ball all the way to his goalkeeper - The Barcelona keeper does not catch the ball but simply knocks it to the feet of Pique - Pique takes a reverse touch to the ball, turns on the touch, moves the ball forward of his penalty area and passes to his left full back.

11 min 52 sec : Pique receives the ball back from his left full back and passes the ball on to his right center half (in their defensive third) - The right center half returns the ball to Pique - Pique in turn plays the ball to Xavi who moves the ball on forward and left of the midfield third.

12 min 40 sec : Pique comes short for the ball from his goalkeeper - Goalkeeper makes a mistake - Takes no chances and plays the long ball - Gives the ball away to a Real Madrid player in midfield - Real player, on seeing the goalkeeper out of his goal, plays a long shot effort but fails to hit the target - Offside given in any case - Possession to Barcelona.

13 min 0 sec : Goal kick to Barcelona - Goalkeeper plays the ball to Pique inside the penalty area - Pique returns the ball to his goalkeeper

13 min 4 sec : Goalkeeper passes the ball on to his right center half who is close to the corner flag to the right side of his penalty area - The right center half plays the ball back to the keeper - The keeper in turn moves the ball on to Pique inside the box to the keeper's left side - Pique keeps the ball under pressure from a Real Madrid forward - He wrong foots the Real player who turns awkwardly and falls to the ground - Pique then plays the ball to his left full back to his left and forward of his defensive area of play.

13 min 21 sec : Time out for an injured player

15 min 4 sec : Game restarts with a throw in to Barcelona - Barcelona in possession - the ball changes hands, both teams win and lose the ball

15 min 52 sec : Throw in to Barcelona - Taken on the right side of the Barcelona half, midway between the halfway line and the goal area - The throw in played to the right center half Puyol - Puyol in turn plays the ball to Pique - Pique moves the ball forward away from the defensive third, then plays the ball to his left to Xavi who is now in the midfield third and on the counter attacking mode of play.

17 min 19 sec : The long ball played by the Real goalkeeper is competed for just past the halfway line and inside the Barcelona half - Xavi first to the ball but is fouled - Free kick given to Barcelona - Free kick taken quickly with a short pass to Messi - Messi plays the ball to Xavi - Xavi passes the ball to Pique - Pique plays the ball down the line

18 min 11 sec : Hand ball by Barca player - Real Madrid take the free kick - They play the long ball, which is won by Barcelona - Barcelona in possession.

18 min 28 sec : Head tennis - The ball is headed on by 3 Real players and ends up at the feet of Pique - Pique does a Cruyff turn and plays (passes) the ball on to his right center half (Puyol) - Barcelona in possession.

19 min 12 sec : Pique moves up in support of attacking play - The attack breaks down - Real Madrid on the counter attack - Pique tracks Ronaldo - Ronaldo moving fast with the ball down the left side - Pique stays with Ronaldo applying pressure - Ronaldo shoots for goal, low shot is intercepted by the right center half Puyol - Barcelona clear the danger, not by playing the long ball but by a sequence of short passes out of the defensive area and into the midfield area of play - Barcelona have possession.

Highlighting the difference again between Real Madrid and Barcelona - Casillas, the Real goalkeeper has plenty of time to do whatever he wants with the ball. What does he choose to do? The Real defense is not expecting the ball from their keeper at this point, unlike the Barcelona defense who shapes up to receive the ball from their goalkeeper at every opportunity. Casillas plays the long ball inaccurately and gives the ball away for a throw in on the far side of the Barcelona half - Throw in to Barcelona - Pique has the ball.

20 min 20 sec : Pique takes his time - Plays the ball wide to his left past the halfway line to Iniesta.

20 min 36 sec : Real midfield puts pressure on Pique who has the ball inside the center circle - He plays the short pass to Xavi - Xavi in turn plays the ball to Busquets - Busquets plays the ball to Pique - Pique plays the short pass to his left full back Abidal - Barcelona have possession.

Note - The priority for Barcelona on 20 min was to keep the ball away from Real Madrid as much as possible, counter attacking when it was on, but in general terms playing deep inside their own half, and they obviously kept strictly to their game plan. The priority was clear - keep the ball away from the Real Madrid players. If the opponents don't have the ball they can't hurt you!

22 min 50 sec : Barcelona on the counter attack - Corner to Barcelona - Played long into the Real Madrid penalty area - The ball misses every player - Goal kick given.

23 min 21 sec : Real Madrid keeper kicks the long ball out of his area - The ball ends up with Barcelona - Barcelona in possession.

23 min 43 sec : The Barcelona goalkeeper is put under pressure and plays the long ball - However, not just any old long ball - This ball from Valdes is played diagonal and to a specific area - Near the touch line - On the right side of the field of play from his point of view.

24 min 35 sec : Ronaldo misses a great opportunity to score a second goal for Real but he misses the target - His effort ends up a goal kick to Barcelona - Valdes passes the ball to Pique - Pique passes the ball on to his left full back - The left full back (Abidal) passes the ball forward of his position to the midfield player Busquets.

Note - The game is 25 minutes old and there is a calm feeling about the way Barcelona is controlling the game. Real Madrid look to have lost their concentration and their confidence.

25 min 4 sec : Messi is brought down inside the Real Madrid half - Free kick to Barcelona - A sequence of short passes between Xavi and Messi keeps the ball for Barcelona.

26 min 31 sec : Barca foul Real Madrid - Free kick to Real - cross comes into the Barcelona box - Messi half-clears the ball - Ball ends up with Alonso - Possession is won and lost in the midfield third and ends up with the Real Madrid goalkeeper who kicks the long ball - Barcelona half-clear their lines and give the ball away to Ronaldo - Ronaldo gives the ball away.

Note - Ronaldo quite in this game - Much was expected of him but he failed to deliver on this occasion. He is a talent though and I am sure he would do better next time.

29 min 32 sec : Pique has the ball well out of his defensive third - He finds a pass to Messi who is now inside the center circle - Messi turns on the touch and moves forward into the opponent's half - He then goes on a dribbling run - Moves the ball (and himself) past the first challenger - Past the second challenger - Stays on his feet and threads a perfect pass through to the right hand side of the striker Alexis - Alexis evades two Real defenders before finishing with a right foot effort that ends up with the ball at the back of the Real Madrid net - Casillas is unable to prevent Alexis from scoring the equaliser.

29 min 50 sec : Real Madrid 1 - Barcelona 1

Kick Off

30 min 27 sec : Ronaldo on the ball - wide and left from his point of view - He crosses the ball into the Barcelona penalty area - Pique clears the ball long out of the defense - Real Midfield wins the ball some 20 yards from Pique - Real in possession.

31 min 18 sec : Real lose the ball to the Barcelona goalkeeper - Valdes takes a quick goal kick and passes the ball to his left center half Pique who in turn plays the ball back to Valdes - The opposing striker tries to put pressure on the goalkeeper, but to no avail - The keeper simply plays the ball back to Pique.

Note - Very often during play, Barcelona move the ball in a 'now you see it, now you don't' style. In other words, they double pass the ball on lots of occasions. Just when the opponents think they have closed a player on the ball down, that player moves the ball on and back to where it came from. So it is difficult for the opponents to get to the ball. Also, Messi can play a passive role one minute but in an instant turn, change pace and run at the defense when they least expect it. A case in point is the way Messi created the pass opportunity for Alexis to score the equaliser.

31 min 25 sec : Pique drives the ball low to Iniesta who is up field close to the half way line - Barcelona in possession.

31 min 57 sec : Real play the ball out of their defense to the feet of Ozil to their left side of the midfield third - Ozil plays the ball to Ronaldo down the left hand side - Ronaldo goes on a run with the ball - He gives the ball away.

Note - If one of the star players is not playing well, it can affect the team's confidence as a whole.

32 min 47 sec : Messi loses the ball close to the Real penalty box, but doesn't give up on the ball - He tracks back and wins the ball back.

Note - This hustle play by Messi is certainly an inspirational moment for his teammates.

34 min 24 sec : Pique on the ball - Plays a short pass to Fabregas just short of the halfway line - Fabregas play a short pass to Messi - Barcelona in possession.

34 min 44 sec : Typical of Barcelona now - The back four is now moving forward in support of attacking play and are now inside the opponent's half - Pique passes the ball to his full back who is overlapping him on the left side in the opponent's half now - Developing attacking play.

35 min 32 sec : Barcelona in the attacking third - Real on the defensive - Pepe takes out Alexis on Casillas' right hand side and just outside his penalty area - Free kick to Barcelona.

36 min 34 sec : Free kick taken - Real Madrid keeper punches the ball clear - Ball reaches Pique some forty or so yards from the Real Madrid penalty box - Pique plays a short pass to Alexis (forward) - The attack fails - Real Madrid keeper has the ball and uses the length of his penalty box to play the ball long - The ball ends up with the Barcelona keeper.

36 min 53 sec : The Barcelona goalkeeper on catching the ball played by his counterpart in the Real Madrid goal doesn't return the favor but rolls the ball by hand to his left full back - The left full back, who is now in Pique's place (playing as a left center half for a moment), lets the ball roll past his position to Pique, who has taken up the left full back position - Pique in turn plays the ball to Abidal (now playing in Pique's position) - Abidal moves forward into the midfield third where he in turn plays the ball to Iniesta - Barcelona in possession.

37 min 32 sec : Iniesta plays the ball to Messi - Messi in turn plays the ball to Pique - Pique in turn plays the ball to his right center half.

37 min 43 sec : The ball is with Pique - Pique, under pressure from the Real player Benzema, plays the long ball down the line (a rare sight) and on this sole occasion of playing the long ball naturally gives the ball away.

38 min 28 sec : Hopeful ball forward by Real Madrid ends up with Pique heading the ball forward of his defensive third and as with most high ball clearances, it is not possible to secure possession of the ball - Real wins possession but loses it under the immediate pressure from Barcelona - Throw in to Barcelona - Real win the ball back and counter attack - Ozil takes on Pique - Pique tackles for the ball and wins the ball back for Barcelona.

39 min : Barcelona lose the ball in the opponent's defensive third - Madrid keeper has the ball - He in turn hoofs the ball long and out of play on the far side of the pitch - Barcelona throw in.

40 min : Barcelona in possession in the opponent's half - Foul on Fabregas - Free kick taken short to Messi - Interactive play ends with a throw in to Real Madrid's Ronaldo on the far side of the field of play - He gives the ball away to Puyol.

42 min 26 sec : Real in possession of the ball - Messi fouls Alonso - Free kick to Real Madrid on the halfway line - Ball is played back to the Real goalkeeper, who kicks the ball long into the defensive third of Barcelona - Benzema caught offside - Free kick taken short - Barcelona in possession.

45 min 16 sec : Real have the ball but give away a throw-in to Barcelona near their penalty area.

45 min 33 sec : Real win the ball back in their box and counter attack but give the ball away - The ball is with Barcelona.

45 min 56 sec : End of the first half - Real Madrid 1 - Barcelona 1
Barcelona are the away team and as such did not make this an open game in the first half, but simply set their stall out to keep the ball away from Real Madrid as much as possible and to rely on the counter attack. I believe that Barcelona did succeed in keeping the ball away from Real Madrid and because of that Real Madrid lost its way and were beginning to be less effective - Let's see if anything changes in the second half of this game - Will Barcelona defend from as deep a position in their defensive third as they did in the first half or will they push up more into their opponent's half.

The Second Half

The focus is on Pique and on how the back four plus the goalkeeper Valdes play the ball out of their defensive third. How many long balls will Barcelona play in the second half of this game? That is the question that interests me the most, for obvious reasons.

45 min : Straight away the Barcelona team is positioned higher up the pitch than before and the back four is now holding their line of defense some thirty or so yards from their penalty area. The intention is clear - To put pressure on the opponents in their own half of the pitch.

45 min 12 sec : Pique putting pressure on Coentrao out wide near the halfway line - ball goes out for a throw-in to Barcelona.

46 min 12 sec : Real play the ball down the line - Pique moves to the ball and gains possession to the right side of his penalty area - Under pressure from Ozil he plays the ball to Valdes and moves to open up the area of play - He parks himself near the corner flag - Valdes plays him the ball again - Under pressure from Real Pique does a couple of keep ups and dinks the ball over a Real forward but the ball is intercepted by Ronaldo - Ronaldo gives away a throw-in to Barcelona.

47 min 3 sec : Barcelona defense supporting play push up to the halfway line - Pique putting pressure on the ball - Real counter attack

47 min 18 sec : Pique tracks back and gives cover to his right center half Puyol.

48 min 26 sec : Ronaldo takes the ball past Pique - Pique does a back foot lift and clips Ronaldo - Ronaldo falls to the ground - Free kick given plus a yellow card to Pique - Free kick taken in sight of goal.

49 min 45 sec : Ronaldo takes the free kick - Strikes the ball straight at the Barcelona Goalkeeper - Valdes has the ball.

50 min 45 sec : Pique receives the ball from Busquets on the left side of the defense - He dinks the ball over the opponent's heads but gives the ball away for a throw in to Real.

52 min 8 sec : Throw in to Real - Barcelona win the ball back - moving the ball through the midfield third to Iniesta who plays a one-two with Messi - Defenders get a touch on the ball - Ball falls at the feet of Alexis - Alexis shoots for goal - The ball hits Xavi and it is deflected past the stranded Real Madrid goalkeeper - Goal - Real Madrid 1 Barcelona 2 - A lucky goal.

Kick Off

54 min 40 sec : Corner to Barcelona - Pique up for the corner - corner taken long into the Real penalty area - Long clearance by Real is collected by Abidal who covered for Pique - Abidal plays the ball to Valdes - Valdes plays the ball to Alves (almost giving the ball away) - Alves has the ball.

55 min 17 sec : Pique pushes into the midfield third with cover from Busquets - Puts pressure on a Real midfield player in possession - Pique drops back into the defensive third and takes up the left center half position.

55 min 50 sec : Corner to Real Madrid - Taken long to the far side of the six yard box - Ball is headed back towards the center of the six yards box - Pique gets his head to the ball and clears the danger to his goal - He finds his own player with this header - Barcelona in possession.

56 min 47 sec : The back four of Barcelona supporting play are now on the halfway line - The Barcelona right center half receives the ball inside the Real Madrid half and passes to Pique - Pique in turn plays the ball across the pitch to his left full back - Real Madrid on the defensive.

57 min 55 sec : Throw in to Barcelona deep inside the opponent's area of play

Subs On

58 min 41 sec : Throw in taken - Offside given - Free kick - Real keeper plays the long ball.

58 min 47 sec : Pique heads the ball up field - Barcelona in possession.

59 min 32 sec : Real Madrid break out of their defense and counter attack down the left side - Real Madrid forward wrong foots Pique - Alves (the right back for Barca) gives cover and challenges for the ball - The Real forward manages to pass the ball to Ronaldo - Ronaldo plays the ball across the penalty area of Barcelona - Puyol intercepts.

59 min 47 sec : Puyol plays the ball to Pique - Pique plays a short pass to Iniesta - Barcelona have the ball.

60 min 19 sec : Iniesta is brought down at the halfway line - Free kick to Barcelona taken short - Ball played to Pique - Pique in turn plays the ball to his left full back.

60 min 54 sec : Yet another foul on a Barca player in the opponent's half of the field - Free kick taken short to Messi - Messi runs at the defense and ends his run with a shot on goal - Keeper saves - Corner given - Cleared

61 min 41 sec : Messi is brought down again - Free kick given just outside the Madrid penalty area - Messi takes the free kick - Misses the target on the right post - Goal kick to Madrid.

63 min 31 sec : Real have the ball - Counter attack on the right side of the pitch - Marcelo crosses the ball into the Barcelona penalty box - Pique intercepts the ball - Gives away a corner to Real.

63 min 56 sec : Corner taken long - Valdes punches the ball out of the area - Real have the ball - Alonso crosses a peach of a ball to Ronaldo - Ronaldo heads the ball but misses the target wide to his left.

64 min 56 sec : Pique plays the ball out to Iniesta who is in the midfield third now - Iniesta moves the ball forward, avoids one tackle and plays the ball to Messi - Messi plays the ball wide now to Alves reaching the final third - Alves crosses the ball into the Real Madrid box - The ball reaches Fabregas on the far post - A bullet header low to the corner of the Madrid goal seals the game for Barcelona on 65 min 15 sec - Real Madrid 1 Barcelona 3

67 min 6 sec : Real in possession of the ball on Pique's side of the defense - The dink over Pique's head doesn't work - Pique heads the ball down to the feet of Iniesta - Barcelona have ball.

67 min 46 sec : Free kick to Barcelona - A short pass taken - Pique on the ball - Under pressure, gives away a throw in - Real Madrid on the counter attack.

68 min 20 sec : Real lose the ball to Barcelona in the defensive third - Barcelona play the ball out of their defense with a sequence of short passes - Valdes to Pique - Pique to Valdes - Valdes to Alves - Alves plays the long ball out of the defense (rarely seen) and the ball reaches Casillas (Madrid goalkeeper) who in turn returns the favor and in effect hoofs the long ball back and into the hands of Valdes.

68 min 49 sec : The Barcelona goalkeeper rolls the ball out to Iniesta just to the outside of his goal area - Iniesta in turn plays the ball to Pique - Pique plays the ball down the line to Alves - Barca have the ball.

69 min 13 sec : Foul on Messi - Free kick to Barcelona in their attacking third - Short free kick taken - Barcelona have the ball.

70 min 23 sec : Real counter attack - In reaching the Barcelona penalty area, Pique competes for the ball and wins possession inside the box - He clears his area by playing the ball to Busquets - Barcelona have the ball - Barcelona give the ball away - Real keeper has the ball and plays the long ball out of his area - Ball in the Barcelona half is headed backwards by a Real player - The left full back for Barcelona reaches the ball first and plays the ball to his goalkeeper (Valdes) - Valdes in turn plays the ball to Pique - Pique moves forward of his defensive area and plays the ball to Iniesta - The ball is intercepted - Real in possession now - Barcelona foul the Madrid midfield player but the referee doesn't give anything and the loose ball ends up at the feet of Iniesta - Iniesta is fouled - This time the referee stops play - Free kick to Barca.

72 min 43 sec : Short free kick taken - Barcelona move the ball into the Real Madrid half.

73 min 31 sec : Ronaldo on the ball - He runs with the ball down the line - On the right side of the opponent's defensive third he makes an attempt to cross the ball into Barcelona penalty area but Pique intercepts and passes the ball out of his penalty area to his left full back - The full back Abidal passes the ball on to his midfield player Iniesta - Iniesta is fouled - Free kick to Barcelona short of the halfway line.

73 min 59 sec : Short free kick taken Barcelona move the ball forward into the Real Madrid half of the field of play.

75 min 6 sec : Valdes has the ball - Goal kick - Plays the ball to Pique who is positioned to the keeper's right - Pique, close to the touch line, dinks the ball over the head of a Real forward player to Alves - Alves moves forward down the line - Barca have possession.

75 min 44 sec : Pique moves up in support and receives the ball from Alves short of the halfway line on the left side of the field - Pique plays the ball down the line - Alves competes for the ball but loses it - Real in possession

78 min 8 sec : Subs On - Fabregas off

79 min 11 sec : Real play the long ball down the line - Pique shadows the ball out of play - Goal kick given to Barcelona - Valdes plays a diagonal ball to his left close to the touchline and halfway line - Marcelo intercepts the ball with a header - Ball falls to Messi and a couple of passes on Pique has the ball - Pique passes the ball square across the pitch to Pusket (on for Fabregas) on the left side, short of the Real defensive third.

81 min 12 sec : Alexis fouled - Free kick to Barca - Taken short - Real win possession - Real Madrid on the counter attack - Puyol intercepts the ball and clears.

82 min 35 sec : Free kick to Barcelona - Pique notices Alexis in a one on one situation with Ramos - Real clear the danger - Real have possession.

82 min 58 sec : Offside given - free kick to Barcelona - Subs On - Free kick taken - Pique plays the ball short to Iniesta.

83 min 55 sec : Kaka on for Real Madrid - Playing well, so all the more surprising why he doesn't get much of a game for Real Madrid - He works out a shot on goal - Valdes saves but gives away a corner - Corner taken - Pique clears the ball out of the penalty box.

85 min 3 sec : Real on the ball - Pique jockeys Kaka - Kaka gives the ball away - Puyol clears the ball but gives a throw-in to Real - Still deep in Barcelona defensive third - Throw-in taken - Real lose the ball.

85 min 11 sec : Barcelona on the attack - Real Madrid on the defensive.

85 min 41 sec : The ball changes hands frequently.

86 min 16 sec : Real counter attack comes to nothing - Barcelona keeper has the ball and plays it to his favorite link up man Pique - Pique has all the time in the world now - He moves the ball out of the defensive area and forward towards the middle third of the field of play - He then passes the ball to Pusket on the left side of the midfield - Barcelona attacking now - Real give away a corner.

86 min 39 sec : Barcelona take the corner kick - Short this time - The ball is driven hard and low into the Real penalty box - Real defense clear.

87 min 38 sec : Pique on the ball, just short of the opponent's half - Makes a penetrating pass to Iniesta - Iniesta drives the ball to the goalline - Goal kick to Real.

88 min 34 sec : Subs On - Iniesta rested - He played really well deserved his accolades.

89 min 15 sec : Foul on Barcelona player on the right side of the Real penalty area - Free kick taken short - Ball worked back to Pique - Pique plays a diagonal ball to the right side of the field.

89 min 49 sec : Barcelona have the ball in the Real Madrid half - Alves gives away a free kick to Real - Real counter attack.

91 min : Barcelona have the ball - The ball is with Pique - Pique passes the ball short to Puyol on the halfway line - Puyol moves the ball on to Messi - Messi plays the ball down the line to Alves.

91 min 47 sec : Barcelona attack ends with the ball in the hands of Casillas - Long ball kicked and competed for - Throw in to Real - Real give the ball away - Xavi heads the ball to Pique - Pique plays the ball to his goalkeeper Valdes -

Valdes moves the ball on to his left full back wide left of his penalty area - The left full back plays the ball across the box to Pique - Pique in turn plays the ball to Xavi - Xavi plays the ball back to Pique.

92 min 26 sec : Pique plays a forward pass up the field to Alves who is now in the center of the midfield third.

92 min 56 sec : Ronaldo goes on a dribbling run at the Barcelona defense - Pique fouls him on the edge of his penalty area, just left of center - Free kick to Real Madrid.

94 min 18 sec : Free kick taken - Ronaldo strikes the the ball well but hits the wall - Ball rebounds off a Barcelona player and falls at the feet of a Real player who strikes the ball - It hits Puyol and goes out - Corner to Real.

94 min 27 sec : Corner taken long - Ball cleared by Barcelona - Referee blows his whistle - Full time

Real Madrid 1 Barcelona 3

Statistically Speaking

Excluding corners - Real Madrid played **11** long balls in this game - Barcelona just **3**!

Pique - This player was involved with the ball some **65** times and gave the ball away arguably **3** times - Only on the one occasion did he give it away when he had the ball at his feet and might have done better. Players like Pique take the responsibility for what happens to the ball, unlike functional players who are only concerned with clearing the ball out of the defense, not bothering about the fact that on clearing the ball out of their defensive third they give the ball away every time. What players like Pique show is that in terms of their development they are not just functional players but are players that have formal skills and subsequently the confidence to play soccer in a skillful manner, which means keeping the ball rather than just getting rid of it to satisfy one's own functional role.

A Summary Of The Reality

The above stats have shown a completely different game to that of any long ball game mentality. Playing as a single unit rather than individual functional players and taking responsibility for every position in the team, such as giving cover to the central defensive position for Pique or the full backs is normal in this type of team. In this iteration of the Barcelona team, Xavi - Iniesta - Messi - Fabregas - have a free role within the structure, down the so-called spine of the team with support from such players as Puyol - Abidal - Alves - Pique and Busquets. As you have seen in the stats, the pass options are multi directional and players like Pique have a lot to say about how the game unfolds. Only Alexis Sanchez (now with Arsenal FC) kept to one side of the field of play in this first half against Real Madrid. Keeping the ball is the name of the game first and foremost and so it is acceptable, for example, for Messi (in midfield) to turn away from the direct line to the Madrid goal and play the ball back to Pique and Pique in turn doesn't launch the long ball but plays the ball to Puyol - his right center half. Moving the ball back before moving the ball into attacking forward positions is the way for Barcelona and is acceptable, which is something that is not part of the British way of playing. In England the game is forward moving to create a false illusion of a good game of soccer. Constant changes of possession create the effect of a good game of soccer when in fact it isn't. The reason things work for Barcelona is because they don't just think of passing the ball forward or crossing the ball into the box in the hope of getting someone in on the end of the ball, but they actually work hard to create an end product to what they do with the ball, all of the time. The name of the game for Barcelona is as I have said before to keep the ball first and foremost and then make their possession count in terms of creating a goal scoring opportunity.

WHEN THE FIRST BALL GAME TEAM PLAYS

In many ways I have concentrated on the defense more than on any other players because it is the defense and the goalkeeper who actually control the way the game is played. Barcelona use every inch of the field of play and players like Pique work hard in co-operation with their goalkeeper and the midfield to use the space effectively in order to keep the ball. It makes sense to use as much of the field of play as is possible. After all, the opponents cannot close down every inch of space. In terms of keeping the ball, playing only to the forward direction would not make any sense to Barcelona and so Barcelona play the ball to feet and to any direction because the opponents cannot police every inch of the field in any effective numbers, especially in their defensive third.

The above statistics show a first ball game (or possession game) mentality. The first ball game is a skilful game of soccer, one that requires a different approach to player development solutions. The statistics tell it like it is and in conclusion it is simply not possible for any player to simply play his or her way into any worthwhile standard. When it comes to the development of the player, it is important to move away from the forward moving mentality if the quest is to develop the skillful player. Functional solutions are just that, functional. They fail when it comes to the development of the full potential of the player. The way forward lies in the implementation of the lateral angle into the training equation and the relevant information to achieve the correct objectives is found in this book which underpins all my work in video and book form.

With My Best Wishes!
Martin W Bidzinski

www.ingramcontent.com/pod-product-compliance
Lightning Source LLC
LaVergne TN
LVHW081300100826
845148LV00005B/930

* 9 7 8 1 5 9 1 6 4 2 5 2 7 *